TRUST ME,
I'M A JUNIOR DOCTOR

Max Pemberton charts his roller coaster journey from idealism to bewilderment as one of the many hapless medical novices, as he realises that his heady ideals of 'saving people' come a distant second to the more pressing concerns of signing forms, placating tyrannical consultants and working out if people are actually dead – it's not as easy as you think. Max and his fellow newbies grapple with these and many other complicated questions of life, love, washing and mental health in this witty, bittersweet and revealing peek into the hidden world of life and death, and everything in between.

TRUST ME,
I'M A JUNIOR DOCTOR

Trust Me, I'm A Junior Doctor

by

Max Pemberton

Magna Large Print Books
Long Preston, North Yorkshire,
BD23 4ND, England.

British Library Cataloguing in Publication Data.

Pemberton, Max
    Trust me, I'm a junior doctor.

    A catalogue record of this book is
    available from the British Library

    ISBN   978-0-7505-3310-2

First published in Great Britain in 2008 by Hodder & Stoughton
An Hachette Livre UK Company

Copyright © Max Pemberton 2008

Cover illustration by arrangement with
Hodder & Stoughton Ltd.

The right of Max Pemberton to be identified as the author of
this work has been asserted by him in accordance with the
Copyright, Designs and Patents Act, 1988

Published in Large Print 2010 by arrangement with
Hodder & Stoughton Ltd.

Magna Large Print is an imprint of Library Magna Books Ltd.

Printed and bound in Great Britain by
T.J. (International) Ltd., Cornwall, PL28 8RW

Names, identities and circumstances have been changed in order to protect the privacy of the individuals involved.

To my mum, who will be relieved to hear that I wrote all of this while eating properly and wearing a thermal vest (honest).

AUGUST

Monday 4 August

I am scared. I know I'm supposed to be a grown-up now, someone sensible who pays taxes and worries about hair loss, but I'm still scared. I feel like I'm standing at the open door of an aeroplane, about to jump, unsure if my parachute will open and knowing that even if it does, I will spend a significant period of time hurtling towards the ground, my stomach in my mouth, wishing the whole thing were over. And the thing that's really annoying is that I have no one to blame but myself.

I was the one who ticked 'medicine' in the careers box at school. If only I'd missed and ticked 'media studies', I'd be well on my way to being clued-up on thinking outside the box and where to get the best lattes, rather than an expert on anal warts and leprosy. T.S. Eliot was wrong; it's not April that's the cruellest month, it's August, because that's when final-year medical students up and down the country are rudely awoken to the fact that they are now doctors and introduced to exactly what this entails.

Medical school has been rather like a long holiday punctuated by the odd sick person. I can't pretend finals were much fun; memorising whole bookshelves, devouring them like sweets only to regurgitate them back half-remembered in a sweaty exam hall, legs twitching from the combination of ProPlus and triple espressos. But then again, for six years things were fun. It was like playing at being a doctor. When Christmas holidays came and the gauntlet of family parties had to be run, everyone looked lovingly at you. 'Oh, he's training to be a doctor, you know,' was the refrain, a collective sigh would be heard, choirs of angels would chorus from on high, and I would exude a divine light which would bathe the assembled admirers with warmth. People like doctors, or rather, they like the idea of doctors. In fact, they like the idea of knowing a doctor. They only like the *idea* of knowing a doctor because the reality is that knowing a doctor is very dull; they are tired and complain a lot, and are often rather boring because all they do is work. But a medical student is a lovely compromise: all the kudos of being a doctor but without the bags under the eyes or long moaning telephone conversations about how the NHS is going down the pan and how if everyone had to pay for health care they'd soon realise what a bargain they were getting and shut up. And so I have spent the past six years nicely cocooned in 'medicine-lite'. I've never had to work a night shift. I've never had to make a clinical judgement. In fact, I've never even prescribed a drug in my whole life. But as of tomorrow, this will all change. Because as of tomorrow, I start work as a doctor. And I am scared.

Tuesday 5 August

Well, not quite what I was hoping for. Total body count still remains at zero. This is unfortunate because I was hoping to get any deaths that I was to be responsible for over and done with in the first week. Chalk it down to beginner's bad luck, and then wipe the slate clean and move on. A few months into the job, no one remembers and you can still get a good reference. Perfect.

In fact, not only did no one die, but I didn't even see a single patient. Our entire day consisted of lectures and talks about the most tedious things imaginable, which I'm guessing will turn out to be of no use whatsoever. We were addressed by a very efficient-looking lady called Mrs Crook, whose eyes watered every time someone asked her a question. It became clear rather quickly that while she was trying to look incredibly efficient, she was actually teetering on the brink of a breakdown. At point we were having coffee and someone asked if there were spoons. Mrs Crook went bright red and started spluttering and I thought she was going to prolapse right in front of us, until thankfully someone found the spoons where she'd put them: in the bin. This woman, despite her inability to grasp who we were or what exactly we were there for, will be our main point of contact with the administrative side of the hospital.

After we had heard from Mrs Crook, several lectures on health and safety were given by grey people in grey suits: Don't spray the fire extinguishers at the patients, especially not the foam ones; if you are going to vomit on a ward round, please do it in the bins provided; if you are contemplating suicide, please be considerate and do it away from hospital premises.

The only slightly exciting, and I do use that word in its broadest sense, moment, was the 'personal safety at work' lecture. This was given by 'Doug', who used to be a paratrooper but had since left, presumably because it didn't allow him to display his more sadistic side to its best advantage, and had joined the NHS as a safety instructor. He was there to tell us all about what we can and can't do if patients get nasty. Nothing like starting us all off with the right frame of mind. He spent a considerable amount of his talk either rubbing his biceps or playing with his nipples and gave the lecture almost entirely to the cleavage of the woman sitting directly in front of him. Stupidly, I felt the need at this moment to get up to go to the toilet just when he asked for volunteers. Next thing I knew I was being mauled about on a crash-mat. As I struggled to escape, my face turning progressively redder, then bluer, it suddenly dawned on me: this is how I die, snuffed out by a lobotomised Chippendale in a prefab hut in a district general hospital. 'Can't breathe,' I tried to articulate through his hairy armpits, where my head was nestled.

Seeing that he had suitably wowed the female members of the room by suffocating the weakest member of the group, he dropped me and resumed his lecture, flashing up seventies-style sketches of people grappling on the floor which looked as though they had been lifted out of *The Joy of Sex*. 'Try not to break their fingers if you do this one,' he counselled, 'because technically that is not reasonable force.'

'But we're their doctor,' piped up a girl with a ponytail at the front.

Doug looked at her pityingly, said, 'God help you,' and carried on.

We also had a lecture from a man who looked liked he'd died some time ago and someone had forgotten to tell him. Appropriately enough he was from the coroner's office, and delivered a lecture in an impressive monotone about how to fill in a death certificate. There's optimism for you.

By the end of the day we hadn't seen a proper doctor, let alone a patient, and all we had to show was a thick wedge of paper on fire-evacuation procedures, which I promptly lost. I hope there's not a fire any time soon. Although to be honest, if there is, I doubt that I'll have time to consult the pamphlet on how to escape. The same girl with a ponytail, who's called Supriya and who is, like me, working in surgery for the next six months before we change to medicine, asked what we did about the patients in the Intensive Treatment Unit, who after all are ventilated on life-support machines. This seemed a fairly good question, but the answer was a little surprising. Given that we can't get them down the stairs, and we're not supposed to use the lifts, there's not much we can do about them, we were told.

'We just leave them?' Supriya asked, open-mouthed.

'Well, you can stay if you like,' came the reply from the fire-safety woman, whose excessive use of hairspray was surely a fire hazard in itself, 'but if you die you won't be able to make a claim against the hospital.'

Presumably because we'd be dead? But no one felt like pushing this any further.

I have a sneaking suspicion that there are

16

whole swathes of admin staff that view the junior doctors as a pimple to be burst at the earliest given opportunity, rather than an integral part of a working hospital. Looking round at the frosty reception, there is a serious lack of love. Still, we're doing this for the money, not the love, right?

Wednesday 6 August

Ruby, my flatmate who has also got a job working here, has pointed out that despite yesterday's admin hell-a-thon, we still have not been given a contract. I haven't even seen a contract, let alone signed one. But the entourage that greeted us with the enthusiasm of pepper-spray yesterday, seems to have vanished from the face of the earth. We've called personnel, but it appears that they've all gone on holiday, or are off sick, or only work part-time. There was a rumour that Mrs Crook was in her office, but all calls were going to her voicemail. Ruby tried at one point to stage a rebellion with a mass protest, sit-ins and stoppages, something she excelled in at medical school, but we quickly decided that this would certainly end our career before it had even begun. In what other job, especially one as litigious as being a doctor, would people be expected to work without a contract? But then, in what other job would someone be expected to work twenty-four hours on the trot without sleep? Perhaps this is why it's so litigious in the first place.

This was also the opportunity to meet the other two junior doctors working in surgery with me and Ruby. (There are of course the doctors working in medicine, but we're not fraternising with them if we can help it.) There's a Hindu, a Christian, a gay person, a black person, two boys and two girls. It's like a line-up for a politically correct bank advert. Though admittedly Lewis, the Christian, is gay and black, therefore killing three demographic birds with one stone.

Our morning was mainly spent sitting in occupational health, where, should there be a prize for being unable to organise a piss-up in a brewery (or should that be a health screening in a hospital?), they'd surely win. I had already sent in all my forms and certificates, showing that I was not harbouring any hideous communicable diseases and was up to date with my required immunisations, but my efficiency was met with a blank stare from the occupational health nurse.

'You didn't send it in,' she said when I asked why she had no record of one of my forms.

'Yes, I did. I sent it in six weeks ago when you asked for it,' I replied.

'No, you didn't,' she answered.

'Yes, I did,' I parried, getting increasingly frustrated.

'Didn't.'

'Did.'

'Didn't,' and so on. Ruby, who actually didn't send her forms in because she was drunk for the entire six weeks between graduating and starting work, avoided any such grilling by saying that by not sending anything in, she had, in effect, saved them the effort of losing it. They looked genuinely grateful. Myself and a good proportion of the other junior doctors, who had also had their forms 'misplaced', were sent along with Ruby to have them all done again anyway.

'See, I told you that you should have come to the pub rather than filling out those stupid forms,' Ruby smirked.

Thursday 7 August

Oh God. It's dreadful. It's worse than I could possibly have imagined. I can't take it any more. I'm so tired and I haven't even done a week yet. Still, on the bright side, only fifty-one weeks and two days to go and this will be over. That's not too long, is it? How long can a year be?

This morning I arrived at work for my first proper day. The welcome party was far from

19

welcoming. The way it works is that there are two pairs of surgeons, and each pair shares a registrar, an SHO (Senior House Officer) and then two house officers, as we junior doctors are known. This collective hierarchical grouping is called a 'firm', although mine seems anything apart from firm. It was evident right from the start that the SHO and the registrar don't get on. And even more obvious that the consultants and the registrar don't get on. Our first meeting was like a bad family party where everyone hates everyone else but is putting on a united front for the kids. Supriya and I were assigned to Mr Butterworth and Mr Price. They eyed us up as we walked on to the ward where we were due to meet them, surveying us like children about to pick teams for a PE class at school.

The four consultants are a strange bunch: a bizarre combination of professionally high-functioning but socially inept individuals. As they stood in front of us, their respective defects on display, it was hard to know whom I least wanted to be working for. The precocious Mr Grant, who could double as an extra in *Grange Hill*, has a bad reputation for being a nasty piece of work. I can only thank my lucky stars that I'm not spending my six months with him. Ruby has drawn the short straw and is working with him instead. After spending six years of medical school with Ruby, who managed to fall on her feet every time possible disaster struck, I was wondering how she was going to get out of this.

Then, like manna sent down from heaven, her other consultant hoved into view. All the females on the ward stopped. Nurses swooned; yelps of excitement issued forth from assorted female patients; small children touched the hem of his tailored suit and were healed. The man's obviously Housewives' Favourite. Suddenly things weren't looking so bad for Ruby after all.

'Hi, you must be the new house officer?' he said, giving her a slow wink and tossing back his foppish black hair. 'I'm going to be your consultant.' He stared at Ruby, his nostrils flaring slightly while he conspicuously looked her up and down. 'You'll have to excuse me, it's my first day back after a skiing trip. Spent plenty of time off piste', he continued. 'Some great dust. Nothing like the feel of your skis on fresh virgin snow.'

Feeling nauseous, I had to turn away from the sight of Ruby fluttering her lashes and murmuring, 'Well, I doubt I'm as good as you,' and Housewives' Favourite winking at her again before walking off tanned and toned. God, I hate surgeons.

Introductions over, we were cast out on to the wards. No helpful hints, words of support or pep talks here. The two consultants wandered off, with Daniel, the SHO, who has a silver spoon wedged so far down his throat it's a miracle he can speak, bowing and scraping behind them, leaving us with the registrar, Sue, to explain what we were actually supposed to be doing.

Now, this registrar might have got out of bed on the wrong side this morning, though I suspect she's like this permanently. The woman is cold. We're talking Siberia here. The rumour is that she wanted to be a vet, but didn't get the grades. Her love of dumb animals didn't appear to extend to junior doctors. 'I'm not your friend, I'm your registrar. If you don't bother me, I won't bother you,' she began,

Great. Bring on the fun times.

Friday 8 August

Our first full ward round. Chaos. We arrived on the ward, only to find that Sue was already halfway through the patients. No hello or other civil greeting. Having survived a whole half day's work as a doctor yesterday, I had imagined, foolishly, that we'd be greeted with a 'welcome back' or even a 'well done' for having survived thus far. But to veterans like Sue, mere survival isn't good enough. Supriya renamed her 'Sad Sack' due to her uncanny resemblance both physically as well as in attitude to the Raggy Dolls character. Initially I thought this was rather mean, but when she glared at me when I asked her what she was doing at the weekend, her nickname became official.

Supriya and I spent the afternoon wandering round occasionally bumping into other junior doctors, like fellow members of a lost tribe. How do you book an X-ray? Where are the blood forms? How do you get in touch with an occupational therapist? What the hell does an occupational therapist do in the first place? There's just no one to ask. The surgeons are all in theatre operating on patients, the nurses are all busy and all the junior doctors are in the same, rapidly sinking boat of ignorance.

The nurses, who have presumably seen this all before, are unfazed by our complete lack of knowledge. Within seconds of walking on to the ward, we are having things thrust in front of us. 'Sign this', 'Can you review this patient?', 'What's happening with this operation?'

By the afternoon it was all too much. I needed to get away from the constant questions that I didn't know the answer to and didn't even really understand. I went into the doctors' room on the ward and closed the door behind me. I jumped as I heard a noise and was relieved to see Ruby emerging from behind the filing cabinet. 'They just never leave you alone, do they?' she said. 'Patients, nurses, doctors, everyone is on your case.'

A few minutes later Supriya burst in. 'If one more person asks me something assuming I know the answer, I'm going to scream.'

'I know how you feel,' Ruby replied, 'but I reckon we're safe in here for a bit.'

And then her pager went off.

Saturday 9 August

Such high hopes for my first weekend. The washing that has piled up while I was on holiday is still looking at me reproachfully. Somewhere in amongst the debris are my shirts for next week, still unwashed from my last clinical attachment while still a medical student. But not having surfaced from my bed until well into the afternoon, and wandering around in a daze for the rest of the day, I still haven't washed them. After all, if you wash them, they only get dirty again and besides, then they need ironing, something which is pretty low down on my priority list. Surely doctors have more important things to worry about than ironing? Like saving people's lives. Although to be honest, I'm beginning to think that ironing has its benefits.

Ruby has spent much of the day in bed too, and is vowing not to get up until she has developed bedsores. How can we all be so tired when we've only done three days in the hospital? This does not bode well.

There is a sound that every junior doctor learns to dread. It's not the sound of screaming children in A&E, or the sound of abusive drunks or even the bark of their consultant on a ward round. It's the short, sharp, shrill sound of their pager. Affectionately called a 'bleep', because that is all it seems to do from dawn until dusk and actually throughout the night as well, it symbolises the fear of the unknown for the wary junior doctor. You tentatively call the number displayed, unsure of exactly what is about to be asked of you; what question you will be expected to know the answer to. It's like a hideous gameshow, but without the prospect of royalties when it's re-run on UKTV Gold.

And this morning I had the unpleasant realisation that despite living some way from the hospital, our pagers can still be reached by the switchboard. This meant that at 4 a.m. this morning I was awakened by the sound of my pager going off, and then screeching in a computerised voice, 'Cardiac arrest, cardiac arrest'. I fumbled around in my bag, in my coat pocket and in my trousers trying to find it, unsuccessfully. My next memory was waking later this morning to find myself huddled up in the foetal position, clutching my pager to my stomach while it made intermittent beeping noises to inform me that I had missed a call. Later it transpired that Ruby's pager had gone off too – there was I thinking I was special.

Obviously the switchboard just can't be bothered to find out exactly who is on call and responsible for running to the scene of every emergency, and who isn't. Lewis was on call over the weekend, and I wondered how he had managed. Had he known what to do when his pager went off? Had he run to the scene, heroically, or hidden in the laundry cupboard while some 'proper doctors' attended? I breathed a sigh of relief to think that it wasn't me having to answer that bleep last night. Then it occurred to me: it's only a matter of time.

Sunday 10 August

Phone call from Mum. Am I eating properly? Have I done my laundry? Am I still smoking? Yes, yes and no, of course not, I replied, whilst sitting there on my bed, eating mango chutney from the jar, looking at the pile of washing heaped on my bedroom floor. Could I tell her if she had cystitis, she wanted to know. I lit up a cigarette and breathed in, deeply, while my mum nattered away on the other end of the phone.

Monday 11 August

Have spent the entire weekend dreading the thought of having to go back to work. It's only a matter of time before someone realises that I'm a fraud. I should never have been a doctor. There is some horrid mistake.

In desperate need of nicotine, Ruby and I snuck out the back of A&E, and hid behind the bins for a crafty cigarette. Of course, you'd think doctors and nurses would know better than to smoke, but as many people know, they're worse than most. I suppose that given the nature of their job, they become a little blasé about death and dying. But I'm realising now that the prime reason is that it's a good excuse to get away from the ward and the lists of jobs that are constantly piling up. And it's also social. Hey, you might die younger, but at least when you do there are plenty of people at your funeral.

So there we were, gently puffing away at our cigarettes, with only the occasional interruption of our pagers going off, when suddenly, out of nowhere, someone spoke from behind us. 'What a disappointment to see two such young people quietly killing themselves.'

We turned round to see a woman in her early fifties, school ma'am-ish in appearance with her hair pulled up into a bun. Ominously she was wearing a white coat. In the olden days, all doctors wore white coats, but then someone realised that they could potentially spread infection between wards, and they got phased out. These days, the only people that continue to wear them are staunch old-school types, doctors on the telly, and the occasional porter. Certainly no normal, self-respecting doctor would wear one.

'Let's hope you can give up before the neurochemical transmitters in your cerebral cortex become irreparably damaged,' the white-coated woman continued.

Ruby and I looked at each other. 'Hmmm, yeah, let's hope so,' Ruby replied, her eyebrows raised.

'Disgusting habit for weak individuals. I'm watching you two,' the woman said, before disappearing as quickly and silently as she had appeared.

'Who was that cow?' asked Ruby.

'I don't know,' I replied. 'But she shouldn't worry. Unless things change, that place,' I said, pointing at the hospital behind us, 'is going to kill us long before smoking does.'

Tuesday 12 August

Finally finish work hours after we were supposed to. No idea what is wrong with any of the patients on the ward. Not even sure how to go about prescribing paracetamol, which proved pretty embarrassing. The plan had been to read my surgery handbook this evening, but far too tired. Ruby asleep in the bath. Flora, my other housemate who has just started work in another hospital down the road from Ruby and me, has the same feeling of being absolutely out of her depth.

Am going to bed now, as tomorrow have the gut-wrenchingly scary prospect of being on call. A bleep, no hope of sleep and as many sick people as they care to throw at me. What a prospect.

Wednesday 13 August

'You need to come and see Mr Clarke. I'm really worried about him. He's getting worse.'

Silence. I blink. The nurse on the other end of the telephone isn't giving me any slack. 'Er ... hmm. What do you want me to do?' I eventually whimper.

'I don't know, you're the doctor. But you'd better do something and quickly.'

It's a little after midnight, and I've already been working since eight o'clock this morning. This is the sort of call I've been dreading. At this point I have an almost overwhelming desire to cry, but seeing this is my first on-call, I decide it's probably a good idea to reserve that one for a later date. I arrive on the ward. Only the lights on the nurses' station are on, and there are several nurses sifting around writing notes. 'It's OK, the doctor's arrived,' I hear one of them say. My spirits lift but I turn around only to realise that they mean me. Oh dear.

Mr Clarke has got terminal cancer and, I learn from the nurse, is really just waiting to die. He's in his late eighties. His eyes are sunken and his face haggard. He's in lots of pain, is having difficulty breathing and, to top it all off, the nurses think he might have had a heart attack.

'Hello, Mr Clarke, it's the doctor, what's the problem?' I ask, not knowing what else to say. I pray that he'll make a miraculous recovery as I stand there, but instead his breathing appears to be getting worse.

He looks up at me and in a hoarse whisper croaks, 'Help me, doctor. Please.'

My mind goes blank. I have no idea how to help him.

It was for the Mr Clarkes of the world that I became a doctor. I naively thought that after doing a medical degree I'd be qualified to help people, ease their suffering. But as I stare at Mr Clarke all I can think is why does he have to be dying during my shift? Couldn't he have waited?

In medical school we were taught how the body works and how it goes wrong, and then we learned the theory of how to fix it. What no one explained to us is that it's all very well knowing the minutiae of obscure diseases that affect only a handful of people, but that it will be of no use to you when you start work. What you really need to know is the routine stuff: how to put in a catheter, order an ECG, prescribe medication or fill out a blood form, precisely the things that medical school doesn't teach you. I had thought, erroneously, that these gaps in my knowledge would be filled in before I started work but no one has even told me what I'm supposed to be doing, where I am supposed to be, or, most importantly, how to turn my bleep off. I haven't even had a proper conversation with my consultant yet. You would imagine that you'd be eased into starting work as a doctor – some guidance as you performed procedures you had never done before, perhaps even a little course on common mistakes that kill patients. But oh no, that would be too simple. I don't even know how to use the computers yet, which means I can't order blood tests. As I stand on the ward, Mr Clarke and his problems are not my priority. All I'm worried about is not making a mistake; not getting in trouble. It wasn't supposed to be like this.

What should I do first? I open his notes

and my eyes rest on the last entry: 'Contact on-call palliative care team on bleep 0440 if patient deteriorates.' I call the number and with a beam on my face hand over Mr Clarke's care to the doctor on the other end of the telephone. Pass the patient, brilliant. Crisis averted.

A few hours later, just as I finally get into bed in the on-call room, my pager goes off again. I pick up the phone by my side and it's the nurse letting me know that Mr Clarke has died and the palliative care team have just left the ward. 'They've left you the death certificate to write,' says the voice at the other end of the telephone.

'Oh, erm, right. How do I do that?' I ask, trying to remember the lecture we had only a few days ago from the coroner.

'I don't know,' comes the reply. 'You're the doctor.'

Thursday 14 August

I've just survived what must be the most petrifying experience on earth. I've just completed a night on call. All on my own. Well, that's not entirely true. At about midnight, just before I got the call about Mr Clark, Sad Sack Sue, the registrar on call with me, went to sleep. 'Give me a bleep if you run into trouble,' she moped as she

32

made her way to her on-call room. 'But I don't want you waking me up for any crud, you hear?'

I'm not one hundred per cent sure I'm well versed in what constitutes 'crud' and what doesn't. Heart attack: does that count as crud? Haemorrhaging one's entire body volume of blood out of one's mouth, that doesn't count as crud, surely? That counts as an emergency, and one that it is plain I am not competent enough to deal with. Although I'm becoming increasingly curious as to exactly what I am competent to do. Thankfully, aside from Mr Clark, last night was not too bad. Lots of rewriting of prescription charts, which I got the hang of pretty easily as it's really just copying.

And I didn't have to call out Sad Sack, not once. This morning, despite the fact that she had, by my reckoning, a good six hours' sleep, she still looked like she'd been up all night trekking Kilimanjaro. I, on the other hand, bounced on to the ward after only two broken hours – yes, that's right, a measly two – of sleep, in perfect time for the post-on-call ward round, feeling in a celebratory mood. All the team filed in, barely even acknowledging me.

'Let's start,' murmured Mr Butterworth to no one in particular and set off, eagerly followed by Daniel dressed in a smart shirt and tie combo.

I'd just got the notes trolley and started to push it towards the first patient when Sad Sack looked at me. 'Where are the coffees?' she said.

'The what?' I asked.

'The coffee. You're supposed to get coffees before the ward round,' she snapped.

'Ooh, and a Danish pastry if there's one going,' interjected Mr Butterworth, showing more animation in those few words than I'd seen from him during the entire week.

'Erm, I didn't know,' I replied.

Daniel rolled his eyes. 'Can't you get anything right?' Sad Sack huffed under her breath, before heading off to the canteen.

Well, I can do that – buy coffee and pastries. I'm good at that. I'll see if I can get away with only supplying refreshments for the next year. Like one of those people that brings on oranges in football games at half-time, only very well qualified.

Friday 15 August

Suddenly, weekends have taken on a whole new meaning. Being employed, as opposed to being a student, means that all those jobs that there is no time to do during the week have to get crammed into Saturday or Sunday. This would be fine if it wasn't for the fact that everyone else in the entire world is also trying to do the same. I now understand why there are those soul-crushingly long queues round the North Circular to try and get into IKEA – it's not that there's a sudden urge that has taken people to go, en masse, to buy scatter-cushions and unfinished pine, it's just the simple logistic of the weekend being the only time anyone working can get stuff done.

Many things are becoming clear to me, that as a student I had no knowledge of. Dry-cleaners, for example, are expensive, and never open when you want them to be. Currently they are babysitting four pairs of trousers for me, which I have yet to find the time to retrieve. Twice this week I have attempted to get them, and twice I've left work too late to get to the shop on time.

Ruby is having the same problem. She told me that if something drastic doesn't happen on the organisation front for her, she's going to have to turn up to work on Monday wearing items of clothing fished out of the charity clothing-bin at the end of the road.

Monday 18 August

It's occurred to me that we rarely see Daniel, the SHO. Despite only being a few years more senior than us, he manages to avoid any work on the wards and instead scampers off to get 'vital experience' in the operating theatre. This is fine by me, as I'd rather chew my own face off than have to spend time digging about elbow-deep in somebody's abdomen. In addition to the four consultant surgeons, there are two other visiting consultants, Mr Ritchie and Mr Rushmore. As a pair they bear more than a passing resemblance to vampires. They are both worryingly pale and gaunt. Mr Rushmore is perhaps two or three inches taller than Mr Ritchie, but except for the difference in height, they look practically the same. In fact, as I've never seen them together, I suspect that there is only one of them, and that he created the other persona so that he can get double the salary. The evidence: just as one enters the room, the other has just left it; they are never in the same meeting together and both have a peculiar habit of staring into the middle distance when addressing you, as if they're on another planet.

They're vascular surgeons – veins and arteries and things like that to normal people – so they are always off either performing varicose veins operations in their private clinics or trying to stem the flow of blood pouring out of some poor person when something bursts.

Daniel wants to go into this branch of surgery, so he follows them round like a lost puppy, dribbling and drooling. This morning, looking for the secretaries' office, I peered through the window in one of the operating theatre doors, only to see a fine jet of red liquid shoot up into the air and land several feet away. 'Damn, we've got a squirter here,' said Mr. Ritchie as Daniel stood there nodding. I went pale and had to leave, sharpish.

Having to deal with torrents of blood under high pressure is probably why, if you look closely, Mssrs Ritchie and Rushmore always have a few specks of blood somewhere on their person: Either that or it's evidence of their latest victim. It may just be coincidence, but people who have voluntarily gone into such a gory speciality like that can't be normal, can they? I'm going to look carefully next time I'm in the dinner queue behind Daniel to see if there is any evidence of puncture wounds on his neck. And I'm going to have double helpings of garlic bread, just in case.

Tuesday 19 August

My pager never seems to stop going off. Whatever anyone in the hospital's problem is, they page me, and then it becomes my problem. It's difficult to know what the most frustrating thing that we're bleeped for is, but certainly high on the list has to be when the nurses bleep you when you've only just left their ward. 'Can you come and write up some paracetamol for bed 15, Doctor?' comes the disembodied voice at the other end of the phone.

'But I've only just come from your ward,' which is typically met with the nurse merely repeating the request.

Other things that feature high on the list of grievances is when they don't tell you which ward they're calling from, or which patient they are referring to, as if we are somehow telepathically communicating. If that's the case, why bother paging in the first place? The list of grievances goes on and on.

Today I got a page from Lewis. Ruby was on call last night and had had a particularly bad time of it with no sleep, and so she had sneaked off home to bed early, leaving Lewis to fend for himself. 'Max, you've got to help me,' came Lewis's plea at the other end of the phone when I answered my pager.

'Why, what's happened?' I asked, wondering what on earth I'd be able to do about anything that might have gone wrong, especially seeing that Lewis had habitually come top in exams at medical school.

'Someone's died,' came the voice at the other end of the phone.

This puzzled me somewhat. 'Were they supposed to?' I asked. I felt a bit strange after I'd said it, but it's true that there are patients that you expect to die, and there are those that you don't.

'I've got to certify them dead. I mean, they're properly dead. I've never seen a dead body before, except the cadavers at medical school. I've never seen anything that just, you know, died,' he pleaded. 'I don't know what to do. Max, you've done this already, will you come and help me?'

I remembered how horrid it was when I had to certify Mr Clarke. So despite the fact that it was long past going-home time, I met Lewis outside the side room where the body of his patient had been moved to. 'You go in first,' he said, pushing me towards the door. I entered the room and we both stood in respectful silence for a few minutes. Mrs Lipton's body was laid out flat on the bed, her hair gently framing her lifeless face. The nurses had already been and cleaned up the body, and the sheets were pulled up to her chin.

I could see Lewis out of the corner of my eye. Despite him being fifteen stone and a hardened rugby player, I noticed how shaken he looked as his hands softly straightened the bed clothes at the foot of the bed. 'Do you ever think about death?' he asked.

'Sometimes,' I replied.

'It's funny to think that she's not in there any more, isn't it?' Lewis said, and then added, 'Do you believe in God?'

'No,' I replied, feeling that now perhaps was not the time to get into a long theological discussion.

'I go to church, but then I'm not sure. It all seems so convenient, doesn't it?' he continued, undeterred.

'I thought you were a Christian. You were one at medical school, weren't you?' I asked.

I was never particularly friendly with Lewis at medical school, but remembered him once at a Freshers' fair, darting between the Lesbian, Bisexual and Gay Society table, the Christian Fellowship stand and the Rugby Society stall with impressive ease, which made me respect him for not falling into the usual middle-class, dad's-a-doctor category that seems to make up the bulk of people training in medicine. It always struck me that since being a doctor was all about dealing with the general public, who obviously come from all walks of life, the medical profession should reflect this. And while there was a mix of people studying medicine, they were still from a relatively rarefied background. But I suppose six years at university, with fees, no grant and the cost of living to be found, is a privilege that few can afford.

'I suppose I am a Christian, but medical school, and now all this, it makes you think, doesn't it?' says Lewis.

I nod. While other people my age are staring at computer screens or sitting in meetings, here we are looking death in the face and trying to find answers to some of the hardest questions ever asked. I'm not sure if that's a good thing or not.

'I really liked her,' said Lewis. 'She used to be a bus conductor, on a route that went right by my uncle's house. She'd retired before I was even born, of course, but it's a funny coincidence, isn't it?'

And for a few moments we stood quietly, both thinking and not talking. A lump came into my throat. Mrs Lipton didn't die in pain, she lived a good life and had her family round her when she died, but it was still acutely sad, and a lot to grapple with for two junior doctors after only two weeks of work. I glanced at Lewis to see tears in his eyes. I pretended not to notice.

Between us we go through the necessary tests to ensure that she is well and truly dead. Our task done, we leave the room, nodding respectfully at the family waiting outside, not sure what to do or say to them, and leave the ward. 'God, imagine dying somewhere like here,' Lewis said, staring up at the strip lighting and peeling paintwork as we walked down the corridor.

'Imagine having to spend every waking moment of your life somewhere like here,' I replied.

'Fair point,' laughed Lewis, and we caught the bus home.

Wednesday 20 August

On call again today. This means that as well as covering the wards, I am also working in A&E, seeing all the referrals that the casualty doctors think are surgical. It's been scarily quiet for the beginning of the shift, so I had great, irony-free fun watching *Casualty* on TV. They make it look so easy, don't they? There are no doctors wandering around asking where the blood forms are, or how to request an urgent chest X-ray. The computers never seem to break, telephones constantly ring in the background, and yet when there's a dramatic moment, they all seem to silence themselves.

Thursday 21 August

Ward rounds are like trench warfare and it's the junior doctors in the firing line. Every morning Sad Sack leads the troops into battle, whizzing round the patients at breakneck speed, begrudgingly telling us the jobs that need doing that day, which we frantically scribble down on a 'jobs list', whilst writing in the notes, drawing the curtains

42

round the patient, moving tables and chairs and pushing the trolley.

Daniel doesn't deign to help, but stands smirking at our general ineptitude, like an older brother watching his younger siblings getting told off. There's medications to be prescribed on the drug charts, there's wounds to be redressed, samples to be sent. We are supposed to be the lubricant that makes the whole machine run smoothly, although more often than not I suspect we're the spanner in the works. When someone's muttering things you can only half hear and half understand, while a patient is quietly sobbing and the notes trolley is veering off down the ward with a mind of its own, it becomes obvious why this is the case.

Twice a week Mr Butterworth and Mr Price do their ward rounds, invariably while some disaster is taking place. During these ward rounds, even the registrar looks scared, because then they suddenly come into the firing line and the clinical decisions that they have been making about the patients all week come under close scrutiny. While she's far from a bag of sunbeams, during these ward rounds I get a feeling of protectiveness for Sad Sack. The consultants, who have been heard to say she should be at home having babies, either give her a tough time or ignore her point-blank.

This can't be easy for Sad Sack, given that she also has to spend the majority of each day in the operating theatre with them, under their critical eye. The consultants also make an appearance after they've been on call, to do the post-on-call ward round. It's strange to think that consultants are on call as well, although, like a general commanding the troops from well behind the battle lines, they prefer to keep their distance from the action. The registrar on call is supposed to do what operations are required as emergencies, but the consultant comes out if things are getting tricky. I've yet to have the pleasure of seeing Mr Butterworth, shuffling into the hospital in his slippers, still sipping his cocoa from a beaker. Hopefully I never will.

So today's post-on-call ward round was fairly hideous. In the cold light of day, the tiny, stupid mistakes made during the night seem all too obvious. Why didn't I order this blood test? Why did I order that one? Where are the X-rays for this patient? Did I even remember to order them? In theory it's supposed to be a team effort, with the registrar, the SHO and the junior doctor who have been on call the previous night supporting each other. In reality, the consultant asks a question, looking at the registrar, who then turns and looks at the SHO, who then turns and looks at the junior doctor, who then looks at their shoes. The only thing that keeps you going is the thought that once it's been endured, there are days before the next one.

Sunday 24 August

On call again tomorrow. Just as you recover from the last assault, another one comes along. Flora is on call this weekend. The future landscape of my friendships is now becoming clear: whenever I have the weekend off, everyone is either working or recovering from working, and when I'm working, they're off. It's impossible to coordinate seeing each other, which only leaves pottering around the flat trying to remember what it was like when you had a life.

Having finally decided to take action regarding the pile of washing on the floor, which had so grown in size as to require its own postal code, the washing machine appeared to have packed up. Things were getting to the stage were I was seriously considering how I could turn the flock-patterned curtains into suitable attire for the Monday ward round. Ruby, having awoken from a fourteen-hour slumber (at one stage I thought it might be a coma) was near apoplexy. 'Stupid thing,' she screamed, kicking it.

Waited in all day Saturday for the repair

man to arrive, only to get a call at 5 p.m. saying that he'd have to reschedule for later in the week, adding that he worked between 9 a.m. and 5 p.m.

'We all work during the week,' I explained.

'Can't you take a day off?' he asked.

I bit back from explaining that we didn't get time to go to the toilet, let alone time off to let the washing-machine repair man in.

While I was on the phone, Ruby resorted to trying to rock the machine back and forth. Suddenly, the thing started to whir and whoosh, and sprung into life.

'Ruby, you genius,' I said, hanging up on the repair man. 'How did you do that?'

'No idea,' she replied, watching the clothes swoosh round.

If things get too much for her as a junior doctor, perhaps she could carve out a career in fixing washing machines. It's bound to be better paid, and the hours aren't too bad.

Monday 25 August

Mrs Kerrigan can't sleep. It's a shame that it's taken her until 3 a.m. to realise this, and even more of a shame that it's me that the nurses have decided to disturb in order to prescribe her a sleeping pill. The nurses suspect she just wants a chat. I've never prescribed sleeping pills, but the novelty of doing something for the first time wore off some weeks ago.

I go and see Mrs Kerrigan, who's sat bolt upright in bed, reading yesterday's paper. Perhaps she'll have a favourite tablet, which will save me looking through the books.

'Oh, I don't mind, Doctor, whichever one you think is best,' she replies to my question.

'Which ones do you normally take?' I ask, desperate for her just to give me a name so I can write it on her drug chart and go and get some sleep before the 7 a.m. ward round.

'Well, I don't usually have problems sleeping, although I did once when we were moving house, which was very stressful. Have you ever had to move house?'

Mrs Kerrigan is obviously very lonely; after all, she goes on to tell me, her husband died twelve years ago after forty years of marriage and they'd never had children and it isn't easy cooking for one and did I think Carol Vorderman was really that clever and so on and so on.

I sit down on the side of her bed. This is the first time I've had time to sit down in the past fifteen hours, and my feet ache terribly, so I slip off my shoes without Mrs Kerrigan noticing. I've got a feeling I may be here for some time.

My pager goes off and jolts me back into

the real world. I think I've just dozed off in front of Mrs Kerrigan. Did I just dribble down my tie? She doesn't appear to have noticed and is still talking verbosely about meals for one. I'm rather confused about where Carol Vorderman fits into all this. 'I am sorry, I'm just going to have to answer that.'

Phew, that was a lucky escape: a loquacious insomniac with an encyclopaedic knowledge of ready meals – a junior doctor's nightmare come true. I answer my pager. The nurse on the other end of the phone sounds worried. She thinks a patient on her ward has just gone into kidney failure, as he hasn't passed any urine all night. It's an emergency.

Right, don't panic, I tell myself – which makes me panic immediately. I run in the vague direction of the ward where the patient in kidney failure is, and then run back to the ward I came from to pick up my shoes. This never happens on *ER*. Just as I arrive on the ward, my pager goes off again. It's another patient on the other side of the hospital who's got a high potassium level. It's another emergency. I freeze. In the cool, calm atmosphere of medical school we are taught how to deal with emergencies and like good students we memorise the protocol. But what someone omitted to tell us is which emergencies are more of an emergency than others. High potassium causes your heart to stop – that's a bad thing. But then again, kidney failure, that sounds bad too. I'm now very much awake. I run on to one ward, quickly glance at some of the patient's charts and fumble for a course of action. Then I turn on my heels and head to the other ward, the sound of my footsteps echoing down the dingy corridors as I run. I go to and fro in this fashion for some time, getting very little done, until, getting more and more exhausted and seeing that the patients don't appear to be getting any worse, I start to become suspicious. A nurse has just come back from her break. 'Oh, no, sorry, he's not in kidney failure, his urine output is quite good. I just forgot to write it down this evening in his notes.'

She laughs but as I stand there panting with a pile of notes slipping out of my hands, my tie half undone and my shirt un-tucked, I find it hard to see the funny side. And then my pager goes off again. 'Sorry, it's ward 6 here, just to let you know that the potassium levels were actually old ones that had been misfiled in the notes. The levels were taken yesterday and they were normal. Sorry about that.'

On my way back to bed I remember Mrs Kerrigan and pop into her ward. 'Don't worry about her, Max,' one of the nurses says. 'She fell asleep almost as soon as you left.'

I peer over to her bed, and in the dark I can just make out the outline of Mrs Kerrigan, sat bolt upright, but with her head slouched to one side, snoring. I walk out into the dawn and make my way to the doctors' mess. There's only an hour or so before I'm due to start my ward round, so there's no point in sleeping now. Instead, I sit on my own, eat a microwave meal and watch a re-run of *Countdown*.

Wednesday 27 August

Ruby is in trouble. Not with Housewives' Favourite, in whose eyes she can do no wrong and who I suspect has earmarked her as his next sexual conquest, having – according to hospital gossip – already worked his way steadily through all the female members of staff who are continent and with their full complement of teeth. No, she's in trouble with Mr Grant. Lewis was late for a ward round this morning, and while normally the consultants appear oblivious to our presence, let alone show any interest in us, halfway round the ward he turned to Ruby and, in his booming voice, bellowed, 'Where's the darky?'

'The darky what?' asked Ruby, genuinely confused as to what he meant.

Supriya and I, who were waiting for Sad

Sack to finish on the phone, stood motion-less by the nurses' station, listening.

'The black one, you know, the other one that you work with. Gone back up his tree, has he?' he continued, oblivious to the patients and Ruby's open mouth. Surgeons have a bit of a reputation for being reactionary and rude. Mr Grant, who has obviously graduated from the Ron Atkinson school of political correctness, however, is in a league of his own.

Ruby, never one to turn down the opportunity for a fight, didn't let this go. 'What did you say?' she asked, squaring herself up to him.

'Don't make me repeat myself. The other one. There are two of you. Where's the other one?'

'Do you mean Lewis? Your house officer?' asked Ruby, rallying for a fight.

'Whatever his name is, why isn't he here?' replied Mr Grant.

At this point most people hoping, as Ruby is, for a career in surgery would have let things lie. 'You can't call him a "darky". That's racist. It's disgraceful,' she said, ignoring the squeals from the rest of her team for her to leave well alone.

'It would be wise for you to remember your position, my dear,' snarled Mr Grant.

'I'm not your dear, and it's racist to call people "darky". How would you like it if

51

people said "where's that fat ugly spotty one?" when they wanted to know where you were?'

Mr Grant turned on his heel and went to the next patient. 'And if you listen carefully,' said Clive, Ruby's registrar, as they followed behind with the notes trolley, 'you can hear the sound of Ruby's surgical career going down the drain.'

But Ruby doesn't care. And that's why she's my friend.

Thursday 28 August

Another visit from the scary white-coated tobacco fascist again today. I was innocently having a cigarette with some of the nurses before heading back to A&E where I was on call *again*. They'd headed back in while I stayed for another.

'So I see you still haven't found the strength to stop killing yourself, then?' came an eerily thin voice.

I turned round, only to find the tobacco fascist standing directly behind me. I started. 'Oh, you gave me a shock,' I said.

'Not nearly as much of a shock as when you realise you've given yourself lung cancer and are facing a long and painful death,' came her upbeat reply.

Without Ruby I didn't feel so confident.

'Erm, well, I'm planning to give up, just as soon as I finish my first year,' I said in an attempt to get her to leave me alone.

Her nostrils flared. 'Well, I shall be watching you, and that other one that you come out here to kill yourself with,' she continued.

'Ruby, her name's Ruby,' I blurted, in a moment of Orwellian-style treachery. I didn't think it wise to mention the fact that actually it had been I that had first introduced Ruby to cigarettes in our first year of university.

'I trust that I won't be seeing you again out here,' she replied.

I exhaled, and as the smoke dissipated, she was gone.

Friday 29 August

The combination of being gut-wrenchingly tired and constantly worried that you have, at worst inadvertently killed one of your patients, or at best not done a job that means the whole of the next day's surgery list is cancelled, does take its toll. You'd think that your mind would be grateful for the little rest it gets. But rather than indulging in some good old-fashioned deep sleep, I've noticed a worrying trend, and it's one that all the other junior doctors at work have noticed too. Every night I have a dream

53

about work. It's getting out of control. Sleep time is the only time at the moment that isn't taken up with work, so why does my brain see fit to allow work to infiltrate even this area of my life? I dream of running down endless corridors, plagued by the sound of my pager constantly going off, the faces of nurses looming at me asking me things I don't know and don't understand.

Then I wake up to find it was only a dream, until I go back to work where I realise it's a waking nightmare.

Saturday 30 August

My first weekend on call. Saturdays are horrid places in hospitals. You give up your weekend so that everyone else can go out and enjoy themselves and arrive in A&E to get stitched up when it spirals out of control. Thankfully, as a surgical junior doctor, I don't have to come into too much contact with the brawling brainless who make up the majority of people in A&E over the weekend evenings. But picking your way through the barrage of walking wounded, most of which is entirely self-, or rather alcohol-inflicted, is not that easy. The staff in A&E are resilient to pretty much anything. They've seen it all, heard it all, been through it all at some time or another. I'm sure that if there is a nuclear

Armageddon, it would only be cockroaches and A&E staff who would survive.

Walking past a man lying on a bed, surrounded by police, while a nurse took his details, I couldn't contain my horror and amazement. The nurse doesn't seem in the least bit fazed by what the man looks like and is busy chatting to one of the policemen.

'Oi, you a doctor?' the patient asked as I stared at him.

'Erm, yes,' I replied tentatively.

I continued to stare at him. Sticking out of his head, at right angles to his face, was what looked like a short broom handle. A thin trickle of blood had made its way down his temple and on to his cheek, before drying up.

'Can you take this?' he asked. I stared. 'Oh, don't worry, it don't 'urt,' he said. Presumably it had dawned on him that I was finding it hard to pay attention to what he was saying as I was transfixed by the pole sticking out of his head. 'It don't go right into my brain. 'E snapped it in half before 'e lunged at me wiv it. It's stuck in my skull, 'pparently,' he explained.

'Oh, I see,' I replied, convinced that I'd slipped into an episode of *M*A*S*H*. I looked down at what he was trying to hand to me.

'Take this an' take a photo would ya?' he asked, handing me a mobile phone. 'My mates are never gonna believe what this looks like.'

And of course he was right, so I obliged.

Sunday 31 August

End of the first month and total body count remains at zero. Certainly six years at medical school have paid off, Admittedly, total amount of people that I have heroically saved, *Holby City*-style, also remains at zero. You win some you lose some, I suppose.

SEPTEMBER

Monday 1 September

It seems unbelievable that we have been working for nigh on a month already and things don't appear to be getting any better.

The irony is that the actual amount of medicine required to work as a junior doctor is startlingly small. All the main decisions are made by the consultant or registrar. All that is required of the junior doctor is that the show runs smoothly. Each of my consultants operates once a week. We have to ensure that nothing untoward happens to the patients before they have their operation, that all the required tests are done, the results are in the notes and that after the operation, they don't get sick, This should be relatively easy, shouldn't it? Someone tells you what to do, and you do it. Hardly rocket science. Or even brain surgery. But the unknown variable in this equation, the spanner in the works, is that while we make every effort to get the jobs done, there always appears to be some malevolent force at work which is hell-bent on ensuring our failure.

Take X-rays, for example. Mr Price, who is

a breast surgeon, won't operate unless he has personally seen the report from the radiologist saying that the chest X-ray of the woman who is having the breast operation is clear. A week or so before the operation takes place, the woman attends one of the pre-op clinics, run by one of the junior doctors. We personally order the chest X-ray, give the woman the card, and take her along to the X-ray department. At the end of the day, a neat pile of X-rays is carefully placed inside the radiologists' pigeon hole for reporting ... and they then promptly disappear, no one knows where. I suspect that there is a room somewhere with a mountain of X-ray films, neatly placed in envelopes, and labelled with Post-it notes saying, 'Urgent: please report'. If there isn't, I fail to see where they are all going. And believe me, I've spent enough time trying to find out.

Every week it's the same. The day before Mr Price's operating list there is a desperate scramble to find the X-rays and reports for the next day. We have an immediate success rate of usually one, possibly two. Which still leaves four or five reports missing. This is when years of medical school go out of the window, and years of watching afternoon reruns of *Columbo* come into their own. The radiologist, when they are eventually tracked down, will be convinced that they have no knowledge of what you are talking about.

This is obviously not true, because every single week so far it has been clear as day that the radiologist was the last person to clap eyes on the damn things. Today, we had three missing. One was found under the radiologist's desk. 'Well, I didn't put it there,' he said indignantly when confronted, as if I had deliberately hidden it there. This is the golden rule of medicine: if someone is senior to you, they are right. Always.

The third one was located by Maxine. Now exactly what Maxine is supposed to do all day is a mystery. But what she actually does is find X-rays. And as she's been working in the hospital for over twenty years, she's very good at it. 'Have you tried behind the radiator?' she'll ask, as if this were the normal place for diagnostic images to be filed. 'If Dr Palache had it for reporting, that's where it will be. They're always dropping down there in his office.' It evidently takes years of experience to build up that sort of knowledge. It has been rumoured that her actual job is to file away the X-rays once they have been finished with and the patient has been sent home. But every time I see her she's on her knees, covered in dust, stretching and contorting herself behind a filing cabinet in search of one of the lost X-rays.

Apparently she always wanted to be an archaeologist, and it's obvious that where that profession has lost out, the NHS has gained. All she needs is the name and what sort of X-ray it was, and if it's been through her hands, she'll remember it. 'Oh, now I think he had a wrist a couple of months ago, but I haven't seen his pelvis,' she said on my first encounter when I asked about a patient's X-ray that had gone walkabout. But by this afternoon, even Maxine was failing to produce the goods on the final X-ray. After turning the entire radiology department upside-down, I was about to admit defeat.

At which point Dr Palache, tall and slim, with a slightly pinched nose on which sat a pair of designer glasses, walked past with a pile of reports in his hand. We'd already quizzed him. We were sure he'd done the report, but no one could prove it.

'You – no, of course not – but, you wouldn't have happened, by any chance, to have seen the chest X-ray for Mr Weston? Would you, Dr Palache?' Maxine asked and then, in true *Columbo* style, said before be could answer, 'No, of course not, how silly of me.' She was just about to sit back down and resume her work when she looked up. 'Oh, Dr Palache, sorry to bother you again, I was just wondering if you had the keys to the main reporting room?' He felt in his pockets. 'Let me take those from you,' Maxine said.

It was poetry in motion. Before he could do anything, she'd taken the pile of X-rays out of his hand and as he looked for the keys in his pocket, she quickly rifled through the envelopes. 'Found it!' she exclaimed.

Dr Palache had indeed had it last. In fact, he had been carrying it around with him all day. 'Oh, that. Yes, I've had it for reporting. Been a bit behind. Why didn't you say that was the one you wanted?' he said, embarrassed.

'We did say, we've been asking you all day,' I said. He looked at me.

'Erm, perhaps I wasn't clear,' I said. 'Sorry. Well, now that it's found, I wonder if you'd be kind enough to report it for me now, urgently, so I can go and get it typed up for tomorrow's theatre list?' I said, remembering the golden rule, and that I was now having to ask him for a favour, even if it was his fault I was put in the situation in the first place.

He huffed and puffed for a token period of time, just long enough for me to start panicking again, before he agreed.

'Next time you're looking for an X-ray,' said Maxine, as I went to follow Dr Palache into the reporting room, 'there's one more place you might want to try because I might have put it there.'

'Oh yes?' I said, innocently.

'It involves him and a very tightly rolled X-ray film, and I'd recommend that you wear gloves,' and she laughed.

Tuesday 2 September

Met Ruby at the back of A&E for a crafty cigarette. She's having a shocker of a time with her consultant, Mr Grant. Her comments last week about his racism haven't been forgotten. It appears that he's going out of his way to ensure that things are as difficult as possible for her. He completely ignores her on the ward round, and refuses to acknowledge her existence when talking to the team. Given that he evidently doesn't like Lewis either, whether because he's black, gay or friends with Ruby, the team atmosphere is altogether somewhat strained.

As we leave, Ruby turns to me. 'What's the difference between Mr Grant and a sperm?' she asks.

'What are you talking about?' I reply, puzzled.

'A sperm has a one-in-a-million chance of becoming a human being,' she laughs, and walks off.

Wednesday 3 September

Mrs Crook in admin is, once again, having a crisis. We haven't been paid. Now, this clearly is cause for concern for the doctors involved. After all, we are the ones that have sweated blood for the past month. Unsure exactly who to ask about this administrative error, Lewis thought a good first point of contact should be the administration department. Not an earth-shattering conclusion, it must be said. The first hurdle though is that this means trying to have a reasonable, rational conversation with Mrs Crook, when even the slightest problem sends her into a blind panic.

But while Lewis was, in theory, correct in his assumption that Mrs Crook should be in charge of our pay slips, or at least have some dealings with them, it transpires that things aren't that simple. Trudy is in charge of them. Who the hell is Trudy? we all asked. Mr Butterworth's secretary, it transpires. Baffled as to why a surgeon's secretary would be in charge of paying us, I went to her office this morning to see if she could shed any light.

Trudy, in complete contrast to Mr Butterworth, is lovely. She is in her forties with dyed blonde hair in a bob, and wears very short skirts with black tights and black knee-high boots. She's mutton dressed as lamb, but in a similar way to how mutton must have been viewed in the Second World War, we're grateful for whatever we can get, and you could do a lot worse. 'He's a prick, isn't he?' she said when I mentioned Mr Butterworth.

I'm not sure how to respond to this one;

but I ended up asking, 'How do you manage to work with him?'

'Well, you get used to it, and besides, when you get to my age you realise that most bosses are tossers, and at least Mr Butterworth is so uncomfortable talking to people I'm pretty much left to my own devices here.' She got up and I noticed that in the corner of her office was a fridge, with a tea-towel neatly placed on top, a kettle and mugs. She took one of the mugs and rooted in her handbag for a teabag. 'You can't trust the cleaners here, they'd nick anything that wasn't nailed down. Whole box of tea they had off me when I first came here. I tell you, only fell for that once. Now I keep everything in my bag.' She produced a carton of milk. 'Want one?' she said over her shoulder as she poured the boiling water.

'I can't, I've got to get back to the ward. I came to find out about our pay.'

'Oh,' she exclaimed, I presumed at the mention of pay, but I was wrong. 'Of course you can stay for tea. There's always time for tea. That's what I always say. You can't come in here and not have a cup of tea.'

It's pointless to resist, so I sit down and have a cup of tea. I realise that not only is this is the first time I've sat down all day, but the first time since starting work a month ago that I've had a cup of tea at the hospital. Usually there's not time for the kettle to boil

64

before my pager goes off. And on cue, there's my pager. I scramble for the phone in the usual panic. But Trudy picks up the phone instead.

'Yes, it's Mr Butterworth's secretary here ... yes ... Dr Pemberton's in a meeting at the moment ... no, I can't disturb him. OK, thank you,' and she hangs up.

'Some nurse wanting you to write something up on a chart. She said she'll get another doctor to do it.'

I sit back in the chair. I could get used to this.

Saturday 6 September

Ruby is thinking of applying to Social Services for a home help. We're floundering. There is no food in the cupboards. When we leave for work in the morning, the shops are not open yet, and by the time we get home, they are all shut. We are currently living on condiments, because that's all we've got in the fridge.

Mayonnaise can be very filling when eaten in suitable quantities. But we can't go on much longer like this. Surely we qualify for a UN food parcel drop sometime soon?

Sunday 7 September

On call again. Another weekend ruined by the ailing masses. But I'm actually getting quite used to not having a life. After all, I'd only be out having fun and spending money, so it's a great way to save. I'm sure this is why being a doctor has the reputation for being well paid. It isn't actually that good when you consider the amount of hours we do, but because we never get the time to spend it, it just sits in our bank accounts until we become consultants. At which point it's used to fund acrimonious divorces from spouses that are fed up with never seeing you.

But today wasn't too bad – quite a bit of sitting round in the doctors' mess watching MTV and eating takeaways with only the occasional call from A&E to see a patient. Sundays are an interesting day in A&E. Now, while statistics was never my strong point, it would seem to me that ailments are relatively arbitrary. No one can pick the day that they have a heart attack or burst appendix, can they? In which case, Sundays in A&E should see around one seventh of the total amount of cases in any one week. This is absolutely not the case. It seems that as God rested on the seventh day, disease follows suit. It's so noticeable that we don't start the morning ward round until 9 a.m., so we can have an extra hour in bed. Perhaps the reason for this is that people who would otherwise be stricken down with sickness are in church repenting for their sins and so are given a second chance by divine intervention. Either way, it makes you think.

Monday 8 September

Mrs Sankaraja's blood pressure is dropping rapidly and she hasn't passed urine for several hours. Her feet have swollen and it looks like her heart is failing. Supriya and I look at each other, bemused. The nurses look at us expectantly. While Supriya leafs through her pocket textbook to see what we should do, I take affirmative action and seek senior assistance.

Not too senior, of course; I don't want to get shouted at. Instead I try and find Daniel. He is, after all, supposed to help us instead of just ingratiating himself to the consultants. I page him a few times but he doesn't respond. Ruby, who is busy in the doctors' office, says she thinks he's assisting Housewives' Favourite in theatre this morning. I leave the ward and walk down the corridor to the operating theatres.

Through a little glass window I can see Daniel and Housewives' Favourite in surgical scrubs, bending over a patient in the anaesthetic room. I'm not sure if I should enter this room without having scrubbed up myself, but since the anaesthetist is talking on a mobile phone in the corner, I presume it's not supposed to be that sterile. I enter the bright room with its strange smells and gentle white noise of whirring machines.

Housewives' Favourite looks up but doesn't say hello, while Daniel glares at me. I venture further into the room and ask Daniel what we should do. He grudgingly tells me a few tests we should do and that he'll be along later.

Housewives' Favourite pulls back the anaesthetised patient's gown to reveal her breasts. 'Look at them,' he exclaims.

Daniel titters like a naughty schoolboy.

'Imagine if she walks into A&E, eh? Prime candidate for a TUBE,' Housewives' Favourite says.

Daniel turns to me. 'You know what TUBE means, don't you, Max?'

I shake my head. 'Ah, I don't know what they teach them at medical school these days,' he laughs.

Daniel is only a few years ahead of me. He makes me feel nauseous.

'Totally Unnecessary Breast Examination,' he snorts and looks to Housewives' Favourite for approval. A nurse ushers them out of the way and tactfully replaces the gown while the patient is moved through to the main operating theatre.

I make it obvious I'm not impressed, which Housewives' Favourite clearly doesn't like. I can forgive Daniel: he is career-driven, impressionable and easily led. But Housewives' Favourite should know better. I hope all the nurses that think he's such a Casanova find out what he's really like.

Tuesday 9 September

The word 'surgery' derives from the Latin *chirurgia*, which in turn comes from the Greek *cheiros* (hand) and *ergon* (craft). So surgery is handicraft. Rather like basket weaving but better paid. Along with surgeons, the only other people I know that are happily employed in handicrafts are Girl Guides and psychiatric patients. Surgeons like to think that they are doing something incredibly clever, when in actual fact, it's rather straightforward: something's wrong, so we'll cut you open, cut it out, and sew you back together again. If we can't cut it out, we can't help you.

Not that I'd ever say this to Mr Butterworth. He's from the old school of medicine, where the consultant is the omnipotent, omniscient master of all. He's from a time when patients listened to their doctors and did what they were told. This would be all very well, except that nobody seems to be able to understand him, which makes unquestioning compliance rather tricky for the patients and life on the wards a nightmare for me. I spend a good portion of every ward round trying to decipher exactly what it is that Mr Butterworth is saying, or rather, muttering. He refuses to look patients in the eye, and tends to direct instructions for their care either out of the window or to the soap dispenser at the side of their bed, before rushing off leaving the patients and me none the wiser as to what's going on. He obviously feels more at ease with the unconscious.

Mrs Sheridan has come in with vague stomach pains and we can't find anything wrong with her. She's had all the investigations available and still nothing. She's rather anxious and straightens herself as we approach her bed. Without a word of introduction, Mr Butterworth pulls the sheets off the bed and inspects her exposed abdomen while I desperately try to draw the curtains round her, despite battling with the notes trolley. This man has all the social skills of a colostomy bag. He prods her belly and mutters, 'Endoscopy was clear. Send home.' He doesn't take kindly to having to repeat himself, and before I know it he's marching off to the next bed. I smile apologetically at Mrs Sherridan and race off.

A few hours later I'm asked to come up to the ward by one of the nurses. 'Mrs Sherridan would like to speak to a doctor.'

This phrase strikes dread into every junior doctor's heart. What it usually means is that a patient has got a string of questions they want to ask and you won't know the answers to them. I've realised that it's easier just to make something up than try to track down someone who does know the answer. I go up on to the ward and find Mrs Sherridan near to tears. She's not the only one. 'I don't understand what's going on, doctor,' she says. 'What did the consultant say this morning? What was wrong with me? Am I all right to go home?'

I refrain from replying that her guess is as good as mine. The fact that the surgical team have no idea what is actually wrong with her, doesn't really matter. There's nothing surgically wrong so she can go home. She's better now. But I can't say that to Mrs Sherridan. Instead, I hide behind the doctor's friend: jargon. The word virus actually translates as 'poisoned liquid' but in the real world, it's doctor speak for 'we don't know what it is, but it's not that bad and you'll get over it'.

'We've run all our tests and haven't been able to find anything, which suggests you had a viral gastroenteritis. You body has fought it off while you've been resting in hospital and you're fine to go home now,' I explain.

I throw in a few more medical-sounding words for good luck. I cringe. Surely she's going to see through that old one? But the old ones are the best, and she immediately cheers up. 'Oh, really Doctor? Well, thank you.'

I spend another few minutes reassuring her and giving her some advice about eating fruit and vegetables that I've picked up from morning television. I leave her to pack her bags, another happy customer, and go off to try to explain to another patient exactly what Mr Butterworth said that morning. I'm beginning to realise that the words 'junior doctor' roughly translate as: I may not know the answer, but I do know some fancy-sounding words and I've got a stethoscope.

Thursday 11 September

Ruby cried today. I met her round the back of A&E, in between wards rounds and theatre. She had a daunting list of jobs to do that took up two sides of a sheet of paper, as well as admission clinic that afternoon. She didn't know where to start, and then while I was with her, her pager went off. She called the number from her mobile, unable to face the short walk back into A&E to use their phones. It was the lab. Some of the bloods she had sent had been lost. Mr Grant had been phoning them as he was about to operate on the first patient, the samples weren't registered as having been taken, and he wanted to know why.

'But I took them,' Ruby said, a look of desperation coming across her face. 'I put them in the pod and sent them to the lab this morning.'

Then a pause as the voice at the other end of the phone said something.

'Oh God, he's going to kill me. He's going to be so cross if his theatre list is delayed.'

Another pause. 'OK, I'll re-take them and then walk them over to the lab myself.'

She looked down at the list of jobs and the half-smoked cigarette in her hand and stubbed it out. And then she began to sob – not a torrent of tears, but the sort of crying that comes from being powerless and tired. Then her pager went off again. And then mine went off. And then we both walked back into the hospital.

Saturday 13 September

Met my mum today for dinner. Didn't have a great deal to talk about. She spent a good proportion of the meal complaining about how much weight I'd lost, as if this was

73

something I had done on purpose.

Sunday 14 September

Lie in bed today. Glorious. It's still warm and the late summer sun streams in through my window and on to the bed. Bliss – until it's brutally shattered by my pager screeching: 'CRASH CALL, CRASH CALL. CRASH TEAM TO RESUS, CRASH TEAM TO RESUS.'

While I'm dozing in the sun, someone somewhere is dying.

Tuesday 16 September

The usual ward-round chaos, with Mr Price charging ahead of us while we follow like little duckings behind their mother, desperate to keep up. It's no use. Supriya is floundering as much as I am, despite her matching twin-set and Filofax.

Daniel showed a moment of compassion after the ward round today, and asked if Supriya was OK.

'I'm fine,' she answered, when Daniel mentioned the dark circles round her eyes. 'Really, I'm just so ... so...' she began.

'Tired,' I interjected, knowing exactly how she feels and suspecting that I look as rough as she does, possibly worse given that I look like I've been pulled through a jumble sale backwards.

Wednesday 17 September

I attempt to get some scans booked, and am faced with the recalcitrant radiologist Dr Palache, who merely bats every request back with a further question. Why is it that everyone is intent on making my life more difficult than it already is? 'Come back when you actually know what you're asking me for and why you're asking for it,' says Dr Palache as I attempt to order a scan for a gall bladder.

Maxine looks at me sympathetically.

'Please,' I ask desperately.

He ignores me.

Thursday 18 September

Much of medicine is about trends: patterns are studied and analysed and the results are extrapolated in order to draw conclusions. As a result, it's easy for doctors to make judgements based on appearance. Certain people develop certain diseases. The prostitute with a cough, for example, might have HIV, the eighty-year-old lady with one will have pneumonia, while the immigrant will have TB. This of course is completely wrong, as we were all reminded today.

While on call last night Supriya accidentally stabbed herself with a needle after taking blood from a patient. He had come in with abdominal pains, accompanied by his girlfriend. Supriya had clerked him in and taken bloods. She was tired and somehow, as she withdrew the needle, it slipped and she plunged it into her finger. She left quickly and ran it under water. The nurses in A&E informed her that there was a protocol to follow and that she should return to the patient, explain what had happened and request that he take an HIV test to see if she had exposed herself to it. Supriya didn't panic – here was a sensible, middle-class man, a stockbroker, in a stable relationship, in a district general hospital. He didn't inject drugs, he wasn't a prostitute, he wasn't gay. What was the worry? He agreed to have the blood test done.

'Sorry, just a formality you understand,' Supriya had explained and the man and his girlfriend smiled kindly back.

It was several hours later, while the girlfriend had left the department to get some coffee, that the man asked to speak to Supriya. 'Look, I don't want to scare you, but...' Supriya broke into a sweat. 'Well, the thing is,' he hesitated. 'You asked me those questions about have I injected drugs before and stuff like that...' Supriya grew paler. 'Well, the thing is, I couldn't say anything in front of my girlfriend, but I have slept with prostitutes.' Supriya nodded slowly. 'And I haven't always used a condom. In fact, I've been really worried that I might have, you know, well, caught something.'

Supriya closed her eyes. 'Are you trying to tell me that you think you might have exposed yourself, and therefore me, to HIV?'

The man nodded.

Supriya spent the next ten minutes crying in the toilet. 'I just never thought it. He looked so, well, normal. You'd never know that he was at risk of catching that sort of thing. If it had been someone who looked, well, dodgy, I'd have been extra careful while taking their blood,' she sobbed as she retold the story after the ward round this morning, her small frame engulfed in Lewis's large arms. Her neat ponytail had become loose at the back and strands of hair were dangling down. It was scary to see Supriya, previously a paragon of control, in such a state. It emphasised the seriousness of what had happened; the possible ramifications not only for her health and further personal life, but her career.

I wouldn't have thought that Supriya, so focused and clinical, would have been the sort of person to cry so openly. You should never make judgements based on appearance.

Friday 19 September

Children are like farts: you always think your own are inoffensive but other people's are repulsive. Sick children are no exception, and given long enough in a confined space, even your own start to get a bit too much.

'Just get him better and we can all get out of here,' shouts the man as I attempt to take his son's blood.

The child starts screaming as I approach him with the needle. I look at the man's tattoos and shaven head. He cracks his knuckles.

'Why are you making him cry?' he roars at me. 'Do you have to do that?' he says, pointing with his fat stubby fingers at the needle gently shaking in my hands.

I assure him that if there was any other way to take blood from his son, I would most certainly be doing it. I've numbed the boy's hand anyway, so he's just making a fuss.

Of all the patients I have to treat, it's children who are the worst. Not the children themselves. The parents. All their anxiety, upset, fear is projected straight on to the nearest adult: the doctor. They end up behaving worse than the children themselves. The man looks at me as though it's my fault his son has appendicitis. Then a nurse appears from behind the curtains with something in her hand. Not another procedure to inflict on this poor child? I think.

'There we go,' she says, unwrapping a boiled sweet and shoving it into the child's screaming open mouth.

Silence. The father continues to scowl at me. I wonder if he'd like a boiled sweet too?

Monday 22 September

Supriya burst on to the ward this morning, looking emotionless. We knew where she'd been and we had all been distracted the entire morning, knowing that today was the day when the results would be ready from the HIV test. If her patient was positive, then Supriya faced three months of nail-biting anxiety while she waited for her own blood test. If it was negative, then there was nothing to worry about.

'It was clear,' she shouted, then burst into tears.

We all hugged her while the patients looked on, bemused by this sudden display of emotion halfway through a ward round.

Thursday 25 September

Mrs Mullen has a new hip. She had to wait a year for it, she told me last week, not that she's complaining. In fact, when she was on the ward, Mrs Mullen never made a fuss about anything. She just got on with it. She even ate the food without complaint. 'I think it's marvellous what they can do these days. I was finding it so hard to get to the shops, it hurt so much, and now I could run the marathon, I tell you.'

While grown men have cried when I've taken their blood (I'm being serious here), this woman didn't even like to bother the nurses for her morphine. She even offered to make her bed every morning to save the nurses from having to do it. She's eighty-three for goodness' sake. I'm in my twenties and have fully functioning limbs and I don't make my bed unless my mum's visiting and certainly wouldn't stop nurses from doing it for me.

'I sometimes think that people these days don't know they're born,' she said, after hearing the fuss that Mr Lindley in the next bed made when the nurse removed his stitches. 'To be honest, I didn't like to take up the surgeon's time getting my hip done, but my niece persuaded me.'

I don't think they make people like Mrs Mullen any more. My generation are a generation of complainers. We think the world owes us something. But if the world owes anyone anything, it owes people like Mrs Mullen. She left school at the age of fourteen despite having won a place at the local grammar school. Until she was twenty she supported her mother and four sisters, working in a factory. She worked in the same factory until she retired. She never had a day off sick in her life and never had a holiday. Not even to have her three children.

But Mrs Mullen is no doormat. She makes a fuss when there's something worth making a fuss about. She has been a trade unionist all her life, has fought for equal employment rights for women, and, she told me with a grin, hers was the first factory in the country to get them. She fought for pension rights and disability payments. 'Couldn't take time off in those days to be sick, too much to do. I had to stand up for those girls. The conditions some of us had to work in was dreadful. Wouldn't be allowed now, I can tell you.'

And the reason it wouldn't be allowed now is because of people like Mrs Mullen. I've never worked as hard as Mrs Mullen, and I'll almost certainly never have to.

Being a junior doctor isn't easy. But as far as jobs go, you could do a lot worse. You could work in a factory for fifty years and never have any time off. Perhaps if my generation had watched our mothers die of TB we'd be thankful when we got treated on the NHS and certainly wouldn't swear at nurses who are only trying to take our stitches out.

I couldn't believe my eyes today when I went to buy a sandwich from the hospital Friends shop this morning and who should be standing behind the counter but Mrs Mullen. 'What are you doing here?' I asked, open-mouthed. 'We discharged you last week. You're supposed to be at home taking things easy.'

'Oh I am,' she replied. 'It's only a few hours a week. I saw the advert for volunteers. It's my way of saying thank you for all that this hospital has done for me.'

A box of Terry's All Gold would have done. But Mrs Mullen is the sort of person that gives back more than she takes. It's a dying breed. I ask for a cheese and tomato sandwich. She hands me egg instead, it's all they've got. I hate egg, but decide to eat it anyway and not complain.

Saturday 27 September

If we're all leading lives of quiet desperation, there are some of us who are far quieter about it than others. Over the past two months I have seen and heard many sad things, and I'm actively learning not to let them prey on my mind too much. But the things that stay with me are not always the things one would expect. Sometimes, the real pathos is in seeing people live their day-to-day lives, rather than the dramatic things like seeing people die.

I got up early today as I was going to see my mum for some proper home-cooked food. On my way I decided to stop off and get a newspaper. Shopkeepers were busy opening the shutters on their windows, drivers sped along in their cars on their way to somewhere important. My head was rather muggy from being awake so early, and as I strolled towards the nearest newsagent in the early morning sun, it was a while before I realised that someone was calling my name. It was Mrs Walden. She'd come in with stomach pains the previous week but we'd discharged her after the tests came back normal and the pain had subsided. She's well known to the hospital, because she's also a psychiatric patient. Now in her late thirties, she's been in and out of hospital most of her adult life, thanks to her mental illness. She lives alone in a council flat, she's isolated and depressed. She's got nothing to make her happy, except one thing: her son, Henry.

Henry was put into care when he was two because she couldn't offer him a stable home. It was for the best. She hasn't seen him for six years. 'There's not a day that goes past that I don't think of him, though,' she'd told me while I'd tried to examine her stomach in A&E.

The courts recently agreed that she could begin some supervised contact. He had called her a few weeks ago, and she was hoping to be allowed to see him for a few hours at Christmas.

I crossed the road. 'Where are you off to then?' I asked.

She looked at me with concern. 'It's Christmas soon,' she replied.

Sleep deprivation does funny things to you, and I had a moment of genuine panic before coming to my senses. 'Er, it's only September,' I reminded her.

'I know, but I want to get the best present for Henry, and they always sell out of the thing that kids want, so I thought I should get it early.'

She was waiting for the bus to take her to an out-of-town shopping centre with a toy superstore. She took out a photograph of her son to show me. 'It's still very early, it won't be open yet,' I suggest.

'I want to be the first person there. Get the best for him,' she explained.

The truth is, it's ridiculous – here she is, a good three hours before any shop is open, getting ready to buy a Christmas present three months early for her eight-year-old son, whom she hasn't seen for six years. I have this gnawing image of him opening his present on Christmas Day, from a mother he has no memory of, a moment so insignificant for him, but of such importance to her. This is all she has to hold on to. I look at all the people milling about, starting their day, oblivious. She's just a middle-aged woman standing in the street, anxious about what present she is going to get her son for Christmas. For me this sums up the tragedy of how mental illness ravages people's lives, destroying them piece by piece. And yet Mrs Walden is still, desperately, holding on to the idea of a relationship with her son. She puts the photo back in the bag, waves goodbye and boards the bus.

Tuesday 30 September

We have now completed two months as doctors. It's unbelievable. To celebrate I visit Trudy, on the pretext of giving her some letters for Mr Butterworth to sign. She makes me tea, hands me some cake, then sits filing her nails and ignoring the telephone while we chat. 'So,' she asks in her usual up-front way, 'got yourself any action recently?'

I look at her blankly. 'Well, there was a cardiac arrest the other day on the ward, which I sort of helped in.'

This wasn't entirely true. I cowered behind the curtains while the team of 'proper doctors' arrived and attempted to resuscitate the patient, but I don't want to admit this. 'No, you moron, I don't mean that sort of action. I mean,' and she raises an eyebrow, 'lovin' action.'

I look at her blankly again. She rolls her eyes. 'Do I have to spell it out to you?' she asks and then immediately starts doing so: 'S. E. X.'

I recoil in horror. 'Sex?' I ask, nearly choking on my macaroon.

The very idea hasn't even crossed my mind since starting work. I tell her that I've been too busy running around like a headless chicken chasing my tail.

'Chickens don't have tails,' Trudy points out.

'I'm a doctor, not a vet. Anyway, no, is the simple answer. I'm going to focus on keeping myself and my patients alive for the next ten months, and then I'll think about that sort of thing,' I say emphatically.

'Well, it seems some people have found time to take a look at what the hospital has to offer in that department,' says Trudy. 'How *is* Ruby these days?'

'I don't know, she's fine, what do you mean?' I ask.

'I've heard that she's drawing attention from certain quarters. She'll be silly if she gets involved though,' she says.

'I don't know what you're talking about,' I say, wondering if she means who I think she means.

I push the last bit of macaroon into my mouth and scowl. Please, Ruby, not House-wives' Favourite.

OCTOBER

Thursday 2 October

The monotony of today's ward round was broken by a loud-pitched siren. All junior doctors automatically looked at their pagers and were delighted to realise they weren't being paged for once. It took the squeals of 'fire, fire,' from the nurses to end this brief moment of joy.

It very quickly transpired that Mr Butterworth could indeed outdo the laws of physics and move far faster than his Pickwickian proportions suggest. I remembered vaguely some talk of fire and evacuation at our induction course, although that all seemed such a long time ago. The only clear memory was Supriya asking about the patients in Intensive Care, and getting a less than satisfactory response.

Thankfully, the fire was nowhere near our ward, or even in our part of the hospital, so instead of having to evacuate the entire ward, with all their pumps and drips, we were soon returned to our usual state of mild pandemonium. The added bonus was that it appeared we'd lost Mr Butterworth, although for how long none of us were sure, so Sad Sack, seizing the moment, continued on the ward round on her own.

While I was making a start on the list of jobs, Rachel, one of the nurses, came over 'Fire wasn't anywhere near the ward,' she said, 'Apparently it was over in the admin block, under the stairs and it was only small and didn't spread. The fire safety officer is going to be in dead trouble – there were some papers under the stairs that caught fire.'

I thought back to the lecture from the fire safety officer on my first day. And all the bits of paper that we'd been given to read about evacuation procedure. And how I'd promptly lost them all. And possibly left them under the stairs in the admin block. And then I thought how I wasn't going to mention this to a living soul until the day I die.

Saturday 4 October

I woke up this morning in a panic, scrambled for my trousers, rushed into the bathroom and stared at the gaunt, pale figure that looked back at me. No time for a shower. Cleaned my teeth, washed my face and stumbled downstairs. Sitting at the kitchen table was Ruby, smoking a cigarette and staring at the cup of coffee in front of her.

'Quick, we're late,' I mumbled as I tried to find a clean cup.

'No, we're not,' replied Ruby without looking up, her eyes half-closed.

'What are you talking about? Of course we are, it's 7 a.m. already.'

'It's Saturday,' she replied.

Days have ceased to have any real meaning for me. They are just units of time which have to be endured until I can fall into bed. 'Oh, yeah, of course,' I said, it only just dawning on me that for the first time since starting at the hospital we were both off for the entire weekend. How could such a marvellous occurrence have slipped my mind?

We sat in silence for a few minutes until something dawned on me, 'Hang on,' I said, 'why are you up?'

'I forgot, too,' she said, clearly still crushed. 'I realised about half an hour ago but was too tired to get up and go to bed.'

Sunday 5 October

The problem when you are working from 7.30 a.m. until at least 9 p.m., with twenty-four-hour on-calls thrown in, is that there is absolutely no time to coordinate anything even vaguely resembling fun when you find yourself with time off. Weekends when not at work are frittered away in the pursuit of slumber, of which there never seems to be quite enough, foraging for food and trying to get clean clothes together for the following week.

Food, sleep, clean clothes: these have become my main concerns. Flora, who was also off this weekend, was determined to mark the first time we've all been off at the same time by arranging a trip to an art gallery.

'I'm hungry,' said Ruby after only about ten minutes looking at pictures.

'So am I,' said Flora.

I was already heading for the café.

Monday 6 October

'This is your last chance,' warns Mrs Miles. I break out in a sweat and my hands start to shake. We both want to get to sleep, but before we can, I've got to put a cannula in her arm.

Before becoming a doctor I had just a vague idea what a cannula was, thanks to an hour spent with a plastic arm at medical school. Now, however, I can't seem to get away from them. For those of you who are lucky enough never to have had to come into contact with one, these are tiny little tubes that are put into a vein so that fluid or medicines can go directly into the blood. That's the theory. Unfortunately, the problem is getting them into the vein in the first place.

This tends to be trickier than you'd imagine and it's a job that usually falls to the junior doctors. It requires, as well as a level of skill in actually hitting a vein in the first place, a fair degree of coordination. The first thing you have to do is choose a suitable vein. All the junior doctors I know have their favourites. This doesn't help when you are confronted with a patient whose anatomy deviates from the norm, or who has a layer of fat covering your vein so you can't see or feel it. Then you have a choice – either try to find another one somewhere else, or just stab the needle in and hope you hit gold. Once in a vein, there's a little window at the back of the needle that fills with blood so you know you're in, and then you slide the tube off the needle and into the vein, Hey presto. But Mrs Miles's veins are being particularly elusive this evening. I've been jabbing the needle in for at least twenty minutes. 'Isn't there someone else who could do this?' she asks, for the fourth time. 'Someone who knows what they're doing, perhaps,' she adds under her breath.

'Everyone's in bed, it's just me I'm afraid. I'm really sorry.'

There comes a point when saying sorry doesn't help, and I passed that point about ten minutes ago. I dig with the needle a little deeper.

'Ouch! That really hurt,' she spits through clenched teeth. I suspect that Mrs Miles is going to make sure there's blood this evening but at this rate, it won't be hers.

An interesting fact I've come to realise is that, for some mysterious reason, no one seems to need a cannula during the day, but just as you're about to go to bed in the early hours of the morning, the whole hospital seems to be crying out for them. This is also precisely the time when there's no one else around for you to ask for help. Particularly soul-crushing is that nurses have developed an in-built ability to know exactly the moment that you've got undressed in the on-call room and are about to put on your pyjamas, and choose that moment to page you.

It is hard to convey the feeling of terror as you approach the bed of a patient needing a cannula. Because so much of my nights on call are spent putting these little things in, I've become rather obsessed. On trains or buses or out shopping, I see large, ropey veins everywhere, running up someone's arm, engorged with blood, just ready for me to effortlessly slip in a cannula. I've even developed a rather disconcerting habit of tentatively assessing the ones that run over the wrist by carefully squeezing them when I shake people's hands. People think I've joined the Freemasons, but I can't help myself. At the back of my mind there's always the niggling thought: 'What if I had to suddenly put a cannula in this person? Could I do it?' My friends who aren't doctors look at me as though I were some hideous freak when I start salivating at their prominent vasculature. But if they were with me at three o'clock in the morning, with the curtains closed around a bed containing a bleary-eyed Mrs Miles, with just the little matter of venous access standing between me and a few hours' sleep, they'd understand.

Finally, I get it in. Mrs Miles and I both breathe a sigh of relief. I feel rather pleased with myself, but she doesn't seem too grateful. Just as I'm about to leave the ward, the nurse calls me over. 'Max, there's another cannula to do on bed 16.'

I make my way over to his bed and gently wake Mr Marshall.

'I'm Max, I'm the doctor,' I say. 'I've got to put a cannula in your arm so we can give you your medicines.'

Mr Marshall looks down at his hand as I shake it and then up at me. 'Are you a Mason or something?' he asks.

Wednesday 8 October

Only yesterday I was standing in exactly this

spot talking to Mrs Riaz, and now I'm poking her in the eye. 'Yeah, she's not responding to that one is she?' says the nurse absentmindedly as she busies herself around the bed.

'No,' I reply, 'she's not.'

I poke a little harder, just to make sure. 'Yep, definitely dead, I'd say.' I fill out the death certificate and cremation form and leave the ward. My pager goes off and when I answer it, it's the radiology department asking if we still need the urgent X-ray we requested a few hours ago for Mrs Riaz. 'No,' I reply, 'she's died, it's OK, thanks anyway.'

I put down the phone, knowing that her name at this moment is being crossed off a list somewhere, one less person to worry about, one spare slot for another sick person somewhere. Everything moves on.

A few hours later I walk past her room again and it's already got another patient in it, a young woman in her twenties. A young man, presumably her boyfriend, is holding her hand and there's a bunch of flowers in a vase on the windowsill. Mrs Riaz's name is no longer above the bed. Soon I won't even remember who she was. This is the nature of hospitals; this is the nature of medicine. Everything moves on, and it never seems to stop, not for one moment.

Thursday 9 October

I can see someone's loitering outside the window of the doctors' mess, 'Who's that?' I say, pointing to the shadowy figure darting out of sight. Lewis shrugs and goes back to dictating his discharge letters. Ruby looks up, and a strange expression comes over her face. 'Oh, erm, I think it might be someone for me,' she says as she gets up and goes outside.

A few minutes later she returns. 'Who was it?' I ask. She pretends not to hear me, but she looks guilty. I look at her suspiciously and ask if it was Housewives' Favourite.

'Erm, yes, he just came over to...' She hesitates for a moment. '...to see if I wanted to go to a lecture this evening with him about keyhole surgery. He's got a spare ticket.'

I raise an eyebrow. 'Why didn't he just come in here and ask you, rather than skulking around outside?'

Ruby looks at me for a moment, searching for an answer. 'He ... he didn't want to disturb you all,' she says, rather unconvincingly. 'Anyway, I've said I'll go, so don't wait up for me. We're going for dinner afterwards,' she says and quickly gets up to put the kettle on.

I bet you are, I think. And I'm sure that's not all he's got planned.

Friday 10 October

Mrs Miles was discharged today. But not before the ward round, when Mr Butterworth explained in his indomitable style that she had pancreatitis and that she is now cured and can go home. 'Are you an alcoholic?' he blurted out apropos of very little.

'I beg your pardon?' she spluttered.

He ignored her. 'Probably gallstones. What did the scan say?' he continued, looking at Sad Sack, who looked at Daniel, who looked at Supriya and me.

'Erm,' we said collectively, then scrambled to find the results in the notes. But Mr Butterworth had already moved on to the next patient. We decided to chase the results and write to Mrs Miles's GP to tell them what happened and what the follow-up should be.

'Is that it then?' she asked. 'Can I get out of this place?' she almost spat out.

'Yes,' I beam. 'You can go home now.'

As the ward round finished she beckoned me over. I was touched. Here was I, thinking that she was a miserable, ungrateful misanthrope when in fact, she is really a sweet, appreciative and kind soul, grateful for the care she has received from our team. She's going to give me a present, isn't she? I thought. Maybe even a thank-you card. I smiled warmly and walked over.

'Before I go I want to show you this,' she said.

A letter, I suspected, to the Queen, recommending me for knighthood. I prepared my reply: Oh no, I don't do it for the glory, I do it for the love of seeing my patients' faces when they are well. She rolled up her sleeve.

'Look! Look at the size of it. That's your fault, that is. You did that to me,' she shouted as she jabbed her fingers towards the large purple-blue bruise which had spread across her forearm. 'Huh, some doctor you are.'

Oh. Right. I mumbled an apology and turned round while she showed the patient in the next bed. 'Look, look at the size of it,' she continued.

I don't do it for the glory, I do it for the love of seeing my patients' faces when they are well, I said to myself again and again as a scowling Mrs Miles left the ward.

Saturday 11 October

A weekend off but both Ruby and Flora are on call. I stalk around the silent house, looking for something to eat. I wander into Flora's room, heaped with junk, paper, piles of washing and long-forgotten textbooks strewn on the floor. I listen to the radio. I read the paper. I decide I must do something today, reclaim something from the dying embers of the week. But what? Just as I sit wondering if it is too pathetic to go to the cinema on my own, my phone rings. It's my sister.

Now, my sister Ellen is far more intelligent than I am. For this reason, she never became a doctor. Not for her a life of death, depression and sleep deprivation, oh no. She went into recruitment and spends her days finding people their ideal job. Matching employers with ideal employees. It's a normal, 9-to-5 job, sitting at a desk with her own telephone and lunch breaks. Lunch breaks! Imagine that. A whole break, just to eat lunch.

'What're you up to?' she asks with all the bounce and enthusiasm of someone who hasn't spent yesterday with a digit up various strangers' rectums.

'Nothing,' I say.

'Cool!' she replies.

God, I hate happy people.

'Want to go out tomorrow for lunch?' she asks.

'Let me just check my diary, oh no, sorry I can't, I'm dying of exhaustion tomorrow,' I say.

She ignores this. 'So, is my big brother going to let his little sister take him out for Sunday lunch tomorrow then?' she asks. I smell a rat. My sister is only fifteen months younger than I am and only ever acknowledges that I'm older when she wants something.

'What do you want, Ellen?' I ask.

She acts wounded. 'What, isn't your little sister allowed to care about her brother? Isn't she allowed to be worried that he isn't eating properly, now that he's a responsible doctor? Isn't she allowed to take him out for lunch in order to build up his strength?'

I'm too tired to bother to remind her that I know her all too well. 'OK, I'll see you at The Five Bells at 1 p.m. tomorrow,' I say.

I bet she's got a rash or something she wants me to look at.

Sunday 12 October

'Will you just have a look at this?' asks my sister as she shows me a rash on her stomach. I knew it. I look at my watch. It's only 1.10 p.m. She could have at least waited until dessert.

Monday 13 October

On call again and am bleeped for what feels like the thousandth time. I looked at the bleep: ward 4. I walk on the ward to be met by two nurses straight from an audition for the Kray twins. I smile at them and they both curl their lips in irritation. Don't be mean to me, I think as I introduce myself, I haven't done anything wrong ... yet...

'We've got a job for you,' one of them says, raising her eyebrow as she speaks. The other does the same. I wonder if they practise that sort of thing when they're on their breaks. 'Bed 12,' she continues, 'needs a three-way irrigation catheter.'

Hmm, well, better call someone that knows what the hell that is then, hadn't you, I think to myself, but feel it best not to share this with the group. 'Right, well, the thing is, I'm not exactly, how can I put it, *au fait* with that particular piece of equipment.'

I'm met by silence.

'Well, tonight is your lucky night,' says the first nurse.

Does the other one ever speak? I wonder. 'Are you not able to do it?' I ask in the most light-hearted way possible.

'We've tried a regular catheter, but we need an irrigation one, and it's too big. She keeps shouting when we try and force it in.'

The image of it all is becoming almost too much for me. It's 2 a.m. I feel weak at the knees. 'Sorry, did you say "she"?' I ask.

Now, putting a catheter into a man is not a pleasant task. But you'd have to be pretty stupid to be unable to locate the hole. Find the appendage, locate the end, and bingo, there's the hole. Females, on the other hand, are a whole different kettle of fish. I have actually had the joy of doing a few male catheterisations as a medical student, but all the females decline if you're a male medical student. Little do they realise, though, that there's a first for everything and if they don't let us do it in a nice clinic when we're a medical student, with a consultant supervising us, we'll just have to learn how to do it on our own in the middle of the night with two Nazi nurses looming over us.

I make my way over to the bed and the two nurses follow like executioners stalking a condemned man. Mrs Doughty has dementia. She's come in with an obstruction in her bowel, and is now in acute kidney failure as well. She whines as I approach her in the dark. A few of the other patients shift in their beds. Little do they know the pandemonium that is about to ensue...

'Hold her legs or she'll kick you again,' shouts the nurse that speaks. The mute one obliges by grabbing the bent knee and hugging it closer to her chest. I fiddle with the catheter a bit more. It's been over twenty minutes by now.

I'm covered in lubricating jelly, the nurses are covered in lubricating jelly, even the other patients are covered in lubricating jelly by now. 'Can I have another tube of jelly?' I ask.

'What, are you kidding? You've used more of that stuff on one patient than we usually use in a whole week.'

I look up from between Mrs Doughty's legs and am blinded for a moment by the spotlight directly behind me. 'Just get it for me,' I say, aware that it's hard to look authoritative when you have lubricant smeared all over your face. She traipses off and duly returns with a fresh tube. I look closely at my quarry. I can see the hole. I also remember a lecture at medical school where someone said 'aim high'. Apparently the common mistake is to accidentally put the catheter into the vagina, when obviously this is not going to help drain the bladder. 'Aim high,' I say to myself and prod the end of the catheter at the pink fleshy blob in front of me. I'm sorry to have to get technical, but really, it's not nearly as bad as being there yourself. The tip goes in about a centimetre and stops again. Damn it. I don't understand. There's the urethral opening, and here's the catheter, now go in, goddamn you. Nothing. I give up. 'I'm so sorry, Mrs Doughty,' I say, although she looks asleep now. 'I'm going to have to get some help.'

I then make the long walk of shame to the phone and page Sad Sack.

'What?' she says by way of pleasantries.

I explain the problem and she hangs up on me without saying a word. I stand by the phone at the nurses' station. Please come, Sad Sack. Please come. A few minutes later she appears. 'This better be good,' she says.

'Good morning to you too. Yes, I'm fine, thanks for asking,' I mouth as she drags herself past me. I follow her.

'Look,' I say proudly, pointing at the hole. 'I've been trying to push it in but it won't go.'

Sad Sack picks up the catheter and in it goes.

'But, but...' I stutter.

Sad Sack turns to me while the nurses smirk behind her. 'Congratulations, Dr Pemberton. You've just spent the last thirty minutes attempting to insert a catheter into this woman's clitoris.'

I close my eyes in shame.

'With your knowledge of the female anatomy I can only thank God that I'm not your girlfriend,' she says in her gravelly monotone as she drags herself past me and off to bed. 'Don't worry,' I say to myself, 'I'm thanking God you're not my girlfriend as well,' but yet again, feel it best not to say out loud.

Wednesday 15 October

Yes, yes, would all the nursing staff please

stop referring to me as the person that tries to catheterise clitorises. It's not funny any more. George Clooney never got this in *ER*.

Thursday 16 October

It would be nice if everything was fair. In a perfect world, people who are bad would get ill. And good people would be the ones who have long and happy lives and for whom pain is unknown. But things aren't like that. Life isn't fair and it's pointless pretending it is. But it doesn't stop me wanting to rage against this injustice.

Last night Michael was admitted on to the ward. His bowels have stopped working because they've become twisted around themselves. He's also got pneumonia. He had to have emergency surgery last night to untangle his bowel in the first place. We think he might die. He's fourteen. His age, of course, shouldn't matter – after all, it doesn't matter if you're fourteen or forty, a life is still a life. But at the age of fourteen, there is no way you can have done anything to deserve this.

The thing is, this isn't the first time this has happened. Everyone on the ward knows Michael. When he was born, there was a hole in his diaphragm, the muscle at the bottom of the lungs which makes them inflate and deflate. The hole meant that his bowels had herniated through into the space where his lungs should have been. As a result, his lungs hadn't developed properly and his bowel had to be operated on. But while under the anaesthetic, there were complications, and he was left brain-damaged. It was no one's fault, just one of those things. He is unable to use his legs or his upper arms properly. He speaks funny and he's incontinent so he has to wear pads. His bowels have never functioned fully, they cause him constant pain, and because of the operations, he doesn't absorb all his nutrients so he is painfully thin. He's like a sack of bones.

I stood there on the ward round, having read a summary of his problems in the notes. His mum sat by his bedside. She was obviously terrified and upset and restless, fussing over Michael while the surgeons were talking to them both. He was staring up at the ceiling, not interested. He signalled for some of us to go – he doesn't like the whole entourage standing over him and prodding him like some Victorian freak show.

I remembered myself at fourteen: getting into trouble at school for messing around; going bowling and to the cinema; sneaking into pubs with friends and getting promptly thrown out again. Michael's whole life has been hospitals. His mum is his carer and he looks at her as though he's only too well aware of the debt he owes her and with the humiliation that this brings. Being fourteen is all about independence, testing the boundaries and occasionally breaching them. It shouldn't be about having your mum clean you after you've messed yourself or groups of doctors staring down at you for the umpteenth time.

I was overcome with sadness for him, knowing that he had done nothing to deserve this and that there was nothing I could do to help him. But the most poignant thing was this. On top of his lip was the beginning of a moustache; thin, dark wisps of pubescent facial hair. He should have started shaving, but who would have taught him? His mother is focused on her little boy, unaware that he is growing up. It was like a final piece of humiliation, a reminder that he is totally dependent on others and will never grow up, never be normal. It was no one's fault, but it all seemed so unfair.

Friday 17 October

Paid another visit to Trudy for my weekly cup of tea. 'You're looking thin,' she exclaimed as I entered the room. I looked at myself in the mirror on the back of her door. She was right, I had lost weight. For the first few weeks I was aware of being hungry and frustrated at not being able to eat lunch and always eating dinner after 10 p.m., exhausted and barely awake enough to chew, let alone digest, my meal. But I soon got used to skipping lunch, or at best nibbling throughout the day like a hamster on whatever I could find. But that gnawing hunger of my first few weeks has subsided, replaced with an insidious feeling of constant gastrointestinal dissatisfaction that now forms the background to my working day. Even at weekends my eating patterns are so disrupted that I often find myself skipping breakfast and lunch in favour of sleep.

'What you need is angel cake,' said Trudy, producing one from her seemingly bottomless bag. After the first slice my hunger seemed to return and I sat and ate the whole thing, while Trudy answered my pager with her usual, 'He's in a meeting.'

Saturday 18 October

A weekend on call. The nurses seem to be in a particularly bad mood. The barrage of bleeps has been endless. Even the patients seem in bad spirits. The mad scramble on each Friday evening for the doctors to get home and to forget about this place for two days means that the non-urgent jobs often get left for the on-call doctor to do over the weekend. This invariably means rewriting dozens of drug charts. In theory this should just be copying from the full chart on to a nice fresh one. Unfortunately the malicious rumour about doctors' handwriting is actually true – it really is illegible, even to other doctors. So a good proportion of time is spent looking up the medicines the scrawl seems to resemble to see if it tallies with the doses. It's detective work that I could do without. The nursing staff don't appear to appreciate this, and tut loudly when the medical bible, the *British National Formulary* or *BNF* is reached for.

'Haven't you finished that yet?' said Anita, one of the nurses, as I sat pondering what the doctor who had written a squiggly line could have possibly meant. The ward round was like a wake with all the patients' ashen faces staring out from under their bedclothes. Hospitals really can be the most depressing of places.

Sunday 19 October

Today in A&E I saw two appendicitises, one perforated duodenal ulcer, two obstructions and a pancreatitis. Sad Sack shouted at me from one end of the department: 'Can you make sure you've taken an amylase level on the pancreatitis in bed 8?'

I was surprised for a nanosecond to see a middle-aged woman looking back at me from bed 8, rather than a pink, blobby pancreas.

I'm not sure when people started to become defined entirely by their pathology and stripped of any further identity. The reason the woman is here is that she has pancreatitis. The fact that she has three children, a holiday cottage in the Cotswolds, collects Royal Doulton and has a sister called Beryl who lives in Newport Pagnell are inconsequential details. These facts have no place in the medical framework of diagnosis and treatment. Partly it's a function of the pressure we're under. But partly I think it's to distance us from the sheer volume of suffering and fear that we encounter. It's so hard sometimes to see people as people, however much you want to. It's so unbelievably tiring and all-consuming. And it's made all the worse by the feeling that you're not seen as a person yourself either: just another doctor, taking a woman's blood.

Monday 20 October

Overslept. Disaster. Can't believe that happened. Of course, no allowance was made for the fact that I just worked all weekend. I

110

remember waking in the on-call room and vaguely thinking it was time to get up. Then, thirty minutes after the ward round started I awoke with a start. I looked round for my alarm clock, then felt something small and hard digging me in the ribs: my clock, with the alarm turned off. It was displaying the very alarming time of 8.32 a.m. I dashed out of bed, not knowing what to do first. Deciding that clean teeth were low down on my list of priorities, I grabbed my pager, pulled on my clothes and fled. I arrived on the ward, having raced through the hospital at break-neck speed sending patients and nurses flying, only to discover that the ward round had commenced without me. I arrived just as Mr Price and Sad Sack were examining a patient; I could hear them behind the curtain. I waited outside, sick with fear. I grabbed some X-rays from the trolley thinking that I might be able to imply, without exactly lying to their faces, that I had been in radiology all this time. The curtains were flung back and the pair walked straight past me, totally ignoring me. No change there then. No one said anything and the ward round continued. Either they were so cross they couldn't tackle the subject with me, or they just didn't notice I wasn't there.

Tuesday 21 October

Michael, the young boy, deteriorated last night and was transferred to another hospital. I don't know what happened. Supriya was on call and told me at the ward round this morning. This is the nature of being a doctor and I'm finding it difficult to get used to. He was my patient, and now he's not. Simple as that. He's someone else's patient now, someone else's concern. But all day he preys on my mind. It's not deemed 'professional' to let patients get to you so I don't mention this to anyone. And I don't tell anyone about the shaving foam and razor I brought in that now sit, redundant, in my bag.

Thursday 23 October

Mr Butterworth is still our bugbear. I can't work him out. Part of me wants to believe that he is the way he is because of some tragic event in his past. While trailing behind him on the ward rounds I've begun imagining what might have contributed to him turning out like this. Perhaps his mother never loved him or perhaps he was spurned by the love of his life, perhaps he married and his wife ran away with a suave patient that he had brought back from the brink of death. Or perhaps he's just the way he is because that's his nature: a rotten, festering apple in the NHS orchard. Now, while his interpersonal skills leave a lot to be desired, as a surgeon he's supposedly pretty good. Not that I'm able to judge, given that what I know about actual surgery could be written on the back of a postage stamp and still leave room to be licked for postage to the General Medical Council. He's obviously very passionate about cutting people open, so it's fortunate that he became a surgeon because otherwise he'd be doing a long stretch in Broadmoor.

'I'm going to show you something,' whispered Trudy this afternoon, after I'd been trying to pump her for some personal information on Mr Butterworth. 'Have you ever seen inside his office?'

I confessed that I hadn't, and in fact I wasn't even sure where it was. 'Through here,' she said and opened a door to the left of her chest. Inside it undoubtedly smelt of Mr Butterworth, so much so my eyes scanned the room just to check he wasn't in there, loitering in some corner or behind a filing cabinet. There were piles of letters and papers and countless surgical journals on every available surface. 'There,' she said, pointing at a shelf next to his desk. On it stood a bottle and a photograph. The bottle was the sort that I had seen in the anatomy demonstrating room at medical school, containing foetuses or brains. 'What is it?' I asked, not daring to look. 'That,' she said triumphantly, "is the first appendix he ever removed. And the photograph next to it is of his first ever hemicolectomy.'

I looked at the photograph of pink bowel. 'That is gross,' I replied.

'I know, and what else do you notice?'

I looked round the room and shrugged my shoulders. 'No photos of family or a wife or anything. Just this,' she said, picking up the jar of pickled appendix and waving it around so that the contents sloshed about inside. 'The man is married to guts. It's his life. I tell you, he's weird,' she said, a conclusion I'd already come to.

Friday 24 October

The public, I suspect, have rather a warped idea of medicine and hospitals thanks to the endless nauseating television programmes on the medical profession, so let's set the record straight. I don't look like George Clooney, being a doctor is not glamorous, and no, we're not all dashing around saving people's lives. I can barely even muster the energy to clean my teeth sometimes.

What the public doesn't see on TV is patients like Mrs Davies. That's largely because they don't want to see patients like Mrs Davies, who's a patient on the psychiatric ward. And this sentiment is shared by Mr Butterworth. He's been asked to see her as she's having problems with her bowels. 'Nutters and weirdos,' he mutters.

This from the man who wears a bright-red bow tie, trousers six inches too short and smells of pond water and KitKats. 'I bet there's nothing wrong with her. I'm not seeing her. You go and see if she's got an actual surgical problem,' he mutters to Daniel.

Mr Butterworth can't be bothered to make the ten-minute trek out of the bright shiny surgical wards to the other side of the hospital grounds where the psychiatric ward is situated. I suspect he'd rather sit in his office and think up jokes about abscesses. Daniel, ever thoughtful of his future career as a surgeon, refuses to go anywhere where Mr Butterworth is not. So it falls to me to make a trip to the hospital's psychiatric ward.

Mrs Davies is sitting in her room with a few of her things lying around. It looks rather bare. In stark contrast to my surgical ward it's obvious that no one sends flowers or 'get well soon' cards to 'mad' people. She's in her fifties and is wearing a cardigan with flowers embroidered up one sleeve.

She's not wielding an axe or foaming at the mouth. In fact, she's delighted that I've come all this way to see her, and I sit down on a chair while she makes me a cup of tea. To my great annoyance my consultant is right, and Mrs Davies doesn't appear to have a surgical problem – her constipation has resolved and been put down to her change in medicines. So instead I stay for a bit and we talk about art and films and what we'd do if we won the lottery. She'd buy a red ball dress and go to lots of posh parties, she tells me.

I can't help but notice the countless circular burn marks on the furniture where people have stubbed out their cigarettes. There are large cracks going up the yellowed walls. On my way to see Mrs Davies, I had to detour round the building work for the new wing of the hospital. On the billboards covering up the work going on behind them are enormous pictures of sweet, doe-eyed children advertising the new paediatric ward due to be opened next year. The public like the idea that their taxes are being spent on exciting, heart-warming things like helping sick children and the new consumer-led, media-savvy NHS is only too pleased to be seen to be complying.

When psychiatric wards are eventually refurbished, there's no fanfare, no grand openings, no photo shoots. The popular image of psychiatric patients is of doped-up people in straitjackets. Pictures of them on a billboard are never going to be a crowd pleaser. As a nurse once said to me when I was a medical student, 'Try shaking a tin on a high street for sick children or abandoned puppies and see the attention you get. Then try doing it for psychiatric services.'

Mr Butterworth will be starting his ward round soon so I say goodbye to Mrs Davies and walk back to the main hospital. The ward seems even newer and brighter than ever.

'She was fine actually, nothing surgical to be done,' I explain to Mr Butterworth when I return. 'Who? Oh, her. I knew it,' he mutters and marches off with Daniel trailing behind.

I hope one day Mrs Davies gets her red ball dress – perhaps then she'll be seen.

Saturday 25 October

I met up with some non-medical friends for a drink this evening. Ruby was supposed to come too but said at the last minute she had other plans and dashed out of the house, leaving me to go alone. My friends, whom I've known since school and haven't seen since starting work, fell silent as I walked in the bar. 'You look awful,' they chorused. I sat there in a sort of daze while people chatted happily to me. They wanted to hear all the gory stories, funny vignettes and witty anecdotes. I duly obliged. But I could never tell

117

them about the horrors, about the tiredness, about the fear and uncertainty, and the pressure and the feeling of responsibility that almost crushes you on a daily basis. About feeling that your entire life has been turned upside down and now revolves around an out-of-town prefab building where no one knows your name but everyone feels they can call you. Where people shout or swear or spit at you when all you're trying to do is help them, or cry and try and hold your hand when all you want to do is go home to sleep. I didn't tell them any of this. They're my friends, after all, and I couldn't do that to them.

Sunday 26 October

Got up late today and wandered into Ruby's room to wake her up with a cup of tea. She wasn't there. Her bed hadn't been slept in. Strange. I tried her mobile and it was turned off. She eventually turned up mid-afternoon, in the same clothes she was wearing yesterday.

'Hello, where've you been?' I ask.

She looks at me with a mysterious guilty expression I haven't seen since she ate my last Wagon Wheel. 'Nowhere,' she replied, which clearly meant she had been somewhere.

'What's that on your lips?' I ask.

'Nothing,' she says, flushing scarlet, which clearly meant it was something. 'Just some lipstick.'

'You never wear lipstick,' I say, suspicion growing in the back of my mind. 'Last time you wore make-up was at medical school when you were trying to impress that stupid pharmacology lecturer.'

'Oh for God's sake, you're supposed to be my friend, not my mother.' She paused.

I went on with the washing-up, wondering where the snappiness came from. I'm not sure what's going on or indeed whether I really want to know.

'I'm going to have a bath. Is there any hot water left?' Ruby called as she went upstairs.

'Yes, there should be,' I reply, trying not to have to look up at her.

And when eventually I do, she's gone and I can hear the water running upstairs. I thought about what Trudy said a few weeks ago, about Ruby and Housewives' Favourite. Surely not? Ruby has far too much self-respect than to get involved with that sort of man. I plunge my hands back into the grimy dishwater, and wonder what misdemeanour Ruby is trying to scrub away upstairs.

Tuesday 28 October

Another day on call, working through the

night. The atmosphere in a hospital at night, when everyone else goes to bed and you are left walking the dark, friendless stretches of corridor, is almost unimaginably spooky.

The worst bit is the waiting when the pager goes eerily silent. I stand and stare at it like a cowering puppy knowing it is about to be hit and will it to just get it over with. Bleep, I know you're going to, and you know I won't know what to do. I stand in the gloom with only a flickering halogen bulb further down the corridor for light, and eventually decide to go to the doctors' mess and enjoy the apparent reprieve. After an hour of sitting watching late-night television, I become suspicious. Why haven't I been bleeped? Surely it can't be that some almighty power has finally taken pity on me and decided to let me have the night off?

I pick up the telephone in the doctors' mess and page myself. Nothing. I do it again. Nothing. I take a closer look at my pager. Dead battery, I realise in a moment of blind panic. I run over to A&E and am met by one of the nurses. 'Where have you been, Max? We've been bleeping you for hours.'

I knew it was too good to be true. I look at the board. Four patients waiting to be seen. But before I can make a start I should check the wards. I curse my pager as I begin to run through the dark, friendless stretches of corridor.

Wednesday 29 October

He's just smacked her bottom. I mean, he definitely has just done that. I stand at the other end of the ward, speechless, doubting what I have just witnessed. Not so much a smack, more of a lingering-of-hand-on-the-rump sort of thing, with a bit of a flick at the end. I stare in disbelief, not that House-wives' Favourite has just done that to Ruby, but that she hasn't turned round and smacked him one. She's just standing there. In fact, she's not just standing there, she's smiling at him as he sashays down the corridor. What the hell has she got herself into?

Friday 31 October

Lots of discharges today on the ward round, ready for the usual surgical slurry of patients that will be dumped on to the ward over the weekend. Spent most of the day desperately trying to fill out take-home prescriptions. Sign this, sign that; it's all I ever do. I'm just a walking, talking signature. I could have a stamp of my signature made, ensure that designated nurses each had one, and then go shopping in Habitat for the rest of the day. After all, my actual physical presence is not called for, and I seem to just get under people's feet. But then again, if I wasn't there, who would people shout at when things went wrong?

NOVEMBER

Monday 3 November

With three of us sharing a bathroom, it's often a scramble in the morning, but today's different. Ruby has been in there for ages; I don't know what she's doing. Flora left for work some time ago so I go downstairs and pour the remainder of the pot of tea that she made into a cup. It's stewed, but I stopped caring about that sort of thing long ago. When I go back upstairs Ruby is still in the bathroom. 'What you doing in there?' I ask. 'Come on, we've got to get to work and I haven't had a shower yet.'

'I won't be much longer,' comes the reply through the door.

It's oddly silent in there – no sound of running water, no noise of brushing of teeth. That's odd, I think, Ruby never hogs the bathroom. Eventually the door opens. My eyes widen. 'What the hell have you done?' I ask.

'What do you mean?' Ruby says breezily as she pushes past me towards her bedroom.

'I mean your hair. What have you done to it?'

'Nothing,' she says as she sits on her bed and dries her feet.

'What are you talking about? I saw you last night, and you had reddish-brown hair. The same hair that you've had ever since I've known you, and now you've gone orange.'

'It's not orange,' she replies, 'it's blonde, and it went a little wrong, and I don't want to talk about it. OK?' With which she leans forward and shuts the door in my face.

Tuesday 4 November

Having no time to eat, and spending all day running around the hospital, sometimes quite literally, means that pretty soon we will have to be admitted as patients ourselves. Ruby did a blood test on herself the other night while in A&E and discovered that she was technically in acute renal failure because she hadn't had anything to drink for sixteen hours. We wouldn't usually prescribe a can of Tango for acute renal failure, but that was all she could find, and given that she's still here, it must have worked.

On this morning's ward round though, I noticed Supriya drinking something surreptitiously from a carton. Later on I saw her across the ward where she was checking blood tests, again with a carton in hand. How on earth is she finding time to get to the vending machine on the other side of the hospital? I thought. By the afternoon, seeing her with what looked like the third carton of drink, I decided to challenge her. She looked sheepish. 'Erm, well,' she began evasively, 'I found them on the ward.'

I looked suspiciously at her. 'On the ward? Where?'

She led me to a fridge in one of the clinical rooms. 'There,' she said, pointing to shelves stacked with cartons.

I picked one up. 'They're for people dying of cancer,' I laughed. 'You can't drink them. They're build-up drinks. They're like a liquid meal.'

'Yes, I know. And I've lost so much weight recently I can fit into children's clothes,' she replied, snatching the carton from my hand and piercing the top with a straw. Drawing her cheeks in, she took a long hard suck. 'I mean losing weight is one thing, but this is beyond a joke.'

She pulled up her top to show me her trousers held up by a belt. 'Before I started this job they fitted perfectly. Now they fall round my ankles.' She took another drink. 'I was feeling faint the other day, and one of the dieticians gave me one. She said I could help myself if I haven't had time to eat, otherwise I might collapse.'

I could hear my stomach rumbling. 'Are they nice?' I asked casually.

'If you promise not to tell a soul, I'll let you have the strawberry-flavoured ones,' she replied.

Friday 7 November

Medicine is supposed to be upbeat: its aim is to save, improve, extend life. This is what medical school focuses on and it's why I became a doctor. I've been taught about the weirdest and most obscure medical conditions that affect only a handful of people, but death, that most universal of problems? Not a thing. In fact, I'm not even sure how to tell if someone actually *is* dead (it's harder than you'd think).

From my first week, this has provided constant anguish as I am regularly called upon to pronounce people dead. It's further complicated by the fact that dying people often look like dead people, making the exact moment of death rather tricky to detect. Rather than 'pronounce' people dead, which to me sounds rather official, I prefer to 'suggest' that people have died, then leave for a bit and come back. If rigor mortis has set in, then I feel a bit more confident in my diagnosis. This also gives you an added safety net; with any luck another doctor might have taken it upon themselves to pronounce them dead before you have returned. It also means that the nurses will have had time to straighten the sheets and make the body look nice, during which they can keep an eye out for any sudden signs of life.

Because we never actually think about medicine not working and people dying, it comes as a bit of a shock when we're faced with it. But while dealing with dead people is stressful, there's nothing that strikes fear into my heart more than people who are dying. It's hard because we're never taught what to say and what not to say. The subject of death isn't just avoided at medical school, but on the wards too. Dying people are seen as a bit of an embarrassment to doctors – they're reminders that we've failed in our job, despite that fact that dying is an inevitable consequence of being alive. Because of this, doctors tend to avoid dying people like the plague. They run tests and examine, pump them full of drugs and prevaricate, until finally giving them up as a lost cause and referring them to the palliative care team. It's a bit unfortunate that a profession that continually comes up against death hasn't yet come to terms with it. But as a junior doctor there's no escaping it and when the nurse pages me to ask me to see Mrs Bullen, I have to go.

Mrs Bullen is dying. She's had cancer on and off for ten years, and now it's spread all over her body. She has no family, although some neighbours visited this morning. She's been getting worse over the past few hours. 'She doesn't have long,' the nurse tells me as I arrive on the ward. There's nothing more I can do, and I'm perplexed as to why the nurse has called me. Everything that medicine has to offer has been tried and she's still going to die. 'She wants to see you,' explains the nurse. 'I think she knows it's the end and she wants you to be there.'

This is not good news. I don't know what to say to dying people. I feel sure that talking to dying people isn't in my job remit. 'Can't we get a priest or something?' I plead.

'Just pop your head in, Max,' the nurse says firmly.

I gingerly enter the side room where she's been moved to. I have no idea what I will say to her. The curtains are drawn and there's the peculiar musky smell that the nurses tell me is a sign that someone is dying. I stand for a few moments, reluctant to go closer, when Mrs Bullen opens her eyes and beckons me to her side. 'Thank you for all you've done, Doctor, and for being so kind to me,' she whispers through her oxygen mask.

But I don't feel I've done anything for her.

I ask her if there is anything she wants, anything I can do, and she shakes her head but moves her hand closer to mine. I sit for

128

what feels like a lifetime and hold her hand until I realise that she's not breathing any more. I stay with her for a few more minutes and while I sit there it occurs to me that being a doctor is more than just doing exciting lifesaving procedures. What mattered to Mrs Bullen more than the medicines and the operations and the tests, was that someone was by her side when she died.

I quietly close the door behind me and go back on to the ward.

'Well done,' says the nurse, who is just about to have a break, and we go to the canteen for a cup of tea.

While we're supposed to be able to distance ourselves from our patients, sometimes it's hard – especially when you've been there in the last few minutes of their life. Thankfully, when I return to the ward, another doctor has already pronounced Mrs Bullen dead.

Saturday 8 November

On call this weekend. Saw a lovely woman, Mrs Kirsch, with appendicitis today. She smiled and apologised for bothering me. And for the rest of the day, as I arranged for her to go to theatre and ordered her blood tests and X-rays and saw the other patients lined up in A&E waiting to be seen, I forgot it was a Saturday, that I was unlikely to get any sleep that night, that I was missing a friend's birthday party.

'What are you so happy about then?' asked one of the nurses as I walked past to rewrite some drug charts.

I stopped to think. 'Dunno, just in a good mood I guess,' I replied.

And afterwards it occurred to me that Mrs Kirsch had something more than just appendicitis. She had something rare amongst the usual disgruntled patients lying in pain in A&E, something infectious which I had caught: a smile.

Sunday 9 November

The doctors' mess is appropriately named. It's a real mess. It is littered with the debris of those that call it, temporarily, home. It is a place to go to when you need to escape. It is where you steal snatches of waking sleep when you are on call. It is where, in the moments between seeing patients, you can sit down and reflect, or seek unofficial advice from doctors working in other specialities, or catch up on dictating letters or lose yourself for a moment by watching TV. There is bread for toast and the kettle is permanently just boiled. There is always someone on the telephone, speaking to a ward or pleading with a secretary.

Occasionally there are domestic arguments conducted over a mobile phone in the corner, in hushed, hostile whispers, snatches of a relationship gently imploding under the pressure of work: 'I thought your mother was going to pick him up from nursery'; 'Don't shout at me, you knew I was on call this weekend'; 'I said I'll be there, OK? I'll leave earlier tonight, I promise'. There is a constant background noise of people milling in and out and pagers going off. When one does everyone instinctively glances down at their own, then, having been spared for the time being, resumes whatever they were doing whilst some unfortunate reaches for the phone. The evidence of interrupted meals lies everywhere: mugs of cold tea with the teabag still floating in them; half-eaten pizzas; takeaway still in the carton with the lid on, gone cold long ago, its oily footprint creeping out from under the box and onto the table.

At weekends it changes. There are fewer doctors around and those that are in are busy on the wards or in A&E. The mess has a quieter, melancholy air which doesn't suit it.

I woke this morning after a few hours of snatched sleep. I'd been inundated in A&E. Sad Sack was still in an operation which had begun at 5 a.m. Mr Price had been called in.

An ulcer in someone's bowel had perforated and they were close to death. I had watched them from the other side of the department as Sad Sack had explained to the patient what was going to happen. They had signed the consent form and been wheeled up to theatre. It can't be easy for the senior doctors. Other people's lives in their hands, every single day. All I have to worry about really is chasing X-rays and steering the notes trolley in a straight line on the ward rounds.

I sat in the doctors' mess and watched television before making my way over to the wards to start the ward round on my own. Then I heard the outside door open and someone whistle in the lobby. The door slowly creaked open and standing in front of me was an old man, probably in his eighties. He came in, smiled, and started picking up some of the empty cartons strewn around on the floor. I shook my head to see if I was still sleeping. Was he a patient?

He left for a few minutes and came back, carrying a cup of tea, which he put down in front of me. 'There you go, Doctor,' he said. 'Sorry to disturb you. You don't take sugar do you?'

I stared, perplexed, while he continued to clean up. 'I'm not in your way am I, Doctor?' he said after a few minutes.

'Erm, no, sorry, let me help you with that,'

I said, becoming acutely aware that I was sitting with my feet up, drinking tea while a man older than my grandfather was on his hands and knees in front of me, picking rubbish off the floor. 'Really, you don't have to do that,' I said, taking a black bin liner from him. 'Oh, I don't mind, I always do it. Here, Doctor, I've got the Sunday papers if you want to read them?'

There was something about the way he said 'Doctor'. Something old-fashioned about it, like he meant it with the greatest respect, not the way that patients bellow it at you as you walk past in A&E when they want to complain about something or try and assault you. It was as though he was saying 'sir' or 'lord' or some other honorific title. It made me feel awkward.

'Please, call me Max,' I said and offered him my hand. 'Oh, very well then, Doctor. I'm Maurice.' We shook hands. And before I could enquire exactly who he was and what on earth he was doing here at 8 a.m. on a Sunday morning, my pager went off and I was called to the ward, leaving my half-drunk cup of tea behind.

Monday 10 November

Ruby, Flora and I often spend what is left of our evenings sitting round the kitchen table.

The only slight excitement these days is that Ruby has now redone her hair and it's properly blonde – I don't know why she's taken the time to do this when there are far more pressing things on her plate. It seems all our free evenings are spent sitting at home like this. We're too tired to go out, and by the time we arrive home it's hardly worth it. We're usually home too late even to order a takeaway. We are entirely reliant on twenty-four-hour petrol stations for our sustenance (you'd be amazed at the meals you can make out of cheesy Wotsits and Pot Noodles). But the strange thing is, despite feeling crushingly tired, none of us want to go to bed. We sit up, drinking tea and staring into space in companionable silence. It's pointless asking each other how our day was, because we all know the answer as we've been through exactly the same thing. It's a strange feeling, being too tired to go to sleep. But also, we know that once we submit and go to bed, our next waking moment will be getting ready to go back and do it all over again.

Tuesday 11 November

The confusion over the identity of Maurice, our doctors' mess angel, has been resolved. Maxine enlightened me while we searched for X-rays down the back of Dr Palache's radiator. 'Oh, it's quite sad really,' she explained while brandishing a coat hanger she keeps specifically for this task. 'His wife died, oh, I'd say about ten years ago, up on ward 8. Cancer, I think. She was all he had. After that he just started turning up in the doctors' mess, clearing up, and buying the papers every single morning. He even comes in on Christmas Day. He says it's his way of saying thank you for the help the doctors gave to his wife. Little bastard!' she says, breaking away from the topic of Maurice and producing a bent and dusty envelope containing the lost X-ray. 'I knew he had it,' she said. 'You wait till I see that bloody Dr Palache,' and muttered under her breath about what she's going to do to him. As usual, it involved lubricating jelly and one of the X-ray films.

Thursday 13 November

'Are you blind?' asks Trudy as she pours the tea.

'No,' I reply, feeling slightly attacked.

'The whole hospital can see what's happening,' she says emphatically as she hands me the cup.

Trudy, who never appears to leave her office, has an unnerving capacity for finding out every shred of gossip in the entire hospital. Actually, I'm probably doing her a disservice: I imagine she's probably up on the gossip within the entire NHS. 'They're an item,' she says matter-of-factly. 'He took her to dinner last weekend.'

'Who?' I ask. Then it occurs to me: House-wives' Favourite. 'Are you absolutely sure?' I say.

'Wasn't it obvious when she dyed her hair?' asks Trudy. I shake my head. 'Oh Max, really. Everyone knows that he prefers blondes.'

My pager goes off. 'I've got to go,' I say.

'But you've only just got here, you haven't finished your tea, and,' she adds seductively, 'I've got you some Jamaica cake.'

'I can't, really; I've got to get on with some work. I'm so busy today,' I say hurriedly and leave, wondering what could possibly have possessed Ruby to get entangled with that nasty, greasy man.

Friday 14 November

I haven't really spoken to Ruby today. After yesterday's revelation, I don't really know what to say to her. Should I warn her off? Tell her that he's no good and that the whole hospital knows what's going on? Or should I just stay out of it?

It's easy to avoid her; we're both running around after our respective consultants.

When we meet in the radiology department in the afternoon, I pretend I haven't seen her until she comes up to me. 'Just got an urgent abdominal CT off Dr Palache,' she says proudly. 'Can't believe he agreed to do it this late on a Friday. I had to really plead with him, but he caved in eventually. He's a big softy, I reckon,' she says, playing with her hair.

'Why did you dye your hair, Rubes?' I ask casually.

'Oh, no reason. Just fancied a change,' she answers defensively.

Monday 17 November

As a doctor there are, simply speaking, three courses of action available when faced with sick patients: surgery, medication or wait and see. For the junior doctor there is also the fourth option of hiding in the toilets, but the nurses quickly become wise to this one. Waiting to see if the problem spontaneously resolves itself is not that popular with patients. However, more often than not it seems that this is actually the best course of action as the body is a marvellous thing and can correct whatever is wrong with minimal help from doctors. But patients feel that having made all the effort of arranging for someone to feed the dog they would rather

137

something were done.

Surgeons seem to think that everything can be sorted out by cutting, and scoff at the wishy-washy medics, who prefer to use tablets to sort things out. This doesn't mean that surgeons don't like to dabble in the dark side of prescriptions though. In fact Mr Butterworth is rather keen on dishing out the latest drug on the market, which just happens to coincide with which drug company has provided lunch at our weekly surgical meeting. For a few bags of crisps and some doughnuts, a drug company gets ten minutes or so of the entire surgical team's time to push their latest product. They give out free mugs, diaries, calendars, textbooks. Rather than challenge the drug reps, as they normally challenge anyone who tries to tell them something, the surgeons sit there, docile, nodding their heads. Anyone else standing up and trying to tell doctors that their knowledge is out of date would be savaged. Why they listen to someone with an HND in marketing and a chicken tikka sandwich is beyond me.

There's no such thing as a free lunch. For quarter of an hour today I sat in the surgical meeting and was subjected to a barrage of cleverly altered statistics and hyperboles presented by an obsequious drug rep, all white teeth, fake tan and hair gel. The new drug he was peddling is twice as expensive as the current one available and, when you look closely at the evidence, can't even be proved to be as effective. And I think it somewhat suspicious that this brand-new drug comes out just as the patent runs out on this company's current big earner. The problem is that it is presented as scientific research rather than what it really is: promotional material. After all, the research that their data is based on is funded by the company itself, which means it's hardly objective.

You'd think that professionals that have dedicated their lives to the pursuit of knowledge might be a little more discerning, but the drug company is also paying for my consultant and some of the other surgeons to go to a swanky restaurant where minor celebrities hang out and I suspect that this might have something to do with it. But if we'd wanted free stuff, we should have got a job in PR, not the NHS. I decide to skip the free sandwiches.

These are the same doctors that scoff at Miss Miller. We admitted her a few days ago with recurrent stomach pains, and rather than operate, it was decided to wait and see if it got better on its own, which it did. 'I think it's down to my new homeopath,' she says on the ward round, just before we discharge her. Daniel tries to suppress a laugh, while Mr Butterworth doesn't bother and guffaws in her face.

'He says it's because of all the wheat we eat these days,' she continues, anxious to explain. 'Our bodies aren't designed for it. He sees lots of people with the same problems as me. But he's given me a new supplement which I've been taking since I've been in here and it's worked wonders.'

As far as Miss Miller is concerned, she came in with stomach pains, we didn't do anything for her, but she started taking her homeopathic medicine and she got better. Who am I to say it wasn't down to homeopathy? Mr Butterworth isn't convinced. 'New-age rubbish. No, these things just get better on their own, given time. Homeopathy! No reliable evidence that it works at all.' Daniel nods in agreement and they walk off shaking their heads.

'I think it works,' says Miss Miller once they have gone.

'Well, if it makes you feel better, there's no harm in carrying on taking it,' I reply and run to catch them up.

I'm just in time to catch the instructions for the next patient and, no surprises, Mr Butterworth, apparently no longer concerned about reliable evidence, has prescribed the new drug we've just spent lunchtime learning about.

I like to think that I won't be affected by drug company marketing, that I prescribe medicines sensibly and not because someone's paid for my lunch. I like to think that I wouldn't allow myself to be bought by a transglobal company on the promise of supper at a restaurant where Dale Winton goes. But I'm still only a junior doctor, so we'll have to wait and see.

Wednesday 19 November

I first realise that something is happening when I hear Ruby's voice from outside the office. 'Help, I need some help. Anyone. Please.' I ignore her for a few moments, the panic in her voice not really registering at first. The door is ajar and I can hear nurses shouting to one another and then more voices, crying and screaming out. 'Get them out of here, and get someone to help me,' I hear Ruby yell. I rush out the door and see Ruby running past. She stops and without a word grabs me by the arm.

I hesitate. 'What? What is it?' I ask.

'I think she's gone into cardiac arrest,' she shouts at me. 'I can't get a line into her, come and help.'

She hands me some equipment and we both run over to one of the beds. The curtains are pulled halfway round the bed and there are what appears to be dozens of relatives standing round making an awful noise. I can feel my heart beating in my throat.

'Please, Doctor, do something,' says one of the relatives, pulling my arm and staring into my eyes. His face is wet with tears. 'She was just sitting up a while ago, and now she's not speaking.'

There is a small, frail-looking woman lying on the bed, unconscious.

'I've lost the pulse,' shouts Ruby who is crouching at the side of the bed trying to get a needle into the arm. 'Mrs Singh, Mrs Singh, can you hear me?' she shouts.

No response. I stand motionless for a second, frozen to the spot. Ruby looks up at me imploringly and I come round and feel for a pulse in Mrs Singh's neck. Still nothing.

A nurse comes in, wheeling the crash-trolley, followed by more of Mrs Singh's family who begin to wail at the sight of her. 'Get them out of here and get the crash team,' begs Ruby. I check the airways and then look for signs of breathing. Nothing. I get on top of the bed and straddle Mrs Singh's chest. I place my hands on her breastbone and push down. Crack. I push down again. Crack.

Each time I push a rib breaks. It makes me feel sick but I know that if I don't do it, she will certainly die. Ruby has managed to get a cannula into her arm, although she has covered herself in blood in the process. A nurse reappears and attaches a heart monitor to Mrs Singh's chest, while Ruby places a mask and bag over Mrs Singh's mouth to pump air into her lungs. I see the chest inflate and deflate as she squeezes the bag. Having broken all her ribs by this point, there are no more cracking sounds as I resume the chest compressions, just the sound of my own heart in my ears, and the noise from the other side of the curtains of her family wailing and a nurse trying to move them away.

I continue to pump up and down on her chest, sweat pouring down my face. I feel like I'm assaulting her. We stop for a moment. The heart monitor flickers into life. It cannot detect any activity in the heart, which means we cannot attempt to restart the heart with electrical paddles. 'She's in asystole,' shouts Ruby. 'Give adrenaline.' The heart monitor does not change, so we resume. A nurse rushes in to tell us that the crash team – the group of doctors who respond to these emergencies – is involved in another cardiac arrest on the other side of the hospital. At this moment I panic. What are we going to do? Ruby looks up at me. 'It's OK, we can manage this, Max. You're doing fine. Keep going.'

We persevere for another ten minutes until an anaesthetist arrives, out of breath. 'Is it just you two?' he asks as he pushes around the bed. 'Keep going,' he orders and draws up more drugs. Still nothing. Some more doctors from the crash team arrive. After a further five minutes the anaesthetist stands up. 'I don't think we should continue. Is everyone in agreement?'

Ruby and I look at each other and stop. We leave the bed and walk past Mrs Singh's family, our heads bowed low, while the anaesthetist explains to them that she is dead.

After work we decide to go for a drink and sit in the bar silently. The sudden rush, the smack of adrenaline and now the comedown. It all happened so fast. I can recall each moment as though it happened in slow motion. We did everything right. There was nothing more that could be done. But somehow that is no consolation. I can still hear the sound of her ribcage cracking. The way it felt as I pushed down on her chest, knowing that I had to keep on, because if I didn't she would die. And knowing that she had died regardless. That as we sit here, her family are at home crying. It didn't feel heroic or exciting. It felt brutal and extreme. Ruby and I sit in silence, because we each know what the other is thinking. We both want to cry, but we both know that it would be stupid, because what happened today will happen again, and we will see far worse and be involved in far worse. And when we finish our drinks, we walk home in silence, our arms around one another.

Thursday 20 November

Lewis joined Ruby and I for a cigarette round the back of the radiology department today. 'You don't even smoke,' said Ruby as Lewis spluttered and retched his way through one of Ruby's.

'I know, but it's just something to do that doesn't involve someone else's bodily fluids for once,' he said as he exhaled a plume of smoke and coughed.

Dr Palache came out and joined us for a chat. For once he seemed pretty cordial – almost friendly. Perhaps it's just the presence of Lewis, who is one of those people that brings out the best in everyone, or maybe we're finally losing the newbie air that causes the senior doctors such irritation.

Friday 21 November

Damn. Damn. Damn. My sister's birthday. Yesterday. Having realised this morning, I made a mental note all day to try and call her to apologise and wish her a belated happy birthday. Got home at around 11 p.m. this evening, exhausted. I lay on the bed, thinking about the things I had done today and mentally ticking each one off, when I remembered again. Damn. 'Oh, hello, why the hell are you calling me at this time?' she said in a grouchy voice when I called her.

'I missed your birthday and I'm really sorry. Did you have a nice time? Sorry,' I said, in my most apologetic-sounding voice, which I'm getting very good at since becoming a doctor.

Most things you apologise for as a doctor are, in actual fact, not at all your fault. 'I'm very sorry, but it's cancer,' as if I was somehow responsible. And then there are the blanket apologies made by any junior doctor to any senior doctor, regardless of the situation. When an apology is called for it will always be the responsibility of the junior doctor to provide it even if it's not your fault. 'Oh, Mr Butterworth, sorry you accidentally cut through that person's colon, even though I wasn't even in the same room as you at the time.' And then there are the apologies you have to make to the nurses, porters, secretaries, or indeed anyone else with a chip on their shoulder for every doctor that has ever been rude to them.

But this time I really mean it. I really am sorry that I've missed my sister's birthday. 'Why are you calling me at this time of night?' she repeated. 'I've got to be up for work in four hours.'

I look at the clock. I must have dozed off,

because it's now 3 a.m. 'Oh, God, sorry,' I say, and she hangs up. 'Sorry,' I say again as I slip off to sleep.

Monday 24 November

More fun on the ward round. Sad Sack appeared to smile at one moment, but Supriya said it was probably wind.

I met Ruby in the doctors' mess. She had spent the past hour signing cremation certificates. Hooray! She was beaming. 'I'm going to buy a new bike with this batch, I reckon,' she said.

One of the few perks of being a junior doctor is a thing called 'ash cash', which I had never even heard of before I started work. A death certificate is provided by the doctor and is a legal document stating when and how the person died. You can't be disposed of without one. Because it is a statutory legal document, the doctor doesn't get paid for providing it. However, if someone is to be cremated, then a separate document must be supplied by a doctor to the people undertaking the cremation stating that they have examined the body and are happy that this person died of natural causes. For this there is a small charge which the funeral company must pay to the doctor. It's about fifty pounds, which is not to be sniffed at.

Especially not when you think of the volume that we can potentially sign.

OK, it's not going to buy you a holiday home in Marbella, but it might buy you a nice meal out every so often, or a new suit. For this reason a priest giving the last rites is bad news – although clearly good news for the dying person's eternal soul – because most Catholics get buried, not cremated. But had a run of atheists and Protestants? Ker-ching. It feels slightly bizarre to be making money out of the fact that someone has died, but then again, undertakers make their entire living from this.

You sign the forms in a room called 'Patients' Affairs'. Generally a trip to Patients' Affairs is considered a celebratory event as it means a bit of pocket money. But there's a wistful side to it as well. It's a time when you are faced with all the people you have just watched die, their names neatly printed on a piece of paper, strangely disconnected from the people you knew. You come across names of those you really liked, who you'd known perhaps over weeks, who you'd developed a relationship with; and then there are those whose names you don't recognise, those that were admitted and died before they ever had the chance to make an impression.

Either way, it's a strange ending to your professional relationship with someone. Visiting the body in the morgue, and then

signing a piece of paper in a room somewhere. 'I signed Mrs Singh's certificate
today,' Ruby said.

I smiled at her, knowing how deeply what
had happened had affected us both.

'I'll give you half the money,' she said
quietly. 'You helped me with her, didn't
you.' It sounded peculiar and she looked a
little embarrassed after she had said it. But
we both knew what she meant, and what she
was trying to say. She was just trying to say
thank you.

Wednesday 26 November

Poor Mrs Stoffels, I think as she stares at me
intently, her head tilted back and resting on
a pillow while she tries to talk. Her eyes are
wild and wide, like large saucers of milk
perched above her cheeks. She's just been
transferred up from A&E. She's breathless.
Her hands shake as she reaches out for the
jug of water. I pour her a glass and hand it
to her.

She had breast cancer a few years ago.
After surgery and radiotherapy she was
given the all-clear and it had all been going
so well for her until just a year ago. Then she
noticed she was becoming breathless. She
went to the GP, who referred her to the hospital, who did scans and tests and prodded

and poked her, and referred her back to Mr Price, the breast surgeon who had first operated on her. She tells me how, one early spring afternoon earlier this year, she learnt that the cancer had returned. But this time it had spread. It was now in her liver and her lungs. She had been given chemotherapy over the summer, but the cancer continued to march on, undeterred, inside her body. 'It was too late,' she said, 'they can't do anything for me now except manage the pain.'

Where the cancer has begun to grow into her gullet though, it is making swallowing difficult. Mr Price has admitted her to try and remove some of it and place a stent – a small plastic tube – inside her gullet to keep it open for as long as possible.

'Desperate times call for desperate measures,' she said, managing to raise a smile.

Desperate, I thought, that's the word. That's what the look in her eyes was: pure desperation.

Thursday 27 November

It is disgusting, I'll grant you, but there's nothing quite as satisfying as lancing a boil. Mr Fisher came in screaming in agony. In his armpit was a large, hot, red lump. 'It's killing me doctor. I think I'm going to die.'

Young men are so melodramatic when it

comes to their health; they are always 'about to die' from the slightest of ailments. After examining it and getting Sad Sack to take a look, I try to arrange for him to be sent up to theatre to have it dealt with. There are no spaces on today's operating list. I tell Sad Sack, preparing to cower in case she some-how manages to blame this on me.

'You can do it here,' she says, not looking up from the notes she's writing at the desk in A&E.

'Sorry, who can do it here?' I ask, assu-ming I have misheard.

She looks up. 'You.'

I gulp. 'Right. But I've never done it be-fore,' I say, beginning to panic. Once again the feeling of dread which I have become so accustomed to washes over me like a tidal wave.

'It's OK, I'll supervise you,' she says.

Erm, someone's been at the happy pills today, haven't they? I think, as I watch her get up from what she is doing and collect the equipment I'm going to need. I'm dumb-founded.

'You've been at this job for a while now, it's about time you got a bit of practical experience of surgery,' and she smiles. She. Smiles. I steady myself on a nearby heart monitor, lest I collapse with the shock. And for the next fifteen minutes she stands over me, gently guiding me, encouraging me as I make an incision and push the rancid, cream cheese-like contents out of the lump. It's like squeezing toothpaste out of a tube, only absolutely revolting. But unbelievably satisfying too. The joy you get from squeezing spots, but on an enormous scale.

After tea and biscuits the man gets up and goes home, thanking me as he leaves. Amazing. There are times when I love this job. And there are times, I think, when I love Sad Sack. I steady myself on a nearby heart monitor again. Easy now, let's not go too over the top here.

Friday 28 November

Mrs Stoffels died today. I was elsewhere in the hospital, dealing with a recalcitrant six-year-old with stomach pains. I got the page from the nurse telling me that she had died. I had meant to go and check in on her myself after the ward round, when it had become clear that she wasn't going to last. I was too late, though. The nurses had called her husband to warn him, but he'd got stuck in traffic and arrived just after she had died. Too late to save her from the cancer and too late to say goodbye. The two saddest words in the English language: Too Late.

Saturday 29 November

I'm going to confess to something very un-fashionable. And I'm not talking about the purple paisley shirt I bought in a moment of madness in the summer sales. I am aware that this was a serious fashion *faux pas* and I'm not even going to mention the match-ing tie. No, the thing that I'm going to confess to is far more shocking given my age and generally liberal outlook on life. It's drugs.

Usually when people confess to things con-cerning drugs there's a policeman present and they're in handcuffs. But my confession is rather different: I abhor illicit drugs and have no time for people who take them. This evening I went to a party. Ruby dragged me along. 'It will be fun. My friend works in PR so there'll be loads of celebrities there. You might meet a nice supermodel,' she said and winked at me. 'Come on, we need to get out a bit.'

After an hour or so there, it became apparent that hordes of people were congre-gating around the toilet. No one batted an eyelid. Drug taking amongst young profes-sionals has become perfectly acceptable. Provided you don't have to bash old ladies over the head to get the money to pay for it, then it's OK to take them. But this is where I get into deep water. It is actually not the smackheads on the street who I look down on but the smug, educated classes who dabble in something a bit 'naughty'. Though I have yet to hear someone pipe up with: 'Oh, I've just been in the bathroom supporting global criminal networks which include child prostitution and gangland murders.' You'd be a bit of a party-pooper, wouldn't you?

There is a fantastic amount of hypocrisy around drugs. While it's perfectly acceptable for the middle classes, come the weekend, to snort and smoke whatever they like, prostitution, gun crime, murder, extortion, burglary or armed robbery are considered unacceptable. But this is what you're supporting when you take illegal drugs.

What strikes me as ludicrous is that lots of my friends who take drugs would never consider drinking anything but the fairest of fair-trade coffee, while happily snorting substances for which innumerable people have died to get it into the country. But the executives and professionals, celebrities and fashionistas, live a rarefied existence, divorced from the more unpleasant aspects of an underworld they are so happy to finance. From cannabis to coke, it's all part of the same underworld and taking them is, quite literally, buying into it. But while it enrages me when I hear about people doing drugs, it's unfashionable to admit it. But then I've never been that good at fashion. And I've got the purple paisley shirt with matching tie to prove it.

DECEMBER

Tuesday 2 December

Yet more of my life wasted looking for X-rays in the radiology department. Over the past few months, this tedious routine has become strangely comforting, contrasting, as it does, with the utterly unpredictable nature of medicine. The radiology department has become a refuge from the rigors of the ward, and even Dr Palache, who used to scare me, has grown on me.

He and Maxine had an argument over a pelvis yesterday which she said he had in his office and he denied, until she found it, once again, behind the radiator. (I'm aware that outside a hospital such an argument could be considered rather surreal.) Now she's not talking to him and is implicitly threatening not to do the extra typing she does in the evening for his private patients. Of course, we all know that she's just brought an Alfa Romeo on hire purchase, so needs the extra money, but periodically the balance of power between her and Dr Palache needs to be re-negotiated. It's a little ritual they go through every so often. It's rather sweet, really. Like a married couple, but without the sex. Well, just like a married couple then.

So Dr Palache is now desperately trying to ingratiate himself with her. 'Oh, let me help you with that,' he keeps saying today as she heaves hundreds of scans off his office floor, flounces out and loudly drops them on her desk to sort through.

'Would you like a cup of tea, Max?' she asks pointedly while walking past Dr Palache's office. I decide not to get involved and shake my head. 'Would anyone else like a cup of tea while I'm making one?' she bellows, ignoring Dr Palache who is waving his cup at her.

He shrugs his shoulders and rolls his eyes, heaving himself up to go and offer to make one for her. She will at first refuse, then he'll offer to go to the Co-Op at lunchtime and buy her a cream puff or something, and she'll agree and then all will be forgiven. I've seen the routine so many times. It's comforting.

Wednesday 3 December

I don't know what is more ludicrous: that someone has just come into A&E with a hairbrush inserted into his rectum or that he is expecting me to believe that he 'fell' whilst brushing his hair and as he put his hand down to break his fall, it lodged in there that way. For today alone, six years at medical school were worth it. Cases like this are called 'one per centers'. This is because, on the board in A&E, rather than write 'man with a brush up his bum', which might be construed as embarrassing for this gentleman, they are referred to by the percentage of the body that the genitals typically represent. I always find this a rather depressing number – one per cent – it's not very much is it? And I'd love to meet the scientist who worked that out.

Perhaps I shouldn't be telling you this, because now if you ever find yourself in A&E and see '1%' written on the board you'll know what it means, thereby defeating the whole purpose. Of course, it's not funny really. It's childish to laugh at others' misfortune, even if it is, whatever they try and tell you, clearly self-inflicted. I do an X-ray, and there, perfectly outlined, is the brush. It has somehow managed to turn itself round so it looks wedged in there for good. I get Sad Sack.

'Oh well, thank God it's not a sink plunger – they're the worst.'

Well of course, who could be so silly to insert a sink plunger when a brush will do? That's just asking for trouble, isn't it? I can only imagine the excuse for that one, 'There I was, unblocking a drain in the nude, as you do.'

The patient is sent up to the ward where he is then prepared for theatre to have his rectum 'explored'. I meet Sad Sack on the ward round in the afternoon and she informs me that it came out very easily, although they found some Lego up there as well. They thought it best not to mention this to save the poor man the humiliation of trying to explain (presumably along the lines of 'I was building a Lego castle in the nude, as you do...').

When we arrive by his bedside we find the man sitting up in bed, with a lady, probably in her early seventies, sitting next to him. She smiles warmly at us. The patient immediately goes bright red as he sees us and Sad Sack, to her credit, appears to understand and manages to conduct the entire review without mentioning exactly why he was here or what they had removed. The man seems grateful and we can see him relax as we finish writing up the notes and tell him he can go.

Then his mother pipes up. 'You know, it was lucky that his friend Claude happened to be in the other room at the time of the accident, otherwise I don't know who would have called the ambulance. He's such a good friend, isn't he?' she says, and as she gets up to collect the man's things, she gives us a quick, but definite, wink.

Thursday 4 December

Flora, ever insistent that we experience some semblance of normal life, despite the concerted efforts of the entire world to keep us at work, had organised for her, Ruby and me to go to the theatre. 'Come on, it's culture,' she said.

Culture used to mean opera, ballet, art trips, evening lectures at trendy venues, but since starting work it's come to mean something you grow from someone's urine.

'Hey, it will be fun!' she insisted. 'it's a French avant-garde dance company. They're doing an all-female interpretation of *Coriolanus*.'

I'm too tired to object, which means I must be very tired indeed. We arrange to meet at the theatre at 7.15 p.m. 'You won't be late will you?' Flora asked threateningly.

'Well, we'll try our best to get out of work,' Ruby replied.

Needless to say, at 7 p.m. Ruby and I were still at work. 'Damn, we're going to be late,' Ruby shouts after me as she runs past carrying a pot of something probably unpleasant.

I am just preparing to leave when a nurse walks up to me. 'Max, you forgot to do a cannula for Mr Katz in bed 7.'

I roll my eyes. Another ten minutes lost.

Ruby emerges from behind a curtain. 'Come on, we can just make it,' she squeals as she grabs her coat. I race over to Mr Katz and begin to push the needle into his arm. I get it in first time. He groans. And groans some more. Then yelps in pain. I look up at him. 'it's OK, I've got it in now – it can't be still hurting,' I say.

'No, son, it isn't the needle that hurts, it's my chest. The pain's going right down my arm now.' I look at him closely: he's looking pale and sweaty. I feel his pulse, rush off and get the ECG machine to get a tracing of his heart. It shows me he's having a heart attack, at which my own heart sinks. I'm not going anywhere.

An hour later Ruby and I arrive at the theatre. We wait for Flora to come out in the interval. We can't see her. Her mobile is off. Ruby and I sit in the theatre bar talking about work, when we see Flora run in. She's startled to see us. 'I'm so sorry, I got delayed at work,' she pants. 'Have you been here waiting for me all this time? I'm so so sorry. I tried so hard to leave on time and then this woman was brought in and I had to see to her and then another woman needed me...'

'It's OK,' said Ruby soothingly, 'we've only just got here as well. We were delayed too.'

'Never mind,' I say. 'It was a nice idea.'

We decide to go and have dinner instead.

It's such an effort now to do things in the evening I'm not even sure if it's worth it. But the prospect of spending the next forty years crashing out in front of the TV with a glass of rosé is too much to bear. Every plan we ever make is ruined. As we walk to the restaurant round the corner I comfort myself with the thought that the only thing worse than missing an avant-garde all-female dance interpretation of *Coriolanus* is, surely, not missing it.

Friday 5 December

Mrs Sheppard died today and the feeling of sadness is overshadowed by the feeling of horror that all of us, in our own way, were responsible for her death. By this I mean everyone, including you.

Mrs Sheppard was admitted for a routine operation to remove a tumour. After the operation, things appeared to be going well: her wound was healing, she was beginning to walk about on the ward. Then, suddenly, she began to deteriorate and her wound began to open again. She failed to respond to treatment and then the results of some swabs confirmed what we had all feared – she had developed MRSA in the site of the operation. Over the past decade, cases of

MRSA have increased in England and Wales enormously. MRSA stands for methicillin-resistant *Staphylococcus aureus*. It is a variety of *Staph aurcus* – a harmless bacteria present on everyone's skin – which has become resistant to the penicillin-based drug methicillin. Whilst many of the general population have MRSA living on them, if it gets into deep wounds, it can grow out of control and the resulting infection can be difficult to treat. So there's a call for the NHS to 'take responsibility' for MRSA infections.

But is the NHS responsible? Politicians would have us believe that it is simply a matter of cleaner hospitals, but since working here I've come to realise it's not that simple. Certainly contracting out cleaning services to external companies hasn't helped. Our cleaners aren't part of the ward team and as a result have no ownership of their work. However, saying that, it takes only three hours for a new colony of MRSA to establish itself on a ward, so guaranteed eradication would require near-constant cleaning of every surface. And moreover, the reasons that MRSA exists in the first place reach beyond the hospital.

Every time a colony of bacteria is exposed to an antibiotic, they attempt to mutate in order to survive. The more exposure, the more chance they'll become resistant.

When people insist on being given antibiotics for minor infections or when the infection is viral, they contribute to this. Also, many people who are given antibiotics fail to complete the course, thus ensuring that those bacteria which haven't been killed can mutate to become resistant. I've also discovered that our desire for cheap, factory-farmed meat means that large amounts of antibiotics have to be used to help keep infections under control in live-stock, another contribution to resistance. In fact, the current prevalence of MRSA is thought, in part, to be the legacy of a decade ago, which saw large quantities of anti-biotics used in cattle as a growth promoter.

While these may be the underlying causes of MRSA, it's true to say that they are spread to vulnerable individuals within hospitals.

It's here that we come up against the wider political issues which implicate government policy in the spread of MRSA. Over the past few years we have seen dramatic cuts in the number of hospital beds available up and down the country as the government has tried to reduce spending and increase prod-uctivity. As a result, bed occupancy rates in hospitals have increased as patients are discharged and admitted with a quicker turn-around. Research has shown that as the bed-occupancy rate increases, so does the rate of infection. MRSA rates, for example, are over 40 per cent higher in hospitals with 90 per cent bed occupancy than those with less than 85 per cent. On the continent, where bed-occupancy rates are lower still, they have far fewer outbreaks. This has been roundly ignored by the government because it does not fit in with its new agenda for the NHS of closing hospitals, introducing PFI hospitals (which typically have 30 per cent fewer beds than non-PFI) and 'streamlining' services, it's no wonder we're in trouble. Of course the actual spread of infection is often from person to person but not just by doctors like me; it is thought that around half of all MRSA infections are actually from visitors, who don't always wash their hands appropriately before and after visiting a patient. If more people did this, it would be enough to break the chain of infection. So I can't help feeling that before we turn to the NHS and point the finger of blame, we should realise that the responsibility for MRSA rests with us all.

Monday 8 December

Ruby is frantically trying to get an abdominal CT scan which Mr Grant has insisted must happen today. She's sitting in the doctor's office on the phone to radiology while I check bloods but is so far failing in her mission. There are absolutely no spare slots for her patient, she's told. Just then, Lewis walks in and, overhearing her conversation, offers to see if he can fare any better. 'I've got a few to book myself and was going to go down now anyway,' he says, smiling sweetly.

Ruby and I look at him amazed. 'Dr Palache will never agree to it. There's not even a good reason why it can't wait until tomorrow anyway,' says Ruby.

Lewis shakes his head and takes the request form from Ruby.

'Consider it done,' he says.

Twenty minutes later Ruby receives a page from radiology to say Dr Palache has agreed to fit the patient in at lunchtime. How does Lewis do it? We both stand looking at each other, astonished.

'Right,' I say, collecting up my X-ray requests, 'Lewis has just got himself a new job.'

Wednesday 10 December

'That Lewis is a nice chap, isn't he?' says Maxine as we go on the usual pilgrimage to locate the holy grail that is this week's X-rays for the operating list.

'Yeah, he's great,' I reply.

'We see a lot of him you know,' adds Maxine with a little smile.

'Oh yeah?' I reply, juggling envelopes and failing to see the significance of this. 'Well, that's probably because his consultants insist on scans for absolutely everyone who walks through the door,' I add as I drop the entire armful on the floor.

Maxine bends down to help me sort through them. 'I suppose that's one reason,' she says with her little smile again. 'And I doubt it's got anything to do with Dr Palache,' she adds, while looking at me out of the corner of her eye.

'You don't mean ... not Lewis and Dr Palache?' I ask amazed. 'I don't believe you. You're making this up.'

'Didn't you think it was a bit odd that Lewis is quite so good at getting all his scans reported on time? Dr P. never loses the scans for Lewis, does he?' she says, sitting back in her chair, clearly pleased with herself.

'Is everyone at it in this hospital?' I ask, feeling rather dejected.

'Why? Who else do you know about?' she asks excitedly.

'Well, there's Ruby...' I hesitate. I don't want to start rumours about Ruby.

Maxine purses her lips in disapproval. 'Oh. She's not with that horrid consultant of hers? He does this every year to his female house officers. You mark my words, she'll be sorry. He'll get bored of her like all the others.'

I shrug helplessly.

'You feeling jealous of everyone getting some loving?' she adds.

I blush.

'Well, if you're looking for a little company this evening...' she says, laughing and leaning forward to stroke my tie.

'I'm going to sue you for sexual harassment,' I say as I take the X-rays and walk away down the corridor.

'Nice bum,' she shouts after me.

I turn round to see Maxine blowing me a kiss and cackling loudly.

Friday 12 December

'Oi, you,' somebody yells at me as I walk through one of the wards with Supriya, 'I'm not eating this.'

We both turn round, rather puzzled.

'Sorry Doctor, I was talking to the nurse, not you.'

Supriya and I both look at each other, rather bemused.

'What nurse?' I ask.

'Her,' he replies, looking at Supriya.

This isn't the first time this has happened to Supriya and it's starting to really annoy her. The man quickly realises his mistake.

'Sorry love, I thought you were a nurse,' he says, a little embarrassed.

'Well, I'm not, I'm a doctor,' she snaps. 'And this isn't The Ivy so just eat what's put in front of you.'

I brace myself for a barrage of abuse, but instead he smiles. 'Yes, of course Doctor, sorry,' he says before looking at me and sitting back down by his bed as we both walk off.

One benefit of being a doctor is that scary people are nice to you. By just having the title 'Dr' in front of your name you immediately command respect. Not always, but sometimes.

Once they become a patient, some of the roughest, meanest people around can be polite and courteous and go out of their way to be pleasant. People who in normal circumstances would be interested in the contents of your wallet are falling over themselves to say good morning to you. There are, of course, exceptions to this observation, and I've found myself having to call security for a few difficult patients who've decided that the best way to get my attention is to try and punch me in the face.

Unfortunately, hospital security is rather difficult to get hold of when you need them. When you park your car outside a marked bay, they descend en masse, but when you're being held up against the wall by a drunk man twice your size who obviously spends too much time cracking his knuckles and not nearly enough time reading books on etiquette, they're nowhere to be found.

In these situations it's usually best to call for a nurse instead. Nurses take abuse on a daily basis and are therefore fantastic at dealing with it. I've seen nurses half my size tackle grown men twice as big as me without even breaking into a sweat. Not only can they deal with all the nasty patients, they are also the ones, not the doctors, who know what's really happening on the wards. Most patients tend to give doctors more respect. But without the nurses the whole thing would fall apart. Countless times it's the nurse who whispers the answers when Sad Sack or Mr Butterworth asks me questions on the ward round or who stands there silently while Daniel takes the credit for something they've done. It's the nurses who are there dealing with the patients day in and day out, but they don't receive a fraction of the respect they deserve – not from the patients and certainly not from the doctors. There is one group who really respect nurses, and that's junior doctors.

Without nurses no junior doctor would last more than a few days on the wards. Not only do they know where all the equipment is, they know how to use it. While for the junior doctor everything is new, the nurses have seen it all before and providing you're in their good books, they'll make sure you don't make any mistakes. And if they like you, they'll make you tea. One particular nurse, Andrea, even makes me sandwiches when I work night shifts.

Tonight, walking through A&E, I suddenly find myself cornered by Mr Ellis. He isn't happy. He got into a fight earlier this evening and suffered a head injury as a result. Because he's still very drunk and aggressive, he's been left to calm down for a while.

'I've been waiting hours, I want someone to see me *now*,' he shouts, pushing his face into mine.

I try to placate him but he's getting more and more irate and grabs me by the tie. At this point I want to call my mum, but instead Andrea appears. She's only just five foot but takes the situation firmly in hand. 'How dare you behave like that to one of the doctors?' she barks and marches him off.

Twenty minutes later she returns. 'I think he's calmed down enough now for you to see him,' she says.

Mr Ellis is sitting sedately in a cubicle. 'Sorry Doctor, didn't mean to be rude. Just don't like hospitals and was getting myself worked up.'

I'm amazed at this transformation. I assess him and as I'm about to leave the cubicle he leans forward. 'Say thanks to that nurse for me, won't you? She was cool. Respect's due,' he says. I couldn't agree more.

Saturday 13 December

A weekend on call. Last week Mrs Fraser was wheeled on to the ward. She was in her mid-forties, her head hung awkwardly on one side and her eyes appeared to roll to and fro. She'd been diagnosed with progressive supranuclear palsy five years previously. One hand hung lifelessly out of the bed. Her nightdress was damp with sweat and as I leant over her to listen to her heart, in barely formed words she said very slowly: 'Let me die.'

Then she seemed angry and frustrated and tried to turn her head away from me. A few minutes later Mr Butterworth appeared. And again she tried to deliver her request. 'What's she saying?' Mr Butterworth asked.

'She's saying that she wants us to let her die,' I mumbled. Mrs Fraser had been transferred to the surgical team from the medical team. She'd had repeated chest infections as her throat muscles had begun to fail. The surgical answer, for which she had been transferred, is to insert a tube directly into the stomach through which the person can be fed, thereby bypassing the need to swallow and its associated risks.

'Let me die,' said Mrs Fraser again. It was clearly taking considerable energy just to utter these few words.

I stood by while Mr Butterworth explained the possible consequences of her refusing surgical intervention. Mr Grant, Ruby's consultant, came the following day and tried to persuade her again to have surgery. Over the next few days a host of medical and psychiatric doctors came and assessed her. She was adamant: she didn't want the surgery and she wanted to die.

On each occasion I stood by, writing in the notes and thinking how desperately I wanted her to get her wish. What life was this? Trapped in a failing body, knowing what drawn-out agony awaited you but unable to end your own misery. She had tried to kill herself two years previously, before she became absolutely incapacitated, but had failed.

My feelings on the subject are complicated. As a doctor I'm not there to save lives, I'm there to alleviate suffering, and sometimes perhaps that means ending someone's life. Part of me is a passionate advocate for assisted suicide. I'm pleased there are places like Switzerland were people can go. It's not in my ethical backyard so I can avoid the moral debates and respect the service they offer with impunity. But allow it in the UK? There's a niggling, possibly illogical, feeling that persists that makes me feel uncomfortable about it. Equally I can't bear the idea of living in a society where someone like Mrs Fraser is forced to live a life of unbelievable suffering.

On Thursday Mrs Fraser was moved from the surgical ward back to the medical ward. This morning, after the ward round with Sad Sack, I bumped into one of the medical doctors and asked how she was doing. He told me that she had got another infection. Last night, after years of drawn-out suffering, Mrs Fraser finally got what she wanted.

Monday 15 December

Ruby and I sneak outside for a quick cigarette after our respective ward rounds finish. We meet Dr Palache, puffing away. For the junior doctor, these moments are like gold-dust; unofficial moments whereby one gets to corner an unsuspecting consultant caught utterly off guard. We both pounce and in the time it takes to smoke a Benson and Hedges, we had all the scans agreed for the day, he'd looked at a chest X-ray that Ruby had with her and wanted an opinion on, and he'd agreed to review a brain scan that I'd ordered but the results of which hadn't come back yet. If we hadn't seized this opportunity, we'd have both spent a good part of the morning chasing the radiologists round the hospital and getting shouted at for interrupting them when we finally caught up with them. This way, we negotiated the day's radiology requests in a civilised, adult manner and Dr Palache felt obliged to help out as best he could so that our patients got their scans when they needed them.

Smoking may be bad for our health, but it's good for the health of our patients.

Wednesday 17 December

Good time management is one of those things that people write down under the 'skills' sections of job-application forms, along with things like languages or a driving licence. But the truth is that when you're a doctor there's no way to manage time because it's quickly eaten up by the totally unpredictable and unexpected. Every morning, after the ward round, I plan my time with military precision, but this plan invariably falls apart as the day progresses and more and more urgent jobs get added to the list of things that must be done before I leave. The problem is compounded by the fact that, although time is so precious in a hospital, everything seems to take twice as long as it should do to get done. Forms have to be filled out in triplicate, X-rays get lost, patients arrive late.

I've been rushing round all day, desperately trying to get my list of jobs done, until a nurse asks me to see Mrs Feathers. She's about to go home but has some questions she wants answered first. I groan. I'm going to have to stay late as it is and now someone wants to ask me questions. My life would be so much easier if it wasn't for patients. I remind myself that I trained to be a doctor because I wanted to help people, not fill out forms all day and here is someone who needs my help.

I arrive at Mrs Feathers' bedside. She's had breast cancer and has come in to hospital under Mr Price to have her left breast removed. 'The consultant seemed really pleased with the reconstruction. But...' her voice trails off. I pull the curtains around the bed and sit down. 'It's my husband,' she continues. 'I'm sorry to take up your time with this, but, well, he can't bear to look at it. He says it doesn't look right, that there's no nipple any more.' I swallow hard. 'Would you talk to him Doctor?'

I couldn't have prepared for this. I've got X-rays to order, discharge summaries to write, letters to dictate. 'Of course I will,' I reply. A few minutes later, Mr Feathers arrives. 'Oh, everything's fine Doctor, don't worry,' but I can tell from his demeanour that this isn't true.

'Look, I need a cup of tea, so why don't we both pop down to the canteen and we can have a quick chat on the way?' I suggest and he acquiesces.

Sitting opposite him in the canteen, there's nothing I can say to make things magically go back to how they were before his wife got cancer. And I know that he knows this. All he really wants is someone to give him a few minutes of their time. While the operation may have been a success, for Mr Feathers the scars are a constant reminder that his wife had cancer, that she nearly died and that he was powerless to save her himself. He thinks it means that things will never be the same again. By the time we've finished talking, I should have been on my way home long ago. But talking to Mr Feathers was far more important than filling out forms. As he gets his wife's painkillers from the nurses, I stop off and say goodbye to Mrs Feathers. 'Thank you so much, Doctor. I know that talking to you will have done him the world of good. It will all get back to normal again, it's just that these things take time,' she says. I nod my head and walk off to get on with the rest of the jobs before finally going home.

Friday 19 December

Despite all the hints and gossip, I hadn't yet

heard Ruby's side of the story on the Housewives' Favourite rumour. Today I went out back through the radiology department for a cigarette. I walk out into the bright morning sunlight and see the two of them standing behind the bins, a little closer together than you'd expect. I hesitate and then decide to approach them and say hello. Housewives' Favourite gives me his usual withering look, which I return. Stubbing out his cigarette he looks at Ruby, deliberately turning his back on me. 'See you later, then,' he says to her in a decidedly intimate tone, and swans off.

Ruby and I stand in an awkward silence for a few minutes, before I decide to come straight out with it: 'Are you seeing him?' I ask bluntly.

'What do you mean?' she asks, her face betraying the fact she knows exactly what I mean.

'Are you sleeping with him? Come on Ruby, we've been friends for years. I know what's going on. You're sleeping with him, aren't you?'

She sighs. 'OK, yes I am. Look, I wanted to talk to you about it, but I knew you didn't approve and he made me promise not to tell anyone. He said it wouldn't look professional,' she added hurriedly.

'He's damn right. Ruby, that man is bad news. He always does this with his junior doctors. I can't believe you've fallen for it,' I say.

She looks at me intently. 'How do you know he's slept with his junior doctor before? Have you been talking to someone about this?'

I panic, not wanting to let her know that her fling with Housewives' Favourite is common knowledge in the hospital, and that yes, I had been gossiping about it. Before I have time to reply, Ruby's pager goes off. 'Look, I'll have to get this, it's probably theatre wanting to know Mr Grant's list for this morning. Don't tell anyone will you, Max, please.'

I nod. She turns to go, then stops. 'Max, I really like him. This place really gets to me sometimes, you know what it's like. I have to work with that bigoted jerk Mr Grant who hates the sight of me and I never seem to get a moment to myself. I'm just so tired and sick of the constant grind of it all, and when I'm with him I just forget about this place and relax. I know he can seem a bit arrogant, but honestly, when we're together he makes me feel so special. It's just so nice to be really wanted by someone.' Her pager goes off again.

'Looks like you're wanted by quite a few people,' I say.

'You know what I mean. He just makes all this more...' she pauses, lost for words

'...bearable, I suppose.'

She smiles and walks into the back of the A&E department, turning and waving before she disappears through the sliding doors. And I'm left thinking that perhaps I was wrong, perhaps he's not that bad after all, if he makes Ruby happy. Perhaps.

Saturday 20 December

I know the sales assistant really hasn't grasped my lifestyle when he begins with the line: 'And what moisturiser do you use at the moment?'

I look at him closely: is this an ironic 'new-man' quip? He doesn't flicker.

'Well,' I begin, feeling like a schoolboy explaining why I haven't done my homework, 'I don't really actually often use a moisturiser, as such.'

He looks like I've just stabbed him in the stomach. 'Well, how often do you use one?' he asks.

'Erm, well, I'd say not that often at all. In fact, I'd say, about,' I pause. 'Never.'

The sales assistant puts his hands dramatically to his neck.

'Look, the thing is, I don't really want moisturiser, I just want some face wash or something, really.'

I've come here in an attempt to make

myself look slightly less like death than I do at present. I'm hoping that I can make up for five months of serious deprivation and neglect by throwing lots of money at the problem, and getting something I can wash my face with that will make me look better. However, things, it seems, are more complicated than that. 'Well, this contains natural flavinoids which are bioradiant as well as dermo-translucent,' he says, handing me a tube. A combination of Latin and Biology GCSE has equipped me with the knowledge I need to categorically declare that this man is talking piffle. I buy two tubes, a moisturiser and a pot of eye cream.

Sunday 21 December

Having washed with my new face products before bed yesterday and after my shower this morning, I am rather dismayed not to be feeling the effects of any flavonoids or multi-axial vitamin-enriched epi-crystaloids. Of course, exactly what the effects are supposed to be, I'm not sure. I just notice that they smell slightly of cat's wee. Very, very expensive cat's wee.

Ruby is up already, and busy making plans to go back home to visit her parents as she has annual leave this week. Flora is sitting at the kitchen table reading the paper. 'I get it!'

she suddenly exclaims.

'What?' asks Ruby as she rummages through her laundry basket, which has been sitting next to the washing machine for the past three weeks.

'I get the meaning of Christmas,' continues Flora.

At medical school Flora did an evening class in philosophy and from then on she has had a habit of giving impromptu philosophical and anthropological analyses of anything that takes her fancy, without any prompting or encouragement from us. 'It's a way of punctuating the monotony of our lives,' she explains. 'It gives it an external meaning. Something on which to hang our lives. Birthdays, Easter, Christmas. They're all the same. It's just something different, something to break up the tedious reality of working life.'

Ruby and I stare at her.

Ruby replies, 'I never thought I'd say this, but given the choice of staying here and listening to you have an existential crisis or spending a week in a house with my relatives, I'm actually looking forward to going back home.' She pushes some of the clothes from the laundry basket into her bag. 'At least they'll do my washing for me.'

We kiss her goodbye.

'Happy Christmas, my darlings,' Ruby calls after us as she slams the door.

'Bah humbug,' shouts Flora in reply.

Wednesday 24 December

I have always thought that everyone can be placed in one of two categories: those that carry umbrellas, and those that don't. It's strange how you can just somehow guess which category people will fall into. A similar division has been observed all week, which clearly separates society in two: those that want to be in hospital over Christmas, and those that don't. I think it's fair to say that all doctors and nurses fall into the latter category, but unfortunately they don't really get much of a choice.

Some people assure you that they are absolutely fine while clearly at death's door, just because they can't bear to be in hospital. 'What's that pool of blood you are standing in?' 'Oh, that, don't worry, that's nothing, just a little bit of haemorrhaging. It will pass, don't you worry.' In sharp contrast to this group are those that, for a variety of reasons, are determined to ensure they spend the season of goodwill nicely tucked up in a hospital bed being waited on by nursing staff. This category is typically comprised of homeless people, the old and the bereaved.

On the ward round this morning we tried to discharge as many people as we could, most of whom were clearly delighted. Mrs Loukas looked at us menacingly as we approached her bed. 'Are you going to discharge me?' she said, before we'd even drawn the curtains around her bed.

Sad Sack looked at the notes and examined her. She had come in with an infected gallbladder and was still having an antibiotic drip. 'Ouch,' snapped Mrs Loukas as Sad Sack prodded her stomach.

Sad Sack looked thoughtful. 'We'll have to do some more blood tests and then we'll let you know this afternoon if the infection has cleared enough for you to go home,' she concluded and then turned sharpish before she was engaged in an argument. We all smiled at Mrs Loukas and quickly turned on our heels as well.

Mrs Loukas has five children and her husband, who works in the army, is home from leave this Christmas for the first time in three years. Supriya took the blood after the ward round, and a few hours later I checked the results. The infection was still raging. I phone Sad Sack who confirms that we can't send her home in this state. 'You'll have to tell her the bad news,' she says and hangs up before I can protest.

'Supriya,' I call out. 'Sad Sack says you have to tell Mrs Loukas.'

'Nice try, Max,' she shouts back from the other side of the nursing station.

Damn.

I walk over towards Mrs Loukas who is lying in bed filing her nails, presumably in preparation for gouging out my eyes when I tell her she'll have to stay in hospital. 'Look, I'm really sorry,' I begin.

She glares at me. 'Yeah, what?' she replies with a snarl. Clearly this woman has graduated from the Slough School of Charm. 'Are you gonna tell me that I gotta stay here over Christmas?'

'I'm really sorry,' I begin again, before she interrupts me. 'Oh, thank God. Honestly, mate, this has been the first break I've had in years. I mean, don't get me wrong, I love my kids, but they drive me up the wall.'

'Oh, I thought you might be cross?' I say.

'Cross? You having a laugh? Lying here is the best Christmas present anyone has ever given me,' she snorts. 'You reckon I could book in here for next year?'

Clearly it's not just depressed, lonely or homeless people that want to be in hospital at Christmas.

I leave Mrs Loukas to file her nails and make my way back to the nurses' station where Supriya is standing. 'Was she really cross?' she asks. I see an opportunity.

'Erm, yeah, she was. I talked her round, though. But I'm feeling a little shaken. Do you mind if I go for a cigarette? I just need to get out of the ward for a moment.'

Supriya looks concerned. 'Of course you can, I'll hold your pager.'

I go to leave.

'Oh, Max, it's raining by the way.' She pauses. 'You can borrow my umbrella if you want.'

Thursday 25 December

Christmas Day. I wake up late at home at my mum's. Eat, have a little sleep. Open my presents. Then in the evening, it dawns on me: tomorrow I have to go to work. And suddenly I'm not so full of Christmas cheer. In fact, I feel downright miserable. I long for the days when I was young and had seemingly endless Christmas holidays. Visiting relatives, decorating the tree, helping to wrap presents. Now Christmas is just an excuse not to have to get up. Supriya volunteered to do Christmas day because she's Hindu, otherwise I'd be working instead. Thank God for Hindus.

Friday 26 December

A truly miserable day on call in hospital. So much for the season of goodwill. I thought hospitals at Christmas time were jolly places – cheeky nurses with tinsel in their hair serving up turkey while whistling 'Jingle Bells', doctors with reindeer antlers, maybe even an impromptu visit from Noel Edmonds. How wrong could I be? There is a palpable feeling of 'I could be at home eating mince pies with my children' coming from most of the staff, and indeed the patients, all of whom seem to feel that it's my fault they're ill.

I admit I was feeling sorry for myself, which takes a certain amount of selfishness and self-indulgence when faced with so many people in pain. Just as I was about to get off the ward to put my head in the doctors' mess oven, which would have been futile as it's electric, Mr Osunde beckons me over.

Mr Osunde has bowel cancer which Mr Butterworth removed a few days ago. Let me guess, I think as I plod over, you're having a heart attack, just to really make my day go off with a bang. Instead he starts to tell me that his bowels still haven't opened. Marvellous, I think as I stare out of the window, now I'm going to have to examine his back passage. What a fitting end to an utterly miserable day. I've already been shouted at by just about everyone employed in the entire hospital, missed lunch because I was in A&E and had a child vomit on my shoe. I wouldn't mind, but she wasn't even one of my patients – I just happened to be standing nearby. I sigh rather too loudly. 'OK, I'll get some gloves and be back in a minute.'

His eyes widen. 'Oh, that reminds me, my

wife bought you this as a Christmas present. To say thank you, you know, for everything you've done,' and he hands me a parcel wrapped in paper with holly on it.

I'm silent for a few seconds, not sure what to say. I feel awful for being short with him. It's not his fault he's ill or that I have to work on Boxing Day or that everyone feels they can blame me for everything that goes wrong. It doesn't matter what day it is or where I'd rather be, I'm his doctor and I'm supposed to be here to help him. I feel slightly ashamed of myself faced with his kindness. I take the present and open it: a pair of woolly gloves.

'Probably best not to use those for examining me though,' he jokes. 'You've all been so kind, and it can't be much fun working over Christmas, I'm sure.'

I don't want to tell him quite how miserable I've been feeling today. It seems slightly unfair to be complaining about working Boxing Day to someone who has just had a tumour the size of my fist removed from his guts. I put the gloves in the doctors' office as I go to the clinic room to get the equipment I need and suddenly I feel a bit brighter. Not so sorry for myself. I finish the examination and Mr Osunde rolls over and puts his head back on the pillow. 'Happy Christmas,' he says as I walk off.

'Happy Christmas,' I reply, smiling.

Monday 29 December

Ruby has returned from visiting her family and looks worse than when she left. 'I feel like dying,' she said as she walked through the door.

She's got a raging temperature and cramps in her legs. We looked through our medical books. 'I think you've got flu,' said Flora, triumphantly.

'Give the girl a Nobel Prize,' said Ruby irritably as she made her way up to bed. We spend the evening making Lemsip for her. Ruby doesn't make a good ill person. 'I feel awful,' she kept calling down the stairs from her bed.

'Yes, yes, we know you do,' we shouted back.

'God, I hope she gets better soon, I can't handle much more of this,' whispered Flora.

'I know,' I reply. 'I have my fair share of sick people at work.'

'Lemsip,' shouts Ruby.

'This is nearly as bad as being on call,' Flora mutters.

Wednesday 31 December

I sit on Ruby's bed as she coughs. 'I feel like

someone has rubbed a cheese grater over my face,' she says in her croaky voice, adding, 'I hate being sick.'

From her bed we can see fireworks going off outside her window.

'I can't believe I've got to go to work tomorrow,' she says after a time.

'Phone in sick, Ruby – you're really ill,' I say.

'I know – if I work in this state it's going to kill me.'

We both know that medically this is unlikely, but I nod sympathetically all the same. It's nice to indulge in the fantasy that we could phone in sick, because in reality that would never happen. It's an unwritten rule that hospital doctors don't take sick leave. It's regarded as not being a 'team player', because it means that the registrar and SHO will have to do all the running around in lieu of the junior doctor. Short of actually dying, there's no acceptable excuse for not turning up to work. Even dying would be viewed as inconsiderate by Mr Butterworth. He prides himself on the fact that in twenty-five years of working as a doctor he has never taken a day off sick. 'Clear evidence that the man is so repellent that even microbes avoid him,' says Ruby.

Good to know that flu has not broken her spirit.

JANUARY

Thursday 1 January

Awoke to find that Ruby had dragged herself into work this morning. 'I was just so busy I forgot to be ill today,' she said later. I spent the day watching black and white films and thinking.

I don't know if I can stand much more of this. I don't mean the black and white films – I could watch them all day – I mean work. The whole of today was overshadowed by the prospect of work tomorrow. At work the day just races by: hours merge into days merge into weeks. But as soon as I stop, I start to think: is this what I trained for? Now that I've tried it, do I still want to be a doctor? The months will turn into years and before I know it, I'll be a consultant like Mr Butterworth (well, hopefully not like Mr Butterworth). I could wake up one day and realise that I've given the best years of my life to this profession and I'm not sure what I've got back from it. I just don't know if I'm prepared to sacrifice that much.

I watch another black and white film with its simple ideologies, intent on buoying up a generation recovering from a war. It shows the world in black and white; good things, bad things and nothing in between. And always with a happy ending. The characters just get on with their lives, doggedly, unquestioningly optimistic. No career crisis for them. I wish the world were a bit more black and white sometimes.

Friday 2 January

'One more month to go. Officially thirty-one days to go and then we are leaving the building. Bring it on,' bellowed Ruby as she walked into the surgical meeting this morning, unaware that the rest of the senior surgical team were already assembled: They looked at her disapprovingly.

'Who's counting?' asked Mr Grant.

'We are,' we all chanted back, joyously.

Saturday 3 January

Ruby and I had a heart-to-heart this morning. Not about her relationship with House-wives' Favourite, which has taken on the quality of a love that dare not speak its name. About our jobs. I don't mean the usual discussion about how many patients we've got or how to do a chest drain. We talked about whether or not we want to do it any more. I told her that I wasn't sure this was what I wanted to be doing with my life.

Looking back over the past five months I'm struck with the sudden fear that this is it: this is being a doctor. No heroics, no glamour, no TV crews. Just a never-ending supply of sick people who traipse into your life then leave, having either got better or died. It's monotonous. I suppose it's made me question what I thought being a doctor was going to be like. I knew it would be stressful, I knew it would be tiring and draining, but I never realised what that would actually feel like. Never having time to do the things you like, never being able to go anywhere or do anything, either because you're working or because you're trying to recover from working. I don't know how much of this is unique to medicine and how much is just part of the glorious world of employment. Now that the initial shock of starting life as a doctor is over, I'm left with a question: is this it? I was never naive enough to think that medicine would be a bed of roses, I just never realised there'd be so many nettles.

This morning Ruby said that she wanted to leave, that she didn't want the stress and aggravation and she was tired of being tired. I suspect her attitude is more to do with Mr Grant than any fundamental career crisis. But still, it puzzled me to hear Ruby talking this way. She comes across as competent and confident at work. I watch her doing her job and although she'd never admit it, she loves the pressure. She feeds off the drama, the urgency, the extreme physical endurance. She's too good at it to leave. Her bloody-mindedness won't let anything get the better of her. She'd see it as a failure, and Ruby never fails at anything.

But I don't see it that way. While she ranted about how she was treated like a skivvy and never got any credit for anything and Mr Grant treated her and Lewis like subhumans, I sat there imagining myself with a different job, no stress, nine to five, chats round the water-cooler. I'd like to think it's the patients that are making me stay, but it's not. I've trained for six years to do this job, and although it's become evident that a trained lab-rat could out-perform me on many tasks, I don't know what else I'd do. Which is even more depressing. Can I just turn my back on it all, even if I want to?

Monday 5 January

We're having a crisis. A bed crisis. The hospital has been at full capacity for some time. It's been quite tight at times, but nothing too drastic. But then suddenly, just before Christmas, something happened. A few weeks of cold weather and we are bursting at the seams. Given that more people get ill in winter, and that winter has a strange habit of occurring at about the same time every year, I'm not sure why no one predicted this. The hospital managers, who are usually drinking lattes and doing Power-Point presentations somewhere, have suddenly descended on to the wards in an attempt to make us more efficient.

I can see the predicament: there are sick patients waiting for beds in A&E, and there are lots of beds in the hospital. The only problem is that the beds in the hospital are taken up with other sick patients. My suggestion would be to employ a few more nurses, so that the number of beds could be increased, and therefore avoid a bed crisis in the first place. Surely this is logical? But instead someone decided that it was a good idea to keep the same number of beds and employ people to fiddle the numbers and breathe down the necks of doctors in the A&E to disguise the problem. Hospital managers exist for one thing: targets. The latest A&E target is that no one should be there for more than four hours (unfortunately this doesn't apply to doctors). So from the minute someone walks through the doors, it's a race to get them seen, assessed, tests booked, results reviewed, a decision made and the patient either discharged or transferred to a ward.

Mr Rathman, the patient I'm currently seeing, is a rather complicated case and has my seniors worried, so I've ordered a whole batch of tests to try and find out what's wrong. But the clock's ticking: we've only got an hour left. 'I'm going to transfer him to the observation unit,' decides a hospital manager who's been watching me like a hawk all shift.

The observation unit is intended as a waiting area once the patient has been assessed and is waiting for a bed to become free. It's like purgatory for sick people. Mr Rathman hasn't been fully assessed and until we know what's wrong with him, he's not suitable to be transferred there. He'll receive the best care if he stays in A&E. But the hospital manager is more interested in how his pie chart will look at the end of the month. 'He's going to breach the four hours,' he complains.

Just as I'm about to give in, I hear Mr Rathman's voice from behind the cubicle curtain. 'I'm not leaving A&E. The doctors want me to stay here, and here is where I'm going to stay.'

The hospital manager tries to remonstrate with him, but to no avail.

'I'm old enough to be your grandfather, don't argue with me,' he retorts.

I stand silently watching the manager deal

with this display of patient power. Eventually, seeing that he's losing, the manager frowns at me and walks off. Mr Rathman has his scans and breaches the four-hour rule. We decide to admit him, a bed finally becomes free and we transfer him up to the ward.

On the audit of this month's A&E figures, Mr Rathman will be highlighted as a failure of the system, when in fact he was managed exactly how he should have been. But there is a risk of targets and statistics being given more importance than appropriate patient care. Statistics aren't there for the doctors or the nurses, and they're obviously not there for the patients either. Which leaves the question, who are they for?

My shift over, I crawl into bed, while in A&E the crisis continues.

Wednesday 7 January

'You don't mind, do you?' says Mr Price.

I know he hasn't used my name because he doesn't know it, which only adds to my sense of outrage. He knows that I do mind, but he also knows that I can't say anything. Asking if I mind is a mere formality.

What I am about to describe happens on a twice-weekly basis, sometimes more. My indignation is thanks to Trudy who told me how much Mr Price makes from private work. She gets to see his paperwork and has a very liberal attitude towards confidentiality. It is only now that I've realised that I am actually an integral part of his private practice, without realising it and despite being opposed to the very concept.

Several times a week, just as I am finishing work, patients arrive on the ward. They do not have any bloods taken, or heart scans, or any of the usual things you would expect for a patient being admitted for an operation the next day. Despite technically having finished work, I am expected to clerk them in, arrange for all the necessary tests, complete all the paperwork and prepare them for theatre the next day. It means I am routinely delayed by hours before I can leave. Why? These are Mr Price's private patients.

Technically I am employed by the NHS and therefore am under no obligation to do any of this work. But because I am Mr Price's junior doctor, he expects me to prepare them for surgery. While Mr Price's private patients pay for their treatment, we still see them on NHS time on the ward rounds and they take up my time when they get sick on the wards.

While at first glance it seems incredibly complicated, it's now fairly straightforward in my mind. We have a system whereby everyone pays into the NHS and it provides free health care at the point of access. This is a fundamental, founding principle of the NHS and we should be proud of it. The care of some of our patients mounts up to tens of thousands, and there's no way that half the patients we see could afford that. It's egalitarian and it's just. But, for whatever reason, some people opt out of this system and go privately. The argument that people use is that this is 'freeing up' space for other people on the NHS. This is fundamentally flawed. What it actually does is undermine the NHS.

It's like transport: there are public forms of transport, like buses. And there are private, like taxis. Now if I decide to take a taxi and pay the extra, I could argue that in fact I have liberated more space on the bus for other people. But if enough people take taxis instead of buses, then bus routes close down, the infrastructure is destabilised and eventually the whole network breaks down. Then everyone either has to get a taxi or walk. In addition to this, the bus driver – Mr Price – is moonlighting as a cab driver as well, therefore there are fewer buses. Which only makes more people want to get a cab because they're seen as being more efficient. And so on and so on.

These late-night patients exist on the blurred boundaries of private and NHS medicine. The hospital welcomes them as a form of revenue, because increasingly hospitals are being run like businesses rather than places were you go to get better. But I, who am paid by the NHS to look after NHS patients, am expected to be the doctor for the private patients too, so that Mr Price and the hospital can supplement their income. By rights I should be paid privately for doing this, but somehow I suspect Mr Price hasn't budgeted for this. He has budgeted, Trudy tells me, for a holiday home in the south of France. So yes, I do mind, Mr Price. I mind being implicated in the undermining of something which I feel is one of the greatest achievements in this country. And I mind having to stay late.

Not that I say that to him. Instead I force a smile and grudgingly go and see the three patients that are due for his private list tomorrow. And then I get a cab home – there's no way I'm going to brave the bus at this sort of time.

Thursday 8 January

Ruby and I are joined by Supriya for a cigarette. Not that she smokes, of course. She's far too sensible. But behind the bins at the back of A&E is a sanctuary for the junior doctors. The doctors' mess is too far away – usually by the time you're halfway there, you've been paged and are faced with the prospect of either retracing your footsteps or continuing to the mess, only to find you have to go back to the hospital anyway. So we stand there for a few moments, smokers and non-smoker alike, regrouping. Without these moments I think I'd go mad. 'It's not that I feel disillusioned by being a doctor. More duped,' says Ruby, resuming our discussion of the other day. 'I was so excited before graduating and now I feel I've been conned. I thought I'd be helping people, holding old ladies' hands in their time of need.'

I feel slightly awkward that Supriya should be overhearing all this. I look at her, at her freshly painted nails, her smart, crisp shirt, her sleek, immaculate hair. She even coordinates her hairband with her shoes. She never complains, never seems to get stressed out. She is always on the ward on time, always seems to know what needs to be done. She never appears to resent staying late or being shouted at or working weekends. She just quietly gets on with things. But today Supriya looks close to tears. She interrupts Ruby. 'I thought I was the only one. I don't know what to do. This really isn't what I thought it was going to be like.'

I'm agog. Surely not Supriya as well? Supriya who finds time to polish her court shoes? My world is collapsing.

'I want to just leave, but there's no way I

can. My dad's a doctor, my mum's a doctor, my brother's a doctor. Everyone's a doctor in my family. Well, my uncle's an estate agent but we don't talk to him. I can't leave. They'd kill me.'

I realise I'm lucky – my family never put any pressure on me to be a doctor, they just wanted me to be happy in whatever I chose to do. But here stands Supriya, the weight of family expectation on her shoulders in addition to everything else she has to deal with as a junior doctor.

While it sounds heartless, I'm relieved that Supriya is finding it hard too. There's a relief in knowing that even the most competent and committed of us is close to breaking point.

Ruby's pager goes off followed a few seconds later by Supriya's. They both head inside, leaving me alone outside for a while longer, not feeling so much on my own.

Friday 9 January

Having been on call last night, I'm woken up this morning by my pager going off. I look at my clock: 8.45 a.m. I've overslept. Damn. Why, is this happening to me? Weeks from finishing this job, and I fall at the last hurdle. I look at the number on the pager: it's the ward. It must be Daniel or Sad Sack. I sit up and dial the number from the telephone in the on-call room. 'Hello,' says someone at the other end of the phone who sounds like Lewis.

'Bloody shitting hell,' I say urgently, 'I bloody well overslept, shitting nightmare. You've gotta help me, Lewis. I'm on my way there now.'

Silence at the other end of the phone.

'Hello, who is this?' comes the voice on the other end. It's Mr Butterworth.

Oh God. I want to die, and quickly, preferably before I am required to reply. Where's a myocardial infarction when you want one? 'Hello?' comes the now distinctive Mr Butterworth tones at the other end.

'Erm, hello, hello,' I say, playing for time, 'are you there?'

'Is that my houseman?' asks Mr Butterworth. 'I think we just had a crossed line. Where is everybody?'

Mr Butterworth obviously hadn't registered that it was me swearing down the phone, and had instead put this down to the anachronistic explanation of a crossed line, which belongs in the age of telephone exchanges and telephonists. God, I love technophobes. Also, if Mr Butterworth has had to call me himself rather than making a minion do it, this can only mean that no one else is on the ward. A plan quickly forms in my mind. 'Well, I'm in radiology at the moment trying to get some scan results. I'm not sure where everyone else is,' I brazenly lie. 'They weren't on the ward when I was there earlier.'

Perhaps I've pushed it a bit with that last comment. I vaguely remember that Daniel and Sad Sack said something about going on a course today and can't believe that of all the days to oversleep, it had to be the day when I was going to be on my own. 'Oh, well done for taking the initiative, I'll come down now and meet you there and we can go straight on to the ward round.' Oh God, I think, looking down at my pyjamas.

'OK, sure,' I say, feeling that now would not be a good time to come clean with the truth. Cut to scene of me rushing round, throwing clothes in the air trying to get dressed and hurtling out of the door and across the car park to the back of A&E, through the department and just in time to see Maxine hanging up her coat.

'Help,' I have time to say and grab her arm before Mr Butterworth, like a slug moving up a garden path, drags himself into view and makes his way up the corridor. 'I need some scans or something.' Perhaps it's the wildness in my eyes, or possibly the fact that my flies are still undone, that tells her that I'm potentially in trouble.

'Here,' she says, handing me an empty X-ray envelope and smiling at Mr Butterworth as he approaches.

'It's empty,' I whisper.

'Well, what do you want me to do about it?' she whispers back.

But rather than stop and ask me to account for myself, Mr Butterworth marches past not even looking at me.

'That man is so aloof,' says Maxine, rolling her eyes. 'He's been like that ever since his wife left him.'

I begin to follow Mr Butterworth through the department but before I've taken more than a few steps, what Maxine has just said sinks in. 'Sorry, did you say wife? Was he married?' I ask, disbelieving that Mr Butterworth is capable of displaying an interest in any human being that isn't anaesthetised with their abdomen splayed open.

'Oh, yes. He was heartbroken. I think it was a classic case of him never being home. But she left him and he's never been the same since. Not that he was ever what I'd call communicative. But it made him much worse.'

Mr Butterworth appears round the corner again and grunts at me to follow him. I go after him quickly, guilty that I know something so intimate about him. As we stand in the lift together in silence, I see on his right hand a wedding ring. Then we get out of the lift and he barks at a nurse for getting in his way.

Sunday 11 January

Flora made me breakfast this morning. No sign of Ruby. My mum phoned and left a message but I was asleep. Otherwise, an uneventful weekend, which I used to think of as being a bad thing, and now, with my days dominated by events, I can't think of anything better.

Monday 12 January

Mr Goodman was admitted last Tuesday after he came to A&E feeling very unwell. He had been to see his GP the week before because he wasn't opening his bowels. He tried laxatives but they didn't work. Then he started feeling really sick. He began shaking and was short of breath. He drove himself to A&E, promptly collapsed in the car park and was brought in on a stretcher. His X-ray showed that his bowels had perforated, that is, they had burst open inside his abdomen,

I watched as Sad Sack stabilised him in the department so that he could be transferred to theatre. He lay quietly while all this was going on around him. I stood next to Sad Sack as she explained that he'd have to have an operation to mend the hole, that it was serious and that it was possible that they would find cancer when they opened him up.

He nodded gently, intently listening without commenting until, after Sad Sack had finished, he sighed and said, 'That's a bit awkward, isn't it?' An understatement that was only emphasised as he continued, 'The thing is, my wife is paralysed, and I'm her carer. She's at home on her own now and I need to put her to bed. She's waiting for me. I told her I'd only be a few hours. She'll need her catheter bag changed soon. Do you think you could give me some tablets for a few days and then I can come back in for my operation once I've made arrangements for my wife?'

Sad Sack interrupted him. 'Mr Goodman, there is a hole in your bowel. If you are not operated on in a matter of hours you will die. You may still die but if we don't operate your chances of survival are zero.'

That's right, Sad Sack, give it to him gently. He was silent for a few moments. 'Oh dear, well that is very awkward indeed.' I stood in silence, a bit stunned by this extraordinary unselfishness.

Somebody made arrangements for his wife to be brought into hospital as well and Mr Goodman was transferred up to the theatre. I continued to see patients in A&E while Sad Sack and Mr Price operated into the early hours of the morning.

The next day we saw Mr Goodman on the ward round. He was still unconscious, having been sent from the operation straight to the Intensive Treatment Unit. I stood at the end of his bed while the surgeons discussed the previous night's operation and looked at his chart. 'Riddled with cancer. Did a good resection though. Chances are slim, I'd say.'

The following day we visited him again. This time he was awake, but he'd had difficulty with his breathing when they removed the tubes so he'd had a tracheostomy which meant he couldn't talk. He lay silently, peacefully staring at the assembled doctors as they looked at his charts and scans and blood results. I wrote in the notes while Supriya scribbled down the list of jobs. Mr Price turned to him after a few minutes and explained the extent of the tumour they had found. 'Do you have any questions at this stage?' asked Mr Price.

Mr Goodman slowly spelt out on a laminated alphabet card: W. H. O. I. S. L. O. O. K. I. N. G. A. F. T. E. R. M. Y. W. I. F. E.

One part of me wanted to shake him and tell him to start thinking about himself for once. And another part of me wanted to applaud him for his gentle but persistent devotion and dedication.

Mr Goodman developed pneumonia over the weekend and died just before the ward round today. Supriya certified the body while I got the notes trolley ready. All his responsibilities, his concerns, his duties: gone. In one moment, wiped out. Someone will tell his wife and she'll probably be put into a nursing home. Very awkward indeed.

Tuesday 13 January

I'm leaving. Well, that's the plan. It's a friend's birthday and if I could only get away on time I'd stand a chance of making it, but hospitals are hard to leave. In fact, Colditz has nothing on this place. In the six months I've been working as a doctor I have yet to leave work on time.

Because I am the lowest of the low, the plankton in the medical food chain, the senior doctors have a tendency to arrive on the ward just as I put my coat on, and reel off a list of things to be done before tomorrow's ward round. Despite this being a daily ritual, I still convince myself each afternoon that today will be different, that today I will leave on time.

It's not supposed to be like this. The Government has imposed limitations on the amount of hours we junior doctors can work. In theory, this is a fabulous idea. After all, who wants to be catheterised by some-one who's just worked a ninety-hour week?

209

But unfortunately somebody forgot to put the order in for more doctors, so what actually happens is that junior doctors work the same amount of hours as they used to, but only get paid for a fraction of them.

Regardless of how hard and fast I work during the day, I can guarantee that as the clock reaches six and I think about going home, something will happen. It always does. This is because once the mountain of jobs are done, there's the gauntlet of nurses and patients and family to run. As I stroll purposefully towards the glowing EXIT sign above the main doors, I'm bombarded with calls for help: 'Will you just sign this?' 'Can you have a quick look at this patient?', 'Doctor, can I ask you about how my mother's doing?' To actually leave the building requires more cunning than just walking out the door. I've considered digging an escape tunnel with a kidney dish, but my ward is three floors up. To successfully leave the hospital, it is imperative to remove any identifying features of being a doctor: a stethoscope thoughtlessly left round the neck guarantees that you may never see the light of day again. I've even tried adopting a limp for the journey from the ward to the car park.

But today I catch Mrs Whitcomb's eye as I'm about to leave and she calls out to me. I turn round and go back to her bed. She's been on the ward for nearly a month recovering from an operation for bowel cancer. Her husband died last year and she misses his company. 'It's so quiet at home without him,' she tells me, and asks if she can stay longer in the hospital. Although this isn't a surgical problem, there are still plenty of things that can be done to make going back home easier for her, but at some point she'll have to leave the hospital and the security it offers, so I sit and talk to her for a while and write in her notes.

'I'm sure you've got somewhere else to be,' she says eventually and, seeing the time and remembering the party, I say goodbye and make a break for it.

Finally, I have left the building and I limp across the ear park, my stethoscope carefully concealed in my bag.

Wednesday 14 January

Ruby didn't return home last night. No doubt she was out with Housewives' Favourite. I know lots of people would suspect her of using this as a canny way to progress up the greasy pole of a surgical career, though I don't think Ruby's like that. Surgery is one of the last bastions of male dominance and it isn't easy for a woman to break into this world. Housewives' Favourite could certainly help her in her career, but he must know this and be using it to his advantage. I just hope she knows what she's doing. It's pointless talking to her about it though, she just changes the subject every time it's broached. I can't believe that she's using him for her own benefits, but I could believe that of him.

Thursday 15 January

'Where you going on your holiday then, Max?' asks Trudy as she hands me some Battenberg. I'd completely forgotten that I'm about to go on annual leave. I haven't had time to make any plans. Then I remember all the people that I haven't seen since starting work, all the friends I've forgotten to call back, all the relatives I've ignored. I shall atone for the past six months, I resolve. Alternatively, I'll lie in bed and listen to the radio.

Friday 16 January

My last day at work before my holiday. It's like no other feeling I have ever experienced: pure, unadulterated ecstasy. For a moment I feel a pang of guilt at the prospect of leaving the others to do all the work while I relax for the next week. This feeling quickly evaporates. I wave goodbye to Ruby who is on call as I leave the ward in the evening. 'Take me with you,' she shouts after me. 'Don't leave me here.'

I chuckle as I walk out into the icy air. The lights of the hospital flood out behind me and east my shadow long and sinister before me. I can hear the sounds of an ambulance screeching into the bay in A&E, the sounds of a trolley being rushed to the opening doors and I can imagine the sound of Ruby's pager going. I keep walking, into the darkness of the night.

Saturday 24 January

I haven't written anything for the past week because I haven't done anything. Or nothing noteworthy at any rate. I spent the first few days in bed, getting up after midday, relaxing and indulging in therapeutic cleaning of the entire flat. I even did Ruby and Flora's washing for them. And, finally, I went to the dry-cleaner's and was reacquainted with what seems like an entire new wardrobe.

I visited my mum, who screamed at me from the other side of the train platform about how ill I looked. Several of the other passengers looked at me with a mixture of agreement and sympathy. And I visited my grandparents. While I've been looking after other people's grans, another doctor in another part of the country has been looking after mine. My gran had a heart attack a few weeks ago. My mum had phoned to tell me but I didn't get the message until a few days afterwards. My sister sent flowers and said they were from me – she'll dine out on that one for years. My gran is fine and is now back at home, supposedly taking things easy but instead had laid on enough food to feed a small principality.

'You know, we're all so proud of you,' she said as she adjusted my collar. 'Look at him, Jimmy, he's a proper doctor. Who'd have thought it? Our Max,' she beamed as she paraded me in front of my grandfather. He was clearly torn between celebrating my apparent achievements and watching the sport on telly.

'You deserve it lad,' he said with a nod.

My grandfather has worked hard all his life. He left school when he was fourteen, started work as a mechanic and worked his way up in the company. In contrast I have lived an entirely sheltered and rarefied existence, and it seems rather churlish to shatter his illusions with the truth about my recent reservations about being a doctor. So I didn't tell them about feeling scared or lonely or tired or hungry. Nor did I say anything about not knowing what I was doing or about the people dying or crying out in pain. Instead I told them exciting stories about saving people and how it was difficult but rewarding and how the patients were very grateful and how fulfilling it was. And they nodded and smiled and laughed and nearly burst with pride, and at first I felt like a fraud. But after a few days with them, I almost started to believe it myself

Monday 26 January

Back to work supposedly feeling refreshed and carefree. 'What the hell are you doing?' barks Mr Butterworth at me within two minutes of the ward round starting.

I fall back to earth with a thud. 'Erm, I'm writing what you're saying in the notes,' I reply.

'You're standing in my way,' he says as he pushes past me without looking at me.

Nadine, the young girl Mr Butterworth has just been examining, pulls the sheets up to her chin and pulls a face at him behind his back. I suppress a laugh as he makes his way over to the next bed.

'Come on,' grumbles Sad Sack, as Supriya and I scuttle after them.

I hate it when Mr Butterworth does the ward rounds. Everyone's on edge. The nurses even stop reading *Woman's Realm* at their desk. 'Where is the scan for this abdomen?' he says as Supriya and I trail behind.

We frantically search in the trolley. I can't even remember this patient or why they're here, let alone when we booked the scan, or even if it was done at all. Mr Butterworth turns round and rummages through the notes trolley, huffing and puffing as he does so. He's in a really bad mood today. I try to finish writing in the last patient's notes which he promptly snatches from me, mistaking them for the ones for this patient. I try to explain but he doesn't listen. 'They're not even the notes for the right patient,' he says after a few seconds and pushes them back into my arms. I drop them. They make a loud thud as they land upside down, spewing the contents at my feet. Bits of paper glide across the floor and settle gently all over the ward, like scattered debris from a little bomb. Mr Butterworth turns and draws the curtains round the next bed.

'Max!' snaps Supriya in a whisper.

'It's not my fault,' I snap back.

I bend down to start to pick up the notes and arrange them in the folder again and am helped by a nurse and a patient on his way back from the toilet. I can feel my face going red and my eyes sting. I've been back at work for twenty-five minutes.

Tuesday 27 January

I race through the radiology department in a desperate attempt to arrange a scan. After yesterday's humiliation on the ward round I'm not going to give Mr Butterworth the satisfaction of having genuine cause for complaint.

I eventually track down Dr Palache in the hospital restaurant. 'Please, Dr Palache, you've got to help me. Mr Butterworth will kill me if I don't get this done today and yesterday was awful and I'm already in his bad books and I just need it done and...'

Dr Palache hasn't looked up from his fried breakfast.

'Dr Palache?' I say, peering at him.

He clears his throat. 'It's ten minutes to nine. I haven't woken up yet. Please, speak slowly and clearly and don't shout, there's a good man.'

I take a breath.

'Have you had breakfast?' he asks, raising his head as he loads his fork with baked beans. I shake my head. 'Well then, let's start there,' and he puts down his knife and fork and gets up, returning with a fried egg, baked beans and toast. I realise how hungry I am. 'Now, about your scan,' he begins as I launch into the beans.

If Lewis wasn't already seeing him, I'd marry Dr Palache.

FEBRUARY

Monday 2 February

My penultimate day of surgery. Tomorrow
will be the last day I ever spend working on
a surgical ward, as I, unlike Ruby and
Supriya, have no intention of being a
surgeon. It takes a certain type of person to
succeed in surgery. Theirs is a world of just
two possibilities: to cut or not to cut. I've
come to realise that Mr Butterworth in
particular is very good at this. He's a good
surgeon precisely for the reason that he isn't
good with people. He sees lumps and
tumours and lesions, not personalities. It's
not just an ability to cut into someone that's
important, but to cut through someone; to
ignore the emotion and the impact of what
you're doing and strip it down, focus in. It
takes getting used to, but if it wasn't for the
likes of Mr Butterworth, with his unswerv-
ing ability to remain calm, ignore the chaos
around him while he is operating, and give
all his attention to the job in hand, a lot of
people would be dead. He can forget about
the oddness of what he is actually doing,
slicing through someone and putting his

hands in their body. Outside of this profession, you'd be put away for that sort of behaviour, and quite rightly, too.

After the ward round Sad Sack took me aside. 'You really should see some actual surgery before you leave. I've told Mr Butterworth you'll be assisting him today on the theatre list.'

My world stops. Noooo! I begin screaming inside my head. Anything but that. I try and protest but before I can argue why I shouldn't spend the rest of the day poring over somebody's innards while Mr Butterworth shouts at me, she's gone.

Fast forward two hours and I am standing in theatre, sweat tricking down my forehead. I look down into my outstretched arms as Mr Butterworth scoops somebody's intestines into them. 'Keep still,' he shouts as I try desperately not to let them fall on to the floor. This is truly hell on earth. I'm trapped. And I'm also absolutely petrified. I want to faint, but it's not only pride that won't let me, it's the thought of dropping several metres of intestine on myself in the process. My arms are starting to ache. Now my shoulders are aching, too. And then the unthinkable starts to happen. My surgical scrubs begin gently to work their way down past my waist. I can feel them slowly falling off but I'm powerless to do anything about it. I move my legs apart slightly so they remain just below my hip. Then they slip some more. Now they're at my mid-thigh.

'Stop fidgeting,' grumbles Mr Butterworth without looking up, his hand buried in the patient's abdomen. I wince. The intestines, like a mass of giant moist pink worms, move slightly in my arms. I move my legs further apart to prevent the scrubs from falling any further. I remain in this position for the next hour, sweating profusely. I will never be a surgeon. The likes of Mr Butterworth would have just let his scrubs fall to the ground. He probably wouldn't even have noticed. That's focus for you.

Tuesday 3 February

Tonight, junior doctors up and down the country move jobs. On the first Wednesday in August and February, we all switch, our six-month jobs having come to an end. It's a mass migration that goes unnoticed by the public. This is probably because we don't get any time off to relocate; it happens after we've finished work, in the dead of night when most sensible people are asleep in bed. By late evening, the roads are packed with junior doctors, all their worldly possessions crammed into boxes and suitcases, speeding towards their new hospitals. If you were planning on having a car crash, now would be a good time.

In our first year we must spend time working in general surgery and general medicine to prove our competence before we are allowed to seek further higher training in a speciality. Having finally completed my mandatory six months of surgery, I'm due to be plucked from one ward of sick people and dropped into another to work in medicine. And those that have just completed their jobs in medicine start afresh in surgery. Ruby, Supriya, Lewis and myself are lucky – we are all staying in the same hospital to work and are just moving speciality. Most aren't so lucky. Flora is off to a different hospital 200 miles away. She's staying in hospital accommodation and so this evening was packing up all her belongings into boxes.

I finish work later than usual, but I can't quite bring myself to walk out without leaving some hand-over notes for the poor souls who'll be taking over my job in the morning. In most jobs there's at least a bit of orientation, some slack given for the first week or so, but as a doctor, you're expected to seamlessly pick up where your predecessor left off and by some form of telepathy instantly know each and every patient's clinical progress, blood results and where their X-ray is. So I make some quick notes on each of the patients. It then occurs to me that what my successors really need to know is how to avoid infuriating Mr Butterworth, but I stop after it starts to run to over four pages. They'll soon find out for themselves.

I reluctantly leave my pager on the desk in the doctors' office, not quite believing that after six months of it dictating my life, I'm suddenly free from this little black box and its incessant cries for attention. It's like a newborn baby but without all the cute photo opportunities. Of course, I'll get another one tomorrow with my new job, but this particular one hasn't left my sight since starting work.

On leaving the ward the worst thing happens – I come face to face with Mr Butterworth. Cue socially awkward farewell. 'So, erm, this must be goodbye then, Max?'

I'm touched that he even sees fit to acknowledge my existence, let alone that he knows my name. While the man may have all the social skills of a nut loaf, I've become oddly attached to him, though I can't quite believe it. 'All the best for the future then. We'll miss you,' and he shakes my hand. He still doesn't look me in the eye of course, but who's asking for miracles?

I say my farewells to some of the nurses who have held my hand for the past six months. It seems odd that we're leaving each other after all the things we've been through and it's strange to think that the hospital sees hundreds of junior doctors over the years and soon I'll just be a faded memory.

But there's one last person I must say goodbye to before I leave. Her name is Mrs Chevoux, and she's been in and out of my ward since I started work. She's in her seventies. She's got cancer that's spread to her liver. The prognosis isn't good. But despite this, she's the funniest woman I've met and countless times has sent me into fits of giggles. She would always try and make me lose it on ward rounds, and a number of times succeeded. 'I'm off then,' I say, as I poke my head round the door.

'Good, never liked you anyway,' she beams and we both laugh.

It occurs to me that I'm not her doctor any more, so I kiss her goodbye.

I walk out the main exit for the last time. Tomorrow, though, there will be a whole new set of junior doctors arriving to take over her care; tired, disorientated, and fresh from their cars and motorway service stations.

Wednesday 4 February

Another day of meaningless 'introductory' paperwork, which Mrs Crook is adamant that we haven't completed. 'We've been working here for six months already,' Supriya explains patiently.

'We haven't got you on file,' retorts Mrs Crook.

'You have got my name on your list. It's there,' says Supriya, pointing to Mrs Crook's clipboard.

'Oh.' She is flustered for a second. 'Well, that can't be your name because I've already got it ticked off.'

Mrs Crook's ability to remain alive in the world is a persistent source of amazement, going as it does against every reasoned argument for survival of the fittest. She is single-handedly disproving Darwin; anyone who displays such a lack of coping skills would surely have been eaten by a lion by now. 'Which hospitals have you come from?' continues Mrs Crook.

Supriya manages to smile despite this provocation. 'We're from this hospital, Mrs Crook. I've met you many times.'

Mrs Crook scrunches up her nose and peers down her glasses at Supriya. 'You know, all you juniors look the same to me, dear,' she says.

'That's nice to know,' says Ruby and we decide to leave the induction and go for breakfast in the canteen, leaving Supriya, patient as ever, to prove that she has been working here for the past six months.

Thursday 5 February

'So, what branch of medicine are you planning on going into?' asked Dr Pike, my new consultant. He's a gerontologist. I've learned by now that if you want to get on with consultants, when asked this question, you must always say whatever speciality they work in. Everyone does it. Honesty, particularly in medicine, isn't always the best policy. So I lied. 'Gerontology,' I said.

He smiled and squeaked, 'Excellent,' before heading off on the ward round. Unlike Mr Butterworth, who ignored you except when you were doing something wrong, Dr Pike is disconcertingly interested in everything I do. 'What did you have for breakfast today?' he asked. No, that's a lie, he didn't ask me that, but I bet he wanted to.

But while he's very keen to ask questions, he also hears what he wants to hear. 'Did you manage to get to the induction course yesterday?' he asked as we made our way to see our first patient, Mr Farley.

'Well, yes, but I've already been working in this hospital for six months so there wasn't much to do. I was working with Mr Butterworth in surgery,' I explained.

'Oh him, what did you think of him?' asked Dr Pike.

'Erm, well, he was OK. Took a bit of getting used to but...' I began.

'Yes, my thoughts exactly, absolute brute,' concluded Dr Pike.

I attempted to correct him, to explain that wasn't at all what I meant, but he marched on, only turning to me once saying, 'Yes, I agree, a brute. I think we're going to get on.'

I gave up and got the notes.

Mr Farley has had dementia for the past ten years. His wife has looked after him for all that time, day in, day out. And now, his kidneys and heart have stopped working properly. Medicine has decided to bow out gracefully and admit defeat. There's nothing that can be done. He and his wife are in their eighties. How she's coped on her own all this time is beyond me. His eyes are shut and his mouth wide open.

'It's all right darling, I'm here,' says Mrs Farley.

No response. She looks a little crestfallen. She gently strokes his cheek while talking to him, and he moves his head towards her.

'Look, Doctor, he still knows who I am,' she says to the doctors lined up at the foot of the bed.

But everyone looks slightly embarrassed and Dr Pike says gently, 'We're very sorry, there's nothing more we can do. I think it's for the best.'

Everyone quietly moves on.

Back in the office I accost Barney, one of

the middle-rank 'staff grades'. 'But he recognises his wife, that's incredible, isn't it?' I say.

Barney frowns: 'Oh that, no, of course he doesn't recognise her.'

I'm perplexed.

'It's a rooting reflex,' Barney explains. 'He's got advanced dementia. He hasn't a clue what's going on.'

What this means is that the movement Mrs Farley thinks is her husband recognising her voice is, in fact, a mere reflex. Anyone or anything touching his cheek would induce the same response.

I feel somehow cheated. I think I prefer Mrs Farley's explanation. Medicine can be cruel like this. It reduces things to neural pathways, to reflexes, to physiological mechanisms. In our pursuit of the truth, perhaps we can know too much. It removes the mystery and wonder from things. Mrs Farley doesn't want to live in a world where her husband has primitive rooting reflexes. She wants to live in a world where her husband recognises her voice.

I walk through the ward and see Mrs Farley, still sitting by her husband's bed. I introduce myself. 'Do try and get some rest. Is there anything we can do for you?' I ask.

'No,' she replies. 'I'll just stay here with him, if that's OK. I don't think it will be long now.'

His eyes are still closed and his mouth is

still open. His breathing is getting increasingly laboured.

'I don't want to leave him now,' and she strokes him on the cheek, and once again he moves his head towards her. 'We've been married for over sixty years,' she says. 'And apart from during the war, we've never been apart. And no matter how bad things have been, at least he'll always know that I've been by his side, looking after him, won't he, Doctor?'

She's asking me because I'm a doctor and she wants me to reassure her. What good would the truth do? Sometimes, honesty isn't the best policy.

'Yes, of course he does,' I lie, and walk away, leaving the two of them alone.

Friday 6 February

Ruby is working in the liver unit. 'It's just bloody drunks,' she says when I meet her for coffee in the doctors' mess at midday. 'I know you're not supposed to say that, but you can't help but think that they brought it on themselves. I mean, no one forced them to drink ten cans of Tennent's Super every day for fifteen years, did they?' she says.

We all know that this sort of discussion is not suitable for public airing. As doctors we are supposed to remain morally neutral about the nature of the disease we are treating. But when faced with a ward made up predominantly of people who have brought their current predicament on themselves, it's not easy to remain sympathetic. Especially when some people have liver problems that are nothing to do with alcohol. Aren't they more deserving of treatment?

As a doctor you see a lot of illness brought on by mere circumstance or bad luck. Nobody chooses to get cancer or Parkinson's or have appendicitis. But of course there are some ailments where it's easier to attribute blame than others and alcoholic liver disease is one of these.

'They're not even nice to me. In fact, they're the most ungrateful group of people I have ever come across. And none of them want to stop drinking,' Ruby continues. Some of her patients are so desperate for alcohol that they have been known to suck the alcohol-soaked disinfectant wipes if they are left around on the ward. As a result these are treated like contraband and locked away by the nursing staff.

While it's all very well insisting that doctors remain neutral when treating patients, some medical decisions have moral implications. Who should receive a liver transplant? The mother who accidentally contracted hepatitis, the ex-drug addict who contracted it through injecting with dirty needles or the alcoholic who may or may not remain abstinent?

'One of the good things about being a junior doctor is you don't have to make those sorts of decisions,' says Ruby before her pager goes off. It's the liver unit telling her one of her patients has just pulled all his lines out and wants to self-discharge so he can go to the pub. 'He needn't worry about liver failure. I'm going to kill him instead,' she says, before heading out of the mess.

Saturday 7 February

The flat is strangely quiet without Flora. Her absence is even more noticeable because Ruby is nowhere to be seen again this weekend. I'd hoped that now we've changed jobs and are no longer working in surgery, her affection for Housewives' Favourite would dwindle and die. Oh no. In fact, in a way it's worse, because now they feel they can be more open about it. Or at least Ruby does.

Yesterday we went to the canteen together and while I queued to pay, Ruby spied him sitting with a few nurses so she collected her tray and went over to him. From where I was standing I could see him look at her while she negotiated the tables and, I'm sure, he looked panicked. He shovelled in a few more mouthfuls of food and just as she sat down, he got up to go. 'Hi,' she smiled shyly as he picked up his tray. I thought for a moment he was going to brazenly ignore her, but instead he flashed her a quick, insincere smile before walking away.

Ruby flushed red as she joined me at another table, neither of us mentioning what had just happened. We began to talk about our new jobs, when suddenly Ruby interrupted, 'You don't think he's ashamed of me, do you?'

She stared at me intently and then looked down at her lunch, embarrassed.

'No, I don't think so at all,' I said, which was true. I don't think he's ashamed of her. I just suspect that he's bored of her now and doesn't want anyone to know of their relationship in case it affects his chances with anyone else. He *should* be ashamed: of himself

Sunday 8 February

An unexpected visit from my sister, who is sickeningly healthy and beautiful compared to my current 'just been dug up from a nearby cemetery' look. She burst in through my door and was sitting down with a cup of tea in her hand before I had time to follow her through to the kitchen. 'Hello, what are you doing here?' I asked, rather bemused. 'Is everything all right?'

'Oh, of course it is. I don't need a reason to visit my big bruv, do I?' she said.

I narrowed my eyes at her. Here we go, I thought.

'Well...' she began. 'I've got this sore throat, and I just wondered, you know, why go to the doctor when I've got a big clever brother who can help...'

I made myself a cup of tea and sat down with a sigh.

Monday 9 February

I know something is wrong because Lewis walks past me very quickly staring at the floor and doesn't say a word. He doesn't look up, and I'm not sure if he's even noticed me. I call after him. He doesn't turn round and doesn't slow down, and instead only raises his hand briefly as a wave of acknowledgement. I hesitate for a moment. Shall I run after him?

Lewis is one of the friendliest people in the hospital. Everyone knows him and everyone loves him because he always has time for everyone, whether you're a porter or a consultant. He seems genuinely interested in everyone's business, not in a gossipy, malicious way, but in the way that some people seem to have an inexhaustible thirst for understanding other people and their lives. It's obvious to anyone who has ever had contact with the medical profession that being a good doctor is not simply about what you know, it's about how you interact with people.

And Lewis makes sure that each and every one of his patients feels special; that he is their doctor, and theirs alone.

So I'm rather surprised when, as I stand and watch him storm down the corridor, I am bleeped by a nurse on his ward. 'But I've just seen Lewis walking away from your ward,' I protest.

'Max, just come,' replies the nurse at the end of the phone.

I know by now that nurses aren't to be messed with, so I put the phone down and head over to the ward. The nurse meets me with a rather cold look and speaks in a low, dispassionate voice that I can barely hear. 'Mr Oak in bed 2 needs a cannula and his bloods taken,' she says and hands me a tray with the apparatus laid out in it, some of which has already been opened.

'Has someone already tried?' I asked, trying to unravel the mystery of why I have been called to do this for someone that's not my patient.

'Yes, Lewis tried but...' She stops speaking and looks at Mr Oak sitting up in the chair next to his bed and reading a newspaper.

'He couldn't.'

I presume that he must have tricky veins and if Lewis can't get it, I certainly won't be able to. I introduce myself to Mr Oak. He smiles warmly. 'Oh, thank you for coming, I think I need one of those little tubes put in my arm.'

He puts down his newspaper and rolls up his sleeve. I unwrap the needle and tighten the tourniquet around the top of his arm. I vaguely register that there are no other puncture marks from failed attempts, and fleetingly it occurs to me that Lewis didn't even try to take the blood.

I distract Mr Oak while I push the needle into the vein by asking him about how long he's been in hospital, about his job, about his wife and children. The needle slips in easily and I attach a syringe and draw out some blood. I secure the tube with some sticky tape. 'There you go, the nurse will come along and attach your drip in a minute,' I say as I clear away the tray.

'Thank you so much, I do appreciate it. I didn't like to make a fuss, but you know...' he says, smiling at me conspiratorially.

I look at him quizzically. 'Sorry?'

'That other doctor, well, I didn't want to make a fuss, but I didn't want him touching me, really. I asked if there was another doctor who could do it, but the nurse told me there wasn't. I knew she was lying, I'd seen plenty of white doctors walking around.' He pulls a face.

I can feel myself flushing red. I begin to open my mouth but am utterly lost for words. I definitely haven't misheard him. A wave of anger overcomes me. Have we just gone back fifty years? How dare he? Who does he think he is? I'm furious that because of the colour of my skin, he assumes that I will agree with him. The fact that I have indulged his racism by doing what he wants, albeit unwittingly, makes me feel sick.

'Well, he's a better doctor than me,' I say, and walk away.

Where was the tirade? Where was the venom? I hang my head in shame as I walk towards the nursing station. 'What a horrible man,' says the nurse.

'If he doesn't want to be looked after by a black doctor then he should be shown the door,' I say, still unable to articulate my feelings properly.

'I hope you said that to him,' says the nurse.

I hesitate. 'Of course I said that to him, and lots worse,' I reply.

I walk away disgusted with Mr Oak, but disgusted with myself as well. I should have had the courage to stand up for my friend. Evil prevails when good men do nothing, and racism prevails when white men say nothing. I walk down the corridor knowing that if someone like Lewis is being judged in the twenty-first century by the colour of his skin, it's a sickness I don't know how to cure.

Tuesday 10 February

I spend most of today trying to bump into Lewis, who has been strangely elusive. Someone thought he was in radiology, but when I go there, Maxine hasn't seen him. He's not on his ward, but someone saw him there earlier. By the afternoon I begin to suspect he's actively trying to avoid me. I decide to page him. He answers the phone and we begin a stilted chat about a cardiac arrest that morning until Lewis tries to wind up the conversation. 'Hang on,' I interrupt.

Silence.

'Look, about Mr Oak yesterday, he's a dick-head and I'm really sorry about what happened. You aren't upset about what he said to you, are you?' I ask, aware what a leading question that was.

'It's fine, Max. People have said and done worse to me before. It just upset me cos, you know, when you're trying to help someone, when you're doing everything you can and then they turn round and pull that sort of thing on you....' His voice trails off. 'But I'm really sorry. The nurse told me that you stood up for me, that you had a proper go at him, and I'm really grateful to you.'

I don't know what to say. There's no way I'm telling him now what a coward I was.

'I'll be honest, I was a bit embarrassed that you had to get involved,' Lewis continues. 'It's not your problem, I should be able to deal with it.'

'It's not your problem either, Lewis, it's *his* problem,' I begin with a passion I wish I'd articulated to Mr Oak yesterday.

'I didn't know what to say to you today. I was just embarrassed, so I've been sort of avoiding you. But look, I really appreciate you sticking up for me, thanks. You're a proper friend.'

I hang up, feeling slightly sick.

Wednesday 11 February

I bump into Supriya in the doctors' mess this afternoon. She is sitting dictating discharge summaries. 'How's it going?' I ask as I sit down next to her with a cup of tea and switch on the TV. She doesn't say anything but gets up and switches it off. She doesn't resume her dictation and sits in silence for a few moments. 'You all right?' I ask,

Since changing jobs I haven't seen Supriya as much as when we did surgery together. She's working for a different team to me, based on a different ward, so I haven't spoken to her properly for quite a while. She turns to me. 'I feel so miserable, Max. I really don't think I want to keep going with this. It's just not what I want to do with the rest of my life,' she says.

'Come on, Supriya,' I reply, getting up to make her a cup of tea, that universal panacea. 'It's not long to go now. We're over halfway through, and then you'll be able to go into surgery and do exactly what you want to do. Things will get much easier. It's just teething trouble, that's all. Everyone knows you just have to get through this year and then things get better,' I say, attempting to convince myself as much as her.

She nods slowly. 'Maybe.'

Then my pager goes off, and I get up and leave her to her dictation and make my way back to the ward.

Thursday 12 February

Ruby and I meet for a furtive cigarette. As if by magic, the white-coated woman walks past and glares at us. A shiver goes down my spine.

'She's a lung specialist,' explains Dr Palache who has joined us. 'Just ignore her.'

I want to talk to him about Lewis, but feel rather awkward. Instead I give him a list of scans to do.

Wednesday 18 February

I pay a visit to Trudy today, and am shocked to see someone else sitting down eating a piece of angel cake. 'I've brought you some letters for signing,' I begin before my mistake dawns on me.

'Aw, darling, that's not for me any more, is it? You'll need to see the medical secretaries down the corridor, they do Dr Pike's stuff Have you met Julie? She's the new junior doctor for Mr Butterworth.'

I look at her and smile coldly. All those furtive tea breaks with Trudy over the past six months, and within a few weeks, I'm simply replaced by someone else.

I suddenly see that this must have happened to someone else when I started work. This is the nature of hospitals; intense, emotionally charged relationships born out of an intense, emotionally charged, but ultimately transient environment. Patients leave, doctors leave, and the few constant variables like secretaries and consultants remain and become used to people moving in and out of their lives. I say to Julie, 'Have fun. Mr Butterworth's not that bad. And she,' I say, looking at Trudy, 'will look after you.'

A pager goes off and I look down before I

realise that it wasn't me. I look up to see Trudy answering it. 'She's not available at the moment, she's in a meeting,' she says down the phone and Julie smiles and mouths, 'Thank you.'

Trudy puts down the phone and as I leave I hear her say to Julie, 'Have you ever seen inside Mr Butterworth's office? Well…'

Thursday 19 February

They are called The Coven. They cackle at me while they tell me this. It is a strange coincidence that all three of them are called Mary. 'We're like…' begins one.

'…sisters,' complete the other two in unison.

'Only Mary's too skinny to be related to me,' says the largest of them to the young thin one sitting opposite her.

'And you're old enough to be my mother,' answers the skinny one to howls of laughter from the other two.

I stand and watch them, apparently only a mild diversion from their constant banter. It's as though they are clockwork toys I've wound up, and now I can sit back and watch them go. These are the medical secretaries. Each of them works for a different consultant, but they share an office. Mary 2, so called because her desk is at an angle between Mary 1 and Mary 3, is the secretary for Dr Pike. 'But we do each other's work quite a lot,' Mary 1, the older, larger one, informs me.

'Her typing is so slow,' interrupts Mary 2, pointing at Mary 3, the younger, thinner one, 'that half the time the patients have died of old age before she's even typed their letters.'

'That's not true,' interrupts Mary 3, feigning horror. 'I'm faster than you any day.' I quietly put the letters and dictation in the in-tray and leave, as they challenge each other to a typing race.

Monday 23 February

Ruby is in a sulk this week because Housewives' Favourite is away on holiday. She had booked time off to coincide with his but it became apparent that he had no intention of going on holiday with her. He said he was going with some friends and she couldn't possibly go with him. It was a boys' thing, apparently, which makes me suspect he's taking his latest junior doctor instead. So Ruby is left to mope around the flat on her own as it pours down with rain outside. At least she can pick up my dry-cleaning. Every cloud.

Tuesday 24 February

Ruby's going to Cuba. Tonight. She can't bear being in the flat for a minute longer, she tells me as I walk in this evening. 'What?' I shout. 'You can't just go to Cuba like that on your own. You might get killed or kidnapped or something. And what about my washing? I thought you were going to cook for me every night and clean the bathroom?'

I am aware I sound a bit selfish, but I thought the deal was that whoever was on holiday could help the other live a more normal life.

'Don't leave me. Think of the children,' I implore.

She rolls her eyes. 'Max, the only reason you want me to stay is because you had some notion that I was going to suddenly become a domestic goddess and look after you. We both know that's not going to happen. I can barely look after myself, let alone you as well.'

On reflection, this is true. Ruby is about as undomesticated as is possible without being actually feral. She quite happily runs out of underwear and just turns the dirty pairs inside out. Perhaps the place will be a bit tidier with her gone. And when I get a take-away I won't have her descend on it like a plague of locusts. And I'll be able to leave the toilet seat up without her moaning at me: the clincher. I help her pack.

Thursday 26 February

I am going to scream. 'Please press three on your keypad now for computer services,' says the electronic voice at the other end of the phone.

'I *am* pressing 3!' I scream into the ether.

Pause.

'We have not detected a response. Please hang up and try...'

'No, no, don't you dare...'

Click. Too late, I've been disconnected again.

Dealing with automated telephone messages is enraging at the best of times, but it's almost too much to bear when you're trying to arrange a blood transfusion for Mrs Ashcroft who's haemorrhaging in front of you. It's getting to the stage where I'm contemplating dialling 999 – after all, this is an emergency and I desperately do need some services. I try the telephone again. 'Press one for hotel services. Press two for portering services. Press three for computer services' and so on. I've no idea what hotel services does, but I'm very tempted to press one just to see if they can arrange a European city break somewhere and get me out of this mess.

I abandon the telephone and decide on the old-fashioned method of grabbing a nurse, getting down on my knees and sobbing, 'You've got to help me.' This one usually works.

'Press the star button a couple of times,' says Rachel, the nurse.

Miraculously I'm connected to a very disgruntled voice. 'Yeah.'

I can hear the smack of gum being chewed at the other end of the phone.

'I urgently need some help. The computer isn't working properly and I've got to order a cross-match for a blood transfusion. And I need a porter to bring the blood over and–'

'What service centre ya calling from?' interrupts the voice at the other end of the phone.

'What?' I ask.

'What's the unit code?' comes the reply.

'The what?' I repeat. I'm close to screaming again.

These are just the choice highlights of a telephone conversation which only succeeded in establishing that I didn't know what a unit code was and that apparently this NHS trust only has computer support during working hours and so I was going to have to fix the problem myself anyway. Unfortunately this was going to be tricky as medical school neglected to teach me anything about computer programming, preferring to focus on medicine. Welcome to the wonderful world of PFI. No, this is nothing to do with the Pet Food Institute. This stands for Private Finance Initiative, the brainchild of brainless governments. Under this scheme, building projects and certain services are run by private companies, which the NHS then rents back from them. The government likes it because the cost of the hospital does not appear as an immediate lump-sum payment in public expenditure. Sick people are not very cost-effective though, and therefore the only way private companies are going to make money is by cutting corners. The service they provide is shoddy. The computer system is run by one company, catering by another, porters and cleaners by yet another, but the telephone system you use to access these companies is run by a totally different company, sub-contracted out by the computer company. None of these companies seem to communicate with each other and trying to get anything done is like banging your bead against a brick wall, which is appropriate seeing that the portering services are run by a building company. But at least the hospital has now got a chill-out area for patients, complete with IKEA scatter-cushions. Although I'm sure Mrs Ashcroft would rather have her blood transfusion.

'It's all right, Max,' says Rachel, who appears holding bags of blood. 'I've sorted it. Here's the blood for Mrs Ashcroft.'

I stare in disbelief.

'I know the chap in transfusion so he let me have it. You need to sign for it though.'

We connect the blood and Mrs Ashcroft gets her transfusion.

'I owe you one,' I say to Rachel.

If I ever do press one and I get that city break, I think I'll take her.

Friday 27 February

Medicine is full of beautiful patterns. It's tempting when studying it to believe in a divine creator because of the way things fit together: the amazingly intricate interplay between chemicals in the body; the unfathomably complex pathways and cascades that underpin physiological function; the translation of genes into proteins; the delicate formation of a foetus from a ball of cells. Everything is in balance, in equilibrium. Medicine is, in fact, all about balance. Too much of one thing, too little of another and pathology, sickness and disease ensue. The ancient Chinese concept of Ying and Yang encapsulates this exactly. But I also sometimes think that in some mystical, unobservable way, it's not just the body that is in balance, but the world.

Of course I've seen enough distress and disease to realise that karma doesn't really exist. Good people get sick, bad people don't. It's random and unfair. But every now and then, there's a slight shift, a subtle twist of fate that makes you smile, that makes you question if things really are always that arbitrary. And that's exactly what happened today.

Once a week we take it in turns to be part of the crash team. We hold a special pager that is called when someone's heart stops working. We rush to the scene and attempt to restart their heart. It's rather exciting in theory, but in reality it's a strange mixture of dullness, because it rarely goes off, and abject fear, because sometimes it does. But the fact that you're in a team, with senior doctors, makes the whole thing more bearable. Today the pager went off. We ran to the ward. 'Bed 2,' shouted the nurse.

I ran into the clinic room and got the heart monitor and wheeled it into the cubicle of bed 2. And there, facing me, was Lewis, doing a chest compression on the patient. The patient was Mr Oak. I stood there rather redundantly while Lewis pushed down firmly on Mr Oak's chest, ensuring that blood continued to be pushed round his body, despite his heart having stopped. Lewis, it occurred to me, had Mr Oak's life in his hands. I wondered if Mr Oak would object now. Technically, I should have taken over, but instead I let Lewis continue.

An hour later, after the metabolic imbalance that had stopped his heart had been corrected and he was sitting up in bed, alive and well, I smiled as he thanked the team for helping him, and shook each of their hands, including Lewis's. And Lewis, the better man, shook his hand and said it had been a pleasure.

MARCH

Monday 1 March

Ruby remains on holiday. The washing is piling up and the cupboards are bare. Of course it's not as if her presence in the flat improves this situation in any way, it's just that when she is here, at least I can have a crisis about what shirt I'm going to be wearing the next day, or what we are going to have for dinner, with someone else. Being miserable is so much more enjoyable when someone else is miserable with you.

Tuesday 2 March

I stood in A&E, horrified at what I'd just done as the man left the department. I watched him walk out into the cold winter night, clutching a blanket. The doors closed behind him.

The man, Mr Searle, is an alcoholic and was actually discharged this morning from a ward, where he's been an inpatient for the past month. Life can be tough and he obviously can't cope the way most of us can.

He copes by downing a litre of vodka a day, which of course is a good way of numbing yourself to the realities of your life, but not a very good strategy for doing anything to change it. He has had numerous admissions and at the end of each one provision is made for him to get into a hostel, to receive counselling about his alcohol use and be followed up as a medical and psychiatric outpatient. He then promptly goes back to the bottle, and isn't heard from again until he reaches crisis point and presents to A&E once more.

When he was discharged from the ward this morning, he'd been booked accommodation in a hostel, had been given the money to pay for it and had an appointment in the afternoon to find him somewhere permanent to live. Unfortunately, on the journey from the hospital to the hostel where he was supposed to be staying, he detoured into a pub, where he stayed for the next twelve hours, meaning he lost his room and missed his accommodation appointment. Clearly the last month as an inpatient had been a waste of time. At last orders, he realised he didn't have anywhere to sleep, and so thought he'd pop along to the A&E department where we'd be able to find him somewhere to live. Yeah, right. En route, however, he fell over, banged his head and was found by a passer-by who called an ambulance. Then he came here, where despite being medically fit, he demanded we find him somewhere to sleep. I spent hours on the phone trying to find somewhere for him to stay, but at 2 a.m., it was futile. I explained to him that he needed to get in touch with the council in the morning and reschedule the appointment about his accommodation. And then, to my shame, I told him to leave.

'Can I have a blanket?' he asked. I handed it over, pretending I didn't know that he was going to spend the rest of the night sleeping outside. I felt heartless and uncaring, but I couldn't see what I could do to help him. I was also angry and frustrated with him that despite the input of numerous professionals over several admissions he was still in a hopeless situation. Can the NHS, with its limited resources, be expected to act as a wet-nurse for such people, scrubbing them up, putting them back on their feet until they revert to their chaotic lifestyle? Isn't part of being human about making choices about your life and taking responsibility for those choices? But isn't part of being a doctor being compassionate, helping those in need?

He walked out into the cold, the doors closed behind him, and I got on with seeing another patient.

Wednesday 3 March

Met with Supriya this morning for a quick coffee in the canteen. I had bumped into her in the corridor and was relieved to see a familiar, friendly face, and one that I knew was having as miserable a time as I was. Or so I thought. But before we'd even sat down she was enthusing about how great medicine was. She'd talked to her consultant about her doubts and to her family and she told me how they'd encouraged her. How she's changed her mind and she's convinced that medicine is exactly what she wants to do with the rest of her life. She's seen the light. Great, this is all I need. She continues with the enthusiasm of a religious convert, trying to convince me that I love being a doctor too.

The more enthusiastic she becomes, the more negative I feel. I listen to her passionate speech about how she's going to work in medicine instead of surgery, about how the detective work involved in diagnosis is so enthralling. It's not that I don't want to think like that, I do. It's just that I can't. I can't see past all the pointless bits of paperwork, the protocols, the stress, the fact you never have enough time and how easily patients become a frustrating distraction from the endless form-filling and ward rounds. How everything seems so bleak and cold and heartless and empty. I'm pleased for Supriya, but at the same time, I can feel her slipping away to somewhere I just don't recognise.

Thursday 4 March

'Look!' I hear Mary 2 scream as I walk into the office.

They are seeing how many Murray Mints they can put in their mouths. Mary 3 is the clear winner.

In another life, I hope I come back as a medical secretary.

Saturday 6 March

Flora is back this weekend. I'm more grateful than I can express to see her face. 'You all right, Max?' she says.

'It's just so nice to see you,' I say, relieved that she will be here to distract me from thinking about work. We sit down at the kitchen table, like the old days, and reminisce about medical school. Flora is hating her new job and I'm quietly pleased. I don't want the weekend to descend into just a two-day griping extravaganza though. I want to forget about work. I brush her complaints aside breezily.

'It will be fine. Don't worry, everyone

knows this is the worst year and you just have to survive it, and then everything will get better,' I say, reeling off my usual speech like an automaton.

I suspect that Flora is as unconvinced by this as I am, but she doesn't let on. 'I suppose so,' she says with a sigh.

She gets up to make tea then turns to me and says, 'I never think about the dead people any more.'

'What dead people?' I ask. I assume this is the lead-up to some sort of joke.

'The dead people – all the people that we see dead and dying. I don't think about it any more. It used to prey on my mind, when I first started work. Now I just don't really think about them. It's just, well, a part of work. They're dead and that's it. I don't really get upset.'

I nod my head slowly. I know exactly what she means. You're aware that you're surrounded by tragedy, by people upset or in pain. But at some point in the last five months I've become immune to it. It's stopped registering. I think back to when Lewis and I stood in the room certifying that woman – I can't even remember her name now – and we both were so overwhelmed with emotion. Now it's just part of the job. Something which doesn't feature on my emotional radar. I probably see five dead bodies a week. Some I've known, others I haven't. It ceases to have the weight it used to.

'I think it's worrying,' continues Flora. 'It's not normal surely to be so dispassionate about people dying all around you? I don't want to turn into some sort of heartless monster who doesn't care about that sort of thing.'

I nod my head again. This is partly what I don't like about this job either, the slow, subtle hardening of your heart. The slow, insidious infiltration of cynicism and detachment. At the beginning I was worried about being too upset by people dying. Now I'm worried I'm not upset enough.

Sunday 7 March

Flora and I go shopping today. I don't need anything but that doesn't stop me buying things. I don't think about work all day; And then, as we stand waiting to cross the road, the traffic lights let out their shrill beep as they change, and Flora and I instinctively look down and feel for our non-existent pagers before realising our mistake.

Monday 8 March

'What's wrong?' I ask. Matthew is about my

age, with messy brown hair and the beginnings of a beard. While he might come across as a bit odd sometimes, he's polite, well behaved. He sits smoking in the TV room, talks to the other patients.

'I'm lonely,' he replies.

Now, when I'm called to see a patient and I ask them what is wrong, it is, fingers crossed, generally something fairly straightforward. Even if it turns out to be a little complicated, there are always tests to order, scans to book; I can make some attempt to at least start sorting the problem out. Matthew has been admitted because he's developed diabetes as a result of some medication he was given for his schizophrenia. His condition has stabilised quickly and we're waiting for a bed to be free on a psychiatry ward. But the nursing staff on the ward have noticed that he's been acting strangely and are worried about him. He's become more withdrawn, spending longer in his bed and crying in the middle of the night. I'd hoped that it was something medical that was wrong, like an upset stomach. Advice given, medicines prescribed, smiling faces all round, another happy customer. But instead he's lonely.

I know how he feels. It's not just because Ruby is away, and anyway, she's got Housewives' Favourite now. It's that I never seem to have the time or energy to see people any more. I feel like life is just passing me by. I feel so alone sometimes. But I suppose some consolation can be drawn from the fact that I'm not the only one feeling like this.

Matthew hasn't got any friends. I try and suggest some things he could do when he's discharged, clubs and groups he could join. But he shakes his head. He's not stupid, he knows what other people his age do. He knows that other people his age aren't hearing voices, or having toxic medication injected into them to control their psychosis. What he needs I can't prescribe. I can't conjure up a group of ready-made friends who'll accept him for who he is: someone who plays football, who watches *The Weakest Link* (no one's perfect), enjoys going to concerts and who's got schizophrenia. Mental illness is lonely and isolating and I'm not sure what, as a doctor, I can do about it. For people with severe, enduring mental illness it's a life sentence. They don't fit in, they're not normal, and people in the outside world don't want to mix with people like that.

'What about the other people on your psychiatry ward? Have you made friends with any of them?' I ask.

'They aren't my age and none of them are into the same things as me,' he replies. He lowers his voice. 'And anyway, they're mad,' he whispers.

He has a point there; why should he be

expected to be friends with them just because they happen to have mental illness in common?

'Will you be my friend?' he asks after some time.

I don't think anyone has ever asked me that before. I really wanted to say yes, that I would be his friend, but I knew that more than it possibly being 'unprofessional', it would be a lie. I'm not his friend because I'm his doctor. That therapeutic relationship works because the doctor is detached from the patient.

Matthew can tell what my answer is going to be, and before I can find the words for a response he sighs and looks out of the window.

'I wish I was normal,' he says.

I want to tell him that sometimes feeling lonely is perfectly normal.

Wednesday 10 March

Ruby is back! Horrifically brown and healthy looking and generally laden down with Cuban goodies. I was touched that she had thought of me as she unpacked the large box of cigars. I don't smoke cigars, but the thought was sweet. 'Do you think that's a good present for him?' she said.

'Who?' I asked foolishly, then realised she

meant Housewives' Favourite, of course.

I'd hoped she'd have found a nubile Cuban lover while she was on holiday, but no.

'I missed him so much while I was away. I just couldn't stop thinking about him,' she began.

'Have you called him to tell him you're back yet?' I asked, wondering if the affair was still ongoing.

'Oh no, he doesn't like me to call him after 5 p.m. He calls me instead. He's busy a lot in the evenings and can't really be disturbed. His mother's not well at the moment and he goes round to look after her and stuff,' she told me.

I am amazed that someone as intelligent as Ruby can be so stupid when it comes to this man.

Friday 12 March

Housewives' Favourite joins Ruby and me for a cigarette break. Now that I've left surgery I don't have to pretend that I like him, a courtesy he never extended to me in the first place. I nod as he says hello to Ruby, ignoring me.

'How is your new house officer, then?' I ask feigning innocence. 'It's a "she", isn't it? You always seem to get female junior doctors working for you, don't you?'

He pretends not to hear me and Ruby flashes me a look. OK, I'll be civil, if only to please her. I stand in silence for a few moments, sensing the almost tangible desire emanating from Housewives' Favourite for me to leave. But I have an equally strong desire to remain, to protect Ruby from his attentions or possibly just to annoy him.

He is slightly side-on to me, and from where I'm standing I can see the hand with the lit cigarette drop to his side, the furls of smoke climbing gently up his arm. I stare at the cigarette and for some reason, I begin to look at his hand, and it is then that I notice a light mark on one of his fingers. I stare at it more intently as they talk quietly about their respective holidays and how much they missed each other. His hand moves up and I see it, again. A thin, pale mark round the base of his finger, contrasting with his freshly tanned hand.

It has never occurred to me that House-wives' Favourite might be married. I'd just assumed he was a jack-the-lad, someone who liked to play the field. I wonder if Ruby has any idea, and, with a sinking heart, whether I need to tell her.

Saturday 13 March

'I can't tell her. She'll kill me,' I say.

'Why will she kill you? It's not your fault he's married. She needs to know. Look at it this way: if she finds out and then discovers you knew, then she really will kill you, and she'd be right,' says Flora down the phone.

If Flora was still living in the flat I know that, somehow, I would manage to convince her that it was her moral duty to tell Ruby about Housewives' Favourite. But it's just me. 'I don't want to,' I whine.

'Look, I'm on call and can't really speak now. Be a man for God's sake. What's the worst that could happen?' concludes Flora.

'OK. OK, I'll tell her,' I concede.

Tomorrow.

Sunday 14 March

Ruby is laughing at me.

'Married?' she says in between guffaws. 'Is that what you had to tell me? Is that it?'

I hesitate for a moment. This was not the response I had been expecting. 'This is what was so important that we couldn't go to the cinema?' she continues.

I feel rather wounded that my attempts to save her from getting entangled with a married man are being thrown back in my face. 'Well, I'm surprised you're so blasé about it. I thought you were supposed to be an ardent feminist with principles?' I say

261

defensively, possibly aiming a little too far below the belt.

'If you must know, he's told me that he's married. And you might also like to know that he's getting a divorce from her. OK? So I'll thank you to mind your own business from now on.'

With that she gets up and stalks off upstairs and we don't speak for the rest of the day.

Well, could have been worse, at least my front teeth are still in place.

Tuesday 16 March

'Are you and Ruby not talking?' asks Lewis.

I look at him. 'What gave you that impression?' I ask sardonically.

'Well, the fact that she's just walked into the canteen, saw you, and sat on the other side of the room, for starters.'

I sigh. 'Yes, she's in a mood with me.'

I tell him the story of Housewives' Favourite.

Lewis looks at me puzzled for a moment. 'He's still married. He's not getting a divorce. Well, not unless he decided to get one since the weekend.'

'How do you know?'

'Because Mark went out with them for some Royal College do at the weekend. His wife's pregnant. He's not leaving her.'

I'm rather confused by all this. 'Hang on, who's Mark?'

'Mark Palache – he told me that she's pregnant and how he's promised his wife he'll stop messing around. She knows all about his little indiscretions at work. I don't think she knows details or anything, and certainly not the extent of it.' He pauses and takes a sip of tea. 'Ruby should be careful. I don't think she wants to be the woman on the side, but that's the only position that's available.'

I look at Lewis hopefully.

He raises an eyebrow. 'Oh no. No way. I'm not getting involved. You tell her. I'm not going to,' he says shaking his head.

'It's your duty as her friend, her colleague.'

'Not on your life, Max. You're her best friend, you do it.'

I open my mouth but I know he's right. I close it again and sigh. 'She's not talking to me. She thinks it's just because I don't like him or that I'm jealous of him because he's a big successful doctor or something. She won't listen to me.'

'Of course she will, just pick the right time,' says Lewis. He stands up. 'Just don't tell her I said anything. Mark and I are staying out of this,' and he goes back to work, leaving me sitting alone on one side of the canteen, and Ruby, sullenly, on the other.

Thursday 18 March

'We just want a quiet life, Max,' said one of the junior nurses a few days ago.

'I don't understand what the problem is,' the sister of the ward intervenes.

I have come to affectionately call the sister 'The Battleaxe', but not to her face, obviously. She strikes fear into the heart of every junior doctor she comes into contact with. Apparently her bite is actually worse than her bark. This seems hard to believe, as this woman could bark for Battersea Dogs' Home.

In the background I can hear Mrs Linwood shouting. It is annoying, I'll give them that.

'There's not much I can do, really,' I whimper.

'Just sedate her, and then we can all get some work done,' replies The Battleaxe.

I've been dreading confrontations like this since I started work. The nurses on this ward have held my hand countless times when faced with sick patients, so how can I pull rank and use the 'I'm a doctor, you're a nurse' card now?

The nursing staff are being driven up the wall by Mrs Linwood's constant shouts and screams and they want me to sedate her. But

I'm supposed to be there acting in the patient's best interests, not the medical staff's. It's an ethical dilemma and I'm not even sure what's right or wrong any more. I just feel tired. And the frustrating thing is that even if I do stick my neck out and refuse to sedate her, Mrs Linwood won't thank me. Mrs Linwood is severely demented. She won't even know what I've done, or rather not done. And besides, junior doctors are completely reliant on the nursing staff to ensure that everything runs smoothly and if you get on the wrong side of them, they will make sure your life is a living hell. I've seen it happen to some of my friends.

My time in this job is divided between Cardiology and Care Of Older People (which is the new politically correct name for geriatrics, although I'm sure this will change once someone realises that the acronym spells COOP, not a particularly glamorous thing to have as your chosen working environment). But it's the geriatrics side that's the hard bit. I've seen some really dreadful and sad things. Old people get a bum deal in society. And as for people with mental health problems, no one ever stands up for them either. Poor Mrs Linwood has the worst of it: she's old *and* mad. What hope has she got? Nobody is going to reprimand me for sedating her, but my conscience just won't let me.

I go into the side room where Mrs Linwood is. I know from reading her notes that her shouting out is an ongoing problem. Sedating patients is only a short-term solution, though, and the medications have bad side effects if used repeatedly.

She's not in distress. In fact, as I walk over to her bed she stares at me blankly but starts to laugh. Then she starts shouting again. The junior nurse appears, holding a radio. 'We could try this – it might keep her quiet for a bit,' she suggests. I turn it on and tune into a local station. I'll worry about the ethics of making someone listen to Britney Spears later. It works and she's quiet. I leave the ward, acutely aware though that the real issues haven't been addressed.

Then this afternoon, as I queued up in the canteen, Barney came up to me.

'That patient of ours, Mrs Linwood, she's annoying, isn't she? Nurses talked to me about her yesterday,' he said.

'Oh, her shouting? Yeah,' I replied. Proud of my new discovery I added, 'But she's quiet again if you turn the radio on.'

'Oh, I just sedated her. Knocked her out flat,' he retorted bluntly.

I could feel myself burning with rage. I'd like to say that I shouted at him, that I told him it was wrong to sedate someone just because they were annoying the nurses, that

I refused to be quiet, but I'm ashamed to say I didn't. I didn't want to cause a scene, to be branded a troublemaker, so instead I mumbled a few words and sat down at a table and ate my lunch in silence,

There's a part of all of us that, sometimes, just wants a quiet life.

Saturday 20 March

Ruby is now talking to me, sort of. Well, she's eating my muesli, so in a way that's communication. Her behaviour is completely out of proportion for what I actually did – I was only trying to look out for her. Everyone in the world except her can see he's no good, but it's useless trying to convince her. I can't help but wonder if she's actually cross with herself for liking him, and is projecting it all on to me.

Ruby would never accept an explanation like that though; she's a surgeon through and through.

Monday 22 March

Dr Pike is one of those painfully, annoyingly enthusiastic people that you dread being sat next to at dinner parties. They are so excited and happy and manic all at the same time, they inevitably make you feel as if you should be on suicide watch. His frenetic, frantic ward rounds are peppered with squeals of excitement as he remembers obscure details about the functioning of some organ that is relevant to the patient's diagnosis, or yelps of joy as he looks at a blood result confirming his suspicions. He was of course trained in the good old days, when doctors received, he assures me, 'a proper training'.

'I used to work one night on, one night off. You lot don't know you're born.'

He says this a lot. If Dr Pike is to be believed, most people are walking around unaware of their own birth. There's also his annoying habit of saying, whenever he thinks I might be about to say something is unfair, 'that's show business' and then does this really awful smile and jazz-hands move.

I want to reply that, no, this isn't show business. It's medicine. 1 wish it were show business because then I might make a fortune and retire. Instead I have to put my finger up people's bottoms and look at what comes out on the glove. There is no way that that, by any stretch of the imagination, is going to make it on to the silver screen.

This general enthusiasm can even get on the patients' nerves. Dr Pike had suspected that Mr Calwald might have a phaeochromocytoma. It might sound like something you'd pick up from the garden centre to go into that gloomy patch at the end of the lawn, but it is, in fact, a rare type of tumour of the adrenal glands. This morning on the ward round Barney read out the results, which confirmed Dr Pike's suspicions. 'Oh, excellent!' Dr Pike shouted, as Barney explained to Mr Calwald that he had a tumour.

It's not fatal and can simply be removed by a surgeon, although at this point this hadn't been explained to Mr Calwald, who sat looking gaunt and scared.

'There you go Max, what do you know. You don't get to see many of those now, do you? You'll remember this, won't you?' Dr Pike said beaming and wandered off to the next patient, still muttering, 'Marvellous'.

Mr Calwald, understandably, seemed to think it was anything but.

Tuesday 23 March

I remember Molly sitting in the middle of the garden. I was only eight years old. It became one of those famous stories that families accumulate over the years, which are told and retold so many times. Bits are added and details lost so that what I recall now might not be exactly what happened. But still, the fact remains: Molly sat in the garden and died. She found a slight dip in the lawn, settled herself down, and never got up.

'She's upset because George has died,' my mum explained when Molly first started her vigil. For three whole nights my sister and I barely slept. We would get out of bed, press our noses up against the window and see her silhouette, alone, outside on the lawn.

'She'll get a cold,' we sobbed, as we tried to explain why we'd draped the John Lewis picnic blanket over her shoulders on the second evening. And after the third night, when we woke up, she'd died.

For an eight-year-old, the death of your pet chicken is pretty traumatic. The explanation that Mum and Dad gave us was that Molly had died of a broken heart. A few days before this, George, our cat, had died. The two of them had never been friends, exactly. After all, what self-respecting cat would be friends with a chicken? But he would wait each morning to be let out, and sit patiently until the coop was opened. They would chase each other round the garden, and she would peck the top of his head while he ate his dinner. It was more of a love-hate relationship but it obviously ran very deep.

For a few days after George died, Molly stood on the guinea-pig hutch, where he used to sit, basking in the sun. Chickens don't get much credit for being the brainiest of animals, but after a few days she must have realised that wherever he'd gone, he wasn't coming back so she stopped looking for him and, so the story goes, she nursed her broken heart in the middle of the lawn until she died. And so the story of Molly the chicken and her broken heart went down in the annals of our family history; a story told at countless parties, though never while eating chicken drumsticks, out of respect.

I think of this story this morning as I stand on one of the wards, where we are seeing Mr Thomas after he has been admitted with a heart attack. He's also clearly depressed. Dr Pike begins to explain to Mr Thomas that's he's fit enough now to go home and he immediately breaks down in tears. His wife died eight months ago. He doesn't see the point in living any more.

'It broke my heart when she died,' he says, as he dries his eyes. 'I think that's what's made me end up in here.'

I would have dismissed this idea if it weren't for something Dr Pike told me only a week or so ago. He said that for the remaining partner in the first year after a spouse dies, there is a seventy per cent increase in heart attacks, with a forty per cent increase in death rate. It seems you can die from a broken heart after all.

That seemed incredible to me. How can something psychological, like bereavement, be implicated in something as physical as a heart attack? But the mind is obviously more powerful than we thought. There is a strong tendency in medicine to think that things are either physical or psychological, and a denial that there can be an interaction between the two. But looking at Mr Thomas it's obvious that things aren't as simple as that. Doctors need to learn to start seeing people holistically.

After we've talked, Mr Thomas is prescribed an antidepressant as well as some heart medication, and arrangements are made for him to go to bereavement counselling.

I say goodbye, the ward round ends and as I make my way back to my office I pass the canteen and look at the menu: chicken drumsticks and chips. I have the lasagne instead.

Wednesday 24 March

I put my head in my hands. Not another patient to clerk in. I look at my watch; I was supposed to leave two hours ago. 'Sorry Max, he's just been transferred over from the surgical team. He's coming under your team. It should be quite straightforward. Assault, fractured arm and head injury. He's really just for rehabilitation and review of his housing arrangements,' says Rachel.

I sigh. Another elderly, infirm man to add to my list.

I collect his notes. Mr Maurice Goldblatt. Aged eighty-two. He hasn't been transferred with any blood results so I print them off the computer, stuff them moodily in the notes and make my way over to see him. And there, sitting up in bed, a bandage over his left eye, cuts on his face and chest and a nasty bruise on his cheek, is Maurice. Our Maurice, the man who, since his wife died, has unofficially looked after the doctors' mess. Maurice, who was assaulted two weeks ago by thugs who stole his pension and his bicycle.

'Hello, Doctor. I'm so sorry about all this. Really, I'm fine,' he begins as I approach his bed.

I feel awful that none of us knew he was even in hospital, let alone what he'd gone through. And I feel furious that he's here because of the actions of other people who can never know or appreciate what a kind, harmless, unassuming man Maurice is. People who didn't care. But then, I hadn't cared either. I'd seen Maurice as just another patient that needed to be clerked in; another hospital number to be ticked off on my list.

Thursday 25 March

I told Lewis this morning about Maurice,

and by lunchtime he had gone into an organisational whirlwind. A poster had appeared in the doctors' mess asking for donations for a 'get well soon' present and a card was on the coffee table for everyone to sign. There were no teabags, of course, as we'd now realised that it was Maurice who provided these.

'I just thought they were free or something,' said Barney as we reached this conclusion.

I suspect that, coming from a privileged background, Barney assumes a lot of things are free.

Maurice's assault also explains why there haven't been any papers for the past few weeks, or indeed milk. And no one has taken the rubbish out, In fact, without him, the doctors' mess is barely functioning. It's, well, a mess.

Friday 26 March

Dr Palache and Maxine are having another argument. 'He's lost a pelvis and a chest now,' she says as I search on the floor for an X-ray I ordered on one of my patients.

'I haven't lost them,' he shouts from deep inside his office.

Maxine rolls her eyes and mouths, 'He has.'

Dr Palache continues to protest his innocence – but she ignores him.

'Of course, soon he won't be able to lose them,' she says.

'What do you mean?' I ask as I kneel on the floor looking through another pile.

'We're going computerisational,' she says triumphantly.

I'm not sure that's a word, but I know what she means. 'You mean it's going digital?' I ask.

Her eyes light up. 'Yeah, digitalised. The whole department. No more hard copies of scans, just everything on computers. They'll all be stored on some computer chip somewhere,' she says vaguely.

I suspect that Maxine has not fully embraced technology. I also wonder if it's occurred to her that soon she'll be out of a job: no more hard copies of scans means no more sorting and filing. A job she's done for countless years, now redundant. 'Oh, I think they're sending me on a course to learn how to work the new computer system. I mean, I've gone on the...' she stops for a moment. 'You know, the...'

'Internet,' interrupts Dr Palache from inside his office.

'Yes, that's it, the Internet. My daughter showed me. Oh, it's marvellous,' she says, shaking her head in disbelief

'Luddite,' comes the response from the

security of Dr Palache's office.

I leave them to it. As I walk down the corridor back to the ward, I wonder how the steady march of change will affect Maxine, an anachronism in the digital age. Perhaps, instead of shouting through his office door, she'll start sending him emails.

Saturday 27 March

I was wakened this morning by the telephone ringing. I ignored it. It rang again. I ignored it again. My mobile was on vibrate and I could hear the gentle buzz of someone leaving a message. And another one. Eventually curiosity got the better of me and I got out of bed and rooted through my trouser pocket to find it. I'd four missed calls and a text from my sister: 'Gran's had heart attack. Phone ASAP.'

In under ten minutes I was dressed and rushing out of the door to go to the train station.

I arrive at the hospital – a grim district general hospital on the outskirts of a town twenty miles from where my Gran lives – and wander round for ages trying to find the ward. One sign points one way, and when I follow it, another sign points back the way I've come. Do people at my hospital get lost like this? I wonder. I feel strangely exposed and vulnerable – I'm not used to not knowing my way around a hospital.

These feelings are only compounded when I finally find my gran. My sister and mum are already there; my grandfather has gone to find something to eat, and the latest test scores, no doubt. I can't help but look at her drug chart, ask the nurses her blood pressure, take a surreptitious peek at her ECG. I can't switch off, and yet I know that my emotional involvement makes any objective analysis of her condition impossible. I know that the nursing staff want me to assume the usual docile relative role, but I can't help it. Why isn't she on this medication? Why isn't her obs chart up to date? Has she been seen by a cardiologist yet?

All the time my gran lies there, quietly, patiently doing what she's told by the nurses, listens to the frazzled doctor who comes at my request, smiles and nods and is the model patient. I'm a nervous wreck, guilty that I haven't spent more time with her and that it takes a crisis before I do. I hate being on the other side of the bed, impotent and out of control. Now I know how the families of my patients feel. Not for the first time, I'm standing in a hospital and I'm scared.

Sunday 28 March

Gran was sitting up today. She's feeling a little bit better, she insists. My sister has already made friends with a dermatologist who she met in the hospital canteen. He's going to look at her rash, she tells me.

Monday 29 March

I stay with my gran today. 'But what about work?' asks my grandfather.

'I'll phone them,' I say and go outside and call Mary 2. Mary 1 answers the phone instead. I explain what's happened. 'Oh, don't you worry about that. You be with your gran. Family comes first. Give Dr Pike a call and let him know yourself but I'll tell the ward and everyone, don't you worry. Look, I've got to go, Max, Mary's doing her *Titanic* impression and she's fallen out of the window. Hope your gran makes a speedy recovery.'

I telephone Dr Pike. He's not impressed. 'Well, how long will you be? You'll be back tomorrow, won't you?' he asks.

I wonder when he underwent a compassion bypass. After all the hours I've given to that hospital, all the evenings I've sacrificed, all the stress and strain, that's the thanks I get.

'I'll try. It just depends what happens today,' I say firmly.

Sorry, Dr Pike, but that's show business.

Tuesday 30 March

I arrive back at work to the sound of screams. I recognise Lewis's voice, saying, 'Oh my God! Oh my God!'

I tentatively poke my head round the door to the kitchen in the doctors' mess. 'What on earth's going on?' I ask as several other people rush to see what the fuss is about.

'Look,' says Lewis, holding up the collection tin he'd made for Maurice's get well soon present.

For a moment my heart sinks as it occurs to me that someone has stolen the collection. Then Lewis turns the tin upside down, and a fistful of coins clatters onto the table, followed by a thick wodge of ten-pound notes held together with a rubber band.

I move closer. 'Where the hell did that come from?' I ask in amazement, picking up the notes.

Lewis takes them from me and neatly counts them out on to the table. Five hundred pounds. We all stand there, stunned. Barney comes in and starts messing around, throwing them in the air. Lewis glares at him disapprovingly, and Barney picks them off the floor and leaves. I'm guessing it wasn't him who donated them.

'I bet it was Mark,' confides Lewis. I still can't get used to hearing Dr Palache referred to as Mark, even though I know that Lewis and he have now moved in together. 'I told him about Maurice last night and he said he was going to make a donation to the fund.'

I stand open-mouthed. 'That is so kind of him. What an amazing guy. We'll be able to get a replacement bicycle for him and everything now,' I say.

Lewis beams. 'I know. Just wait, Mark's going to get a special surprise tonight,' he says earnestly.

I raise an eyebrow. 'You dirty dog, Lewis. I don't want to know the details,' I laugh.

'What?' he says innocently. 'I'm going to make him my duck à l'orange. What did you think I was talking about?'

I laugh. 'For five hundred pounds that had better be some duck à l'orange, Lewis.'

Then my pager goes off and I leave Lewis neatly counting out the money and shaking his head in amazement.

Wednesday 31 March

Telephone call from my mum: Gran has had another heart attack and is in the coronary

280

care unit. I'm in A&E when Mum telephones, and don't get the message until
midnight.

APRIL

Thursday 1 April

April Fool's Day, and as usual the joke's on me. I'm paged by Mary 2 after the ward round. 'Dr Pike's had a delivery for some medical equipment, Max, can you come over and pick it up for him?' she says.

I can hear the other two cackling in the background. I grudgingly make my way over to the office. 'Oh, we've lost it,' says Mary 3 as I walk in the door.

'I'm sure it was here...' begins Mary 2.

'...somewhere,' interrupts Mary 1.

I'm a little bit suspicious because they're laughing more than usual. In fact, they're barely coherent.

'It was in a big box around here,' Mary 1 giggles. 'I think it was a thing for a pulley device, called a "long weight".'

I've heard this joke before.

'Perhaps it's gone back to the post room,' says Mary 3. 'Would you mind going and asking if they've got a long weight for you?'

Oh, the joys of being a medical secretary. I wonder how long it has taken them to think this one up. Or maybe they try it on the junior doctors each year. It will work like this: I go to the post room, they leave me standing there for fifteen minutes, then come back and say 'There's your long wait.' It's a killer, really.

I decide to play along with them and eagerly leave the office, but pop into the canteen and then make my way back to the ward. An hour later I call Mary 2 back.

'Dr Pike wants to see you,' I say. She begins to laugh as she hears my voice, but quickly stops.

'What do you mean?'

'Somebody died while I was waiting in the post room and he needs to speak to you about why you sent me there. He's blaming you because I should have been on the ward.'

She falls silent. I can hear Mary 1 asking what's wrong. I let her sweat it out for a few more moments.

'April Fool,' I say.

Mary 2 screams at me down the telephone, 'You little bastard, you really had me going then. You wait till I see you, I'm going to kill you,' she laughs.

'Yeah, but it will be a long wait, won't it?' I say and hang up.

Friday 2 April

I am outside smoking a cigarette with

Rachel when Dr Palache joins us. 'That was so kind,' I say to him.

'What was?' he asks as he lights his cigarette.

'What you did for Maurice. And the consultants don't even use the mess, so you really didn't have to.'

He looks at me, rather perplexed.

'Why do people keep asking me about that? Lewis thought I'd given five hundred pounds or something to this fund he's organised. Does he think I'm mad? I was going to give him a tenner, but haven't got round to it yet. I'm not made of money,' he says laughing.

I look at his Rolex, but think it rude to point this out.

'God knows who'd do that sort of thing. But I can categorically tell you it wasn't me,' he says and inhales deeply. 'Still, feel free to spread some more rumours about my philanthropy. Lewis made me the best duck à l'orange before I'd had time to break the news to him that the money didn't have anything to do with me.'

He stubs his cigarette out on the wall and heads back into the hospital, leaving me wondering who on earth it was that donated all that money.

Saturday 3 April

I go with my mum to visit Gran for the weekend, who is now out of hospital. My mum spends the whole train journey saying how much weight I've lost and how ill I look, as if her nagging me about it will somehow reverse this. Eventually I confide in her that I'm really not enjoying being a doctor as much as I thought I would. Until this point I've tried to shelter her from what it's really like, from how I really feel. I know that in one train journey I cannot hope to convey the complexity of my feelings. It's not as simple as being tired or stressed or fed-up. It's about being in your mid-twenties and not knowing what you want to do with your life, even though you always thought you did. It's about having to face the brutal realities of life every day and being ground down by it. It's having your innocence and naivety slowing squeezed out of you.

'Well, you're young, you've got your whole life ahead of you. You've got a good degree so if you don't like it just leave.'

Plain and simple, that's my mum.

'Wouldn't you be upset?' I ask.

'Why would I be upset? It's your life. God, you wouldn't catch me doing it. All that putting your finger in people's bottoms. No thank you. You've given it a go, if you don't like it, then leave and do something else,' and with this she sits back, content that this has solved any problems I have.

In fact, as I stare out the window, I feel even more confused. I think of Supriya, whose parents would have been devastated if she'd told them she was going to leave. Instead, I'm faced with unwavering support whatever I choose, which on the one hand is good, but on the other, provides no excuse to stay. It's going to have to be my decision, and while at work there's always someone else to ask if you're unsure of something, with this, there's no second opinion.

Sunday 4 April

Ruby gave the money. I should have known it was her. She's the only person mad enough. It was something the old Ruby, the pre-Housewives' Favourite Ruby, would have done. 'It was my ash cash. I felt a bit funny spending that money on some shoes when I got it by signing a form to say someone could be burnt,' she explains calmly.

'I thought you were going to buy a bike with it?' I say, pleased that she appears to have forgotten our recent falling out.

'Yeah, I thought about that, but then when I heard about Maurice I thought, well, he can have it for his bike instead.'

Ruby exists on another plane. She doesn't

286

think about paying bills, about washing up, about cooking food. She's an academic through and through. She lives in her ivory tower, and gets takeaway and someone else to do her laundry. And that's what's so appealing about her. For her, money has no real value. It's just something that either she has at that particular moment, or she doesn't. It's this attitude which means her bank account is always freezing, which frequently requires other people to bail her out. It's frustrating, but also incredibly liberating, because she's not beholden to the material world. She must be the only person whose bank manager buys her duty-free cigarettes when he's on holiday because he wants to try and help her budget. But underlying all this is a genuine kindness and compassion. I know that she'd give someone the shirt off her back if they asked for it. Or five hundred pounds for an old man.

Monday 5 April

'Please don't,' I say into the darkness.

I can just make out the silhouette of Gillian's head against the office door. I've been trying to doze, unsuccessfully, whilst sitting in a chair.

Gillian shakes her head. 'It's too late,' she says, wearily.

I turn on the sidelight so I can see her face properly. We've been sitting in the dark, in between seeing patients on night shift.

'I've already written my resignation letter,' she explains, sighing heavily and adding, 'It's a shame. I love my job and I love working here.'

This is a disaster. Gillian is one of the best nurses I've ever worked with. It's a disaster not just for the patients, but for me: she is a joy to work with as she is fantastic clinically and also has a marvellous way with the patients. She's everything you could ever possibly want from a nurse. She's a single parent though, and as the trust has recently merged two wards, it means a significant alteration in the hours she works. Realistically, she can't work the hours she is now required to and also be there to pick her children up from school. She's had to make a choice, and she's chosen her family. Fair enough. But I couldn't help thinking that if I were a manager, I'd do everything in my power to keep her working in the hospital.

The hospital where we work is massively in debt and consistently fails to meet the targets set down by the government. Things clearly aren't improving. In the NHS league tables, it is there in black and white for everyone to see: it is one of the worst performing trusts in the country. Objective assessments of how public services are run are needed, of course.

But nowhere in the league tables was there a provision for evaluating the most important thing in a hospital, the one thing that can really make an impact on the patient's experience of health care: the staff. These tables tell us how the books are being balanced, but there's no assessment of whether someone will hold your hand and stay with you when you're upset or explain your diagnosis in a kind, compassionate way or make you a cup of tea while you wait for a scan. It doesn't take into account the staff staying past their shift because they're worried about a patient. Today is Gillian's last day, and I feel immeasurably sad, not just because the hospital is losing a brilliant nurse, but because none of the managers know it, or indeed, seem to care.

Tuesday 6 April

We are all frantically applying for our next jobs and this dominated all of today. Ruby is applying for surgery and has decided to go for a very competitive, prestigious training rotation in a teaching hospital. Flora telephoned this evening and is thinking about anaesthetics. Lewis is considering becoming a GP and Supriya is following the family tradition and applying for general medicine. I don't know what to do. I've always wanted to work in mental health, but at the moment, I'm more worried about my own than other people's. How can I make a meaningful decision about my future career when I'm not even sure if I want to be a doctor any more?

Wednesday 7 April

Maurice was discharged from hospital today. Supriya and I took him over to the doctors' mess. He was puzzled about why we insisted on it. 'Really, I'll go on my own, there must be so much clearing up to do. You must be out of teabags by now.'

'Stop worrying, Maurice,' said Supriya soothingly. 'We've got a surprise for you.'

In the hallway stood Lewis and a few of the other doctors. They cheered when he walked in and Lewis came forward and gave him some flowers and a card with the money that was left over. Maurice had tears in his eyes.

Then Lewis wheeled in the bicycle and Maurice stood motionless, overcome by the occasion. Lewis had arranged a taxi to take Maurice home and we helped to lift the bicycle into the boot. 'Take it easy, get well soon,' we chorused as the cab drove off with Maurice sobbing quietly in the back and waving.

'Whoever gave that money, they just made

an old man very happy,' said Lewis as we walked back into the mess.

I didn't tell him I knew it was Ruby. She wouldn't like that. She doesn't do things for the glory, she just does them because she wants to. As I walked past A&E on my way back to the ward, I saw her standing having a cigarette with Housewives' Favourite. I didn't stop.

Thursday 15 April

A few weeks ago Dr Pike, seeing how the junior doctors were being driven to distraction by their pagers, suggested that when it goes off, we think of it not as something that is going to delay us from getting our jobs done, but as a little cry for help from someone else in the hospital. I quite liked that as it nicely fitted in with doctors' notions about helping people. It's all very George Clooney, isn't it? The trouble-shooting doctor, here to save the day.

And so there I was, early last week, about to bite into a sandwich at lunchtime, when my pager went off. My heart sank. It was one of the nurses on the ward, asking me to see a patient who has been admitted under the medical team following an overdose. They want my help. I want my sandwich. The nurse lowered his voice. 'Max, she's in a really bad way, I don't know what to do with her.'

I put the sandwich back in its wrapper and make my way over to the ward. I'm met by a greeting party of several ashen-faced nurses. Even The Battleaxe looks worried. I confess for a moment I felt rather proud of myself: here I was, being called upon to save the day. Then I read the notes.

Almost a year ago to the day, Mrs Nelson's two daughters and husband had been killed in a car crash. She had been driving. At some point she had momentarily fallen asleep at the wheel and the car had come off the road. Her husband and youngest daughter had been killed instantly. Her older daughter died shortly afterwards in hospital. Two nights ago, on the anniversary of their death, while at home alone, she had taken an enormous overdose. She had been found by a friend who called the ambulance.

Mrs Nelson was now stable, although not yet ready for discharge. She had been moved to a side room, as if her suffering was contagious. I entered the room. Her head remained turned to the wall. I walked over to the other side of the bed, so I could see her eyes. She still didn't look at me. I introduced myself and began talking, until suddenly she interrupted me. 'I'm not depressed, I'm not ill. I don't want to live any more because all my family are dead,' she said as she stared at the wall.

I didn't know how to reply so I stayed silent.

After a few minutes she began to talk more. She had seen counsellors, she had taken medication, but she still blamed herself. 'It would be my daughter's thirteenth birthday next week,' she said, as tears gently rolled down her face. 'Why was I spared? Why couldn't I have died too? What did I do wrong that I should be punished like this?'

I couldn't answer any of her questions. My job as a doctor is to diagnose and treat. But there isn't a tablet made that cures tragedy. I can refer her to the psychiatry team who'll admit her to one of their wards, prevent her from attempting suicide again for a short time, manage the risk she poses to herself. But perhaps she's right, perhaps the only rational response is to want to die. To simply say this woman is depressed, to attempt to medicalise her is not helpful. How is anyone ever going to make this better? For some people, life is just too painful and sometimes there's no simple answer. Then my pager went off. I made my apologies and left Mrs Nelson alone in her room.

Friday 16 April

Rachel is leaving. First Gillian and now her.

She's retraining as an aromatherapist. 'I've had enough of it, Max. I love my job but I just want something which doesn't grind you down so much,' she says as we stand outside smoking our last cigarette together. She's owed some holiday, so is taking that before she leaves, which means that today is her last day. 'I can earn the same money doing aromatherapy but without the hassle. I'll be my own boss, work when I want, how I want,' she says with a shrug.

The attrition rate in nursing staff is remarkably high. I'm not surprised. They work soul-crushing shifts, get no thanks, and if anything goes wrong management descends on them quicker than you can say 'roll over for your bed bath'. At my interview for medical school I was cheekily asked why I didn't want to be a nurse. The interviewers – all of whom were doctors – knew the answer to this question: because it's an awful job.

Certainly it's rewarding too, but the utter contempt that nursing staff are held in by the management can easily disrupt the fragile equilibrium and make the costs outweigh the benefits. There are bad nurses just as there are bad doctors, but for the good ones, who went into the profession to care for people, the mountain of paperwork and protocols means there is less and less time to spend with the actual patients. It's the same for doctors, but the time commitment with training is greater and the financial rewards larger, so there's more incentive to stay.

I know that Rachel will make a great aromatherapist – she'll listen to her clients, spend time with them and be kind to them. That's what she's so good at. It's just a shame that she has to leave nursing so that she's able to do it.

Monday 19 April

I've been called for an interview for psychiatry. It's in the same teaching hospital as the job Ruby has applied for. I'm not very hopeful and it seems strange to be thinking about our future careers already when I'm only just settling into this job. Ruby has been called in for an interview as well, although on a different day. I really want this job, so am going to keep my fingers crossed. Admittedly, this might make the next rectal examination rather difficult to perform.

Tuesday 20 April

On my way to see the scary Marys I pass Trudy's office and she sees me walk past. She calls out to me, 'Hello stranger, you not got time to speak to me any more?'

I poke my head round the door and smile. I feel a little guilty that I've been neglecting her.

'You heard anything back about your job application?' she says. Apparently Mr Butterworth has received a letter from them asking for a reference. Trudy explains that in reality it will be her that writes it, and Mr Butterworth will sign it. This cheers me up.

'You better be nice about me,' I say, it occurring to me only now that I really should have bought her a Christmas present.

Wednesday 21 April

Being a junior doctor has been a real eye-opener. While I've met fascinating people, heard amazing stories and come into contact with people from all walks of life, one of the things that has surprised me the most is how rude people are. In the 'Good Old Days', I'm told by Dr Pike, everyone was polite. I don't know when the 'Good Old Days' were exactly, but I find this hard to believe and suspect that what he actually means is that way back when, when people were polite to *doctors*. We live in a more tolerant and open society than years ago, which I'm pleased about, but I can understand why Dr Pike looks back on the days when he started working as a doctor with nostalgia.

When he trained, the NHS must have been in its infancy. For the first time ever everyone had free access to health care, regardless of income or social class. That must have been an amazing thing. The public were grateful because within living memory people had died in childbirth because they couldn't afford to call the doctor out; people had had teeth extracted without anaesthetic because they couldn't afford it; people had put up with crippling diseases because the medication needed was too expensive. They remembered a time when seeing a doctor was a luxury available only to the wealthy. They were grateful that, suddenly, health care was free at the point of access. Doctors were seen as the custodians of this brave new world of equality of health care. It must be hard for the older generation of doctors who were trained in this environment of unquestioning respect and gratitude. Particularly when faced with the likes of Mrs Wyatt and her family.

'Mrs Wyatt's family are in a really foul mood. They want their mother to have a side room,' explains the nurse who has come into the doctors' office.

'What can I do? I'm not the bed manager,' I reply wearily.

'They want to speak to a doctor, Max. They're threatening to make a complaint.'

I sigh. I've learned that the people who shout loudest get the most attention, regardless of whether they need it or not. If you're rude, if you kick up a fuss, if you threaten to make an official complaint, everyone runs around you trying to help for fear that they'll lose their jobs or get sued or that it will count against the hospital in the daft league tables, while the patients who don't have anyone making a fuss for them get bumped down on the list of priorities.

'Are you the doctor?' asks Mrs Wyatt's son before I've had time to introduce myself.

'Yes,' I smile.

'Dr what?' he snarls.

'Pemberton,' I reply and continue to smile as best I can. One of the family takes hold of the name badge dangling on my belt and reads it, presumably to check I'm not lying.

With the pleasantries over, they launch into a list of complaints about their mother's care. What this actually amounts to is that she doesn't like the food or the people she shares a ward with. The fact that this is a hospital and not a hotel and that when people are really sick they don't care if they're sharing a ward with Genghis Khan, providing they're getting treatment, appears to have passed them by. I believe that doctors' actions should be open to scrutiny, that people have the right to question us – this isn't the problem. It's the way that they do it that gets me. Even people with perfectly reasonable questions seem to feel it necessary to be aggressive. Perhaps it's because – people have stopped being patients and started being consumers.

Needless to say I spend half an hour with the Wyatt entourage, I explain that there isn't a side room available and even if there was, Mrs Wyatt isn't sick enough to warrant giving her one. They narrow their eyes and prod their fingers at me and threaten to make a complaint and I've wasted thirty minutes with not so much as a thank you.

Bring back the Good Old Days.

Friday 23 April

I am sitting here at the kitchen table, my hands still shaking, still close to tears, knowing that although what happened today was to be expected, I hadn't prepared myself for it. It was, perhaps, almost inevitable. Every doctor is allowed one mistake, one monumental cock-up. Today I made mine. And it's one I shall never forget. Because of me, someone is currently in intensive care. And it's all my fault. Today was the day of My Big Mistake.

I was on call last night, covering the wards. At hand-over Lewis told me about one of his patients, Mrs Lampril, who had just come back from having a stent inserted into her gullet. This is a small plastic tube which keeps the oesophagus unobstructed and stops it closing when something is pressing on it. Apparently she had cancer somewhere and it was pressing in, making it hard for her to swallow and they'd used some sort of special stent; one I'd never heard of. Lewis was in a rush, and I was distracted by my pager going off several times. He explained that the patient had just gone for an X-ray to check it was positioned correctly and when the film arrived on the ward later that night, would I mind checking it. I had no idea what I was looking for, and neither, it transpired, had Lewis. 'My consultant said just to make sure it hasn't slipped down into the stomach at all. Don't worry, it will be obvious if there's anything wrong.'

Fine, I thought, and began to review the other patients that had been handed over to me. At about midnight, I got a page from the ward. I was seeing someone who had been transferred on to the stroke unit. I was trying unsuccessfully to take bloods, as he looked like he had pneumonia.

I took the phone call. The film was back on the ward and would I mind looking at it? 'Looks fine to me,' the nurse said, 'but you're the doctor, so you better have a look.'

I gulped hard – unless it was sticking out of her throat, I wasn't going to know if it was in the right place or not. I went to the ward and Uma, the nurse who had paged me, showed me the film. It looked fine to me. 'What do you think?' I said to Uma.

'Yep, looks good to me too.'

Uma had seen lots of these before, so was eminently better qualified than I was to comment on it. Fine. It's not in her stomach or sticking out of her head, I reckon it's OK. I went back to my patient.

A few hours later I got another page. It was Uma. 'When you've got some time, can you come over and write up some laxatives for Mrs Lampril? She's got stomach-ache and hasn't opened her bowels.'

She's on morphine for the pain from her tumour, and this often makes you constipated. Fine. Uma said she'd give it and I could sign for it later. I busied myself with seeing the other patients. Someone had just had a heart attack and I was connecting the heart monitor when my pager went off again. Uma again: Mrs Lampril was in a lot of pain. She's got cancer, it's to be expected, give her some more morphine and see how it goes. Her obs – the basic observations such as blood pressure, temperature and amount of oxygen in the blood – were due to be done in an hour. Great, let me know if there's any problems, I said, eager to get back to the patient who'd had a heart attack.

An hour later, another page, this time

from another nurse. Uma was on her break. Mrs Lampril's oxygen levels are low, what should they do? Sit her up, give her a bit of oxygen. I go back to seeing another patient. After several more interruptions something in the back of my mind started to niggle.

Uma came off her break and confirmed that she thought something was wrong with Mrs Lampril. I was now back on the stroke unit, a five-minute walk to the ward where Mrs Lampril is. I hesitated.

'She doesn't look right. Her stomach still hurts,' says Uma.

'Has she opened her bowels yet?' I asked, assuming this is constipation. 'Give her an enema and I'll come over now.'

No sooner had I put the phone down when my pager went off again. Someone on another ward has just had a fit, what should they do? I began to panic slightly. Fine, I'll deal with that in a minute, I must see Mrs Lampril first.

I arrived on the ward and Mrs Lampril is sitting up in bed, breathing heavily. The oxygen levels in her blood were now very low. I increased the oxygen. Her stomach was tender. I panicked. Has the stent moved? I looked at the X-ray again. I couldn't see anything obvious.

I called the radiographer and ordered an urgent X-ray to see if the stent had moved. I waited anxiously on the ward while the radiographer came with the portable X-ray machine.

More interruption – the man is having another fit, what should they do? I left Mrs Lampril and went to assess him briefly, then rush back. When I returned she was now very unwell indeed. The radiographer was having difficulty getting her to stay still because she's so distressed. I'm going to call the registrar at home, I decide, but think it best to wait until I get a repeat chest X-ray.

Thirty minutes later and the film had been processed. I felt sick with worry now; Mrs Lampril is on the highest amount of oxygen we can give her on the ward, and still her oxygen levels are dangerously low. I look at the X-ray. The stent is clearly visible and was in exactly the same place. It didn't make sense.

A wave of pure, unadulterated fear swept over me: I didn't know what to do. Without thinking properly I picked up the phone and called the registrar at home. It was 5.45 a.m. He answered in a grumpy, sleepy voice. I explained what's happened. There was silence for a moment. 'There must be something wrong with the stent,' I persevered.

'Have you listened to her chest?' he asks.
No.
'Have you taken a blood gas?'
No.
'Have you examined her calf muscles?'

I haven't done anything, I confess, I just panicked and called him.

'Acute shortness of breath, poor oxygen saturation, immobilised, diagnosis of cancer, recent surgery. What does that history suggest to you, Doctor?'

He spat the last word out as though it were a dirty word.

'Erm,' I say, flustered. 'But the stent' I begin.

'The woman is having a pulmonary embolism,' he said, almost shouting. I began to shake. She's got a blood clot on the lung – one of the most basic medical emergencies but also often fatal. It is one of the first things at medical school that we are taught to recognise. I had done none of the investigations for this, I hadn't started her on any treatment. Instead, I've given her laxatives and an enema. As I stand with the telephone in my hand I can see her across the ward. A nurse shouts to me. Oh God, I think, she's going to die. The registrar was already in his car, having decided that I'm clearly too incompetent to be left to deal with this on my own. In fifteen minutes he was on the ward.

'I just panicked,' I tried to explain to him after he had stabilised Mrs Lampril and transferred her to the Intensive Care Unit. 'I just didn't think.'

'No,' he said slowly, 'you didn't, did you?'

He wasn't cross or nasty. He just looked at me with utter contempt and disgust, as though my incompetence repelled him.

I had no one to blame except myself. I've dealt with dozens of blood clots on the lung over the past nine months. I even got asked about it in my medical school finals. But that's no use to Mrs Lampril if, when faced with it, I get sidetracked by a redherring like her stent. Something going wrong with the stent had been my biggest fear because it was something I knew nothing about. It made me feel vulnerable and exposed because I'd never dealt with that sort of thing before, and I therefore foolishly forgot to step back and assess the situation clinically. It was too easy to ascribe all her symptoms to this mysterious procedure, when in fact, it was the most obvious medical emergency that was happening in my midst.

I left the ward and made my way home. I saw Lewis walking into work, but did not dare to try and explain what an awful night I'd just had. I just wanted to go back home, and get away from the hospital. I was close to tears. I walked out of the main entrance, into the car park and up the road, knowing that as I did, Mrs Lampril's life hung in the balance, because of me.

Saturday 24 April

The start of my holiday and the events of yesterday are still haunting me. I feel sick and embarrassed and furious with myself. I tell Ruby. She's already heard. Apparently everyone knows that I messed up. My Big Mistake, choice extracts of which are available on the hospital grapevine. I roll over in bed and pretend it was all a bad dream.

Sunday 25 April

Ruby was at work today. She's tried to pacify me about Mrs Lampril and even checked up on her – she's out of ITU now and is much better. 'It was an easy mistake to make. You called the registrar when you felt out of your depth and she didn't die. Don't let it prey on your mind.'

But I can't help it. That was too close, too nearly a tragedy, rather than just a humiliating and embarrassing blunder which made me look incompetent. At some point - it's going to happen. Someone will die. It's inevitable; you can't be right all the time. At some point I'll make another mistake but this time someone will die.

I don't know if I can do this job with that knowledge.

Wednesday 28 April

'You're exactly the sort of person we're looking for.'

Suddenly I feel rather excited. I'm exactly the sort of person that other people are looking for. I'm great. Yeah! I compose myself and look round to ensure that no one has recognised me. I shouldn't be here. This man, you see, is trying to make me leave medicine.

A friend of a friend persuaded me to go. 'Just meet them, no pressure,' he assured me. Sure, I thought, what have I got to lose? I didn't really know what a management consultant did, but it was becoming apparent that it involved an emperor and some new clothes. I'd be working in the 'health care' division, giving 'invaluable' advice to the NHS about how to save money.

'What about telling them not to employ management consultants if they want to cut costs?' I say earnestly.

The man opposite me, Simon, laughs. 'Yeah, but then we'd be out of work,' he replies.

Silly me.

He clicks his fingers at a waitress and I wince. I despise the man sitting in front of me, with his slick suit and designer sunglasses (it's April, for God's sake, there isn't any sun and we're sitting in a bar). But I despise myself more. I agreed to this meeting because if I hadn't, I'd have regretted it. I'd have always wondered if I should have left medicine, if there was another pasture somewhere else that was greener, lusher, less stressful. After the fiasco with Mrs Lampril, my desire to leave had never been stronger. But now I'm sat here, faced with the very real prospect of having a job outside of medicine, of not being a doctor any more, I'm not so sure. I'm having doubts about my doubts.

Simon is due at another meeting. He clicks his fingers at the waitress again and she brings the bill. He pays, of course.

'On account,' he tells me and snorts. 'Come and work with us and you'll get one of these too,' he says, waving the credit card in front of me.

He's rude and brash but what he's offering is tempting.

'I'll think about it,' I say as I get up to leave.

He picks up my CV – the CV I've just redone for my application to psychiatry, and puts it in his briefcase.

But I trained as a doctor so that I could work in the NHS, not for a company trying to fleece it. I've got nothing against management consultants *per se* – if companies want to employ them, that's fine. It's their profits they're spending and their share-holders they have to justify it to. But the NHS is a public organisation, so it's the tax payers who have to foot the bill. As far as I can recall, nobody has asked me if I mind having my taxes spent on management consultants rather than, say, nurses.

I did my research before coming to this meeting, and it is estimated that the government; along with individual trusts and health-service bodies has spent £200 million on management consultants. That seems like a lot of cash for not very much in return.

I just don't know. He's offering me lots of money and a company car. And no one was ever killed by a management consultant. Although I wonder if I had to work with this man, if I might not end up killing him.

MAY

Saturday 1 May

I spend the weekend thinking about what Simon was offering me. A new career; an opportunity to escape. Flora telephoned – she's been offered an interview for a job in anaesthetics and was brimming with excitement. It was infectious. I told her about my interview on Monday for psychiatry. I'm at a crossroads. On one path lies a career in psychiatry, on the other, as an office worker. Both paths have their merits, their problems. And it's coming to the point where I have to decide which I'm going to take.

Monday 3 May

This morning I was off work so I could attend my interview. Three psychiatrists smiled at me. I crossed my legs, then wondered if this was sending out some sort of subconscious signal, and uncrossed them again. They asked me questions about my CV, about why I wanted to train in psychiatry, about my future career aims. I don't mention

Simon – that would definitely have sent out the wrong signals. Everything was going well; they seemed interested in everything I said, and I was doing my best not to make them think I was in love with my mother and planning on murdering my father.

And then one of them asked, 'Can you think of a time when you made a mistake at work? Can you tell us what happened and how you dealt with it?'

Oh my God, they really can read your mind. I hesitated. I wanted to tell them a story that wasn't so acute, one that ends nicely, not with me sitting in a bar thinking about leaving medicine altogether. I hesitated again. He leaned forward expectantly. They knew I was hiding something. It occurred to me I might tell them the story about trying to catheterise Mrs Doughty's clitoris.

No, this is a job interview, don't mention the word clitoris. Especially not to a group of psychiatrists.

With a sigh, I told them about Mrs Lampril. They listened intently. When I finished, the man who asked the question sat back in his chair. They looked at each other. Oh God, I thought, I've screwed this up.

'And how did that make you feel?' he asked.

I told him that it made me feel scared and incompetent and a failure. I told him that it felt like the last nail in the coffin of my

311

career, that it made me want to leave even more, that this year hadn't been what I expected. I crossed my arms.

'That's very honest,' said the woman sitting next to him. She smiled warmly at me. And then she began to tell me about a mistake she had made. About giving the wrong dose of a drug and it meaning that someone nearly died and the crisis that it provoked in her. This isn't a job interview, I suddenly thought, it's more like an AA meeting.

'But then I realised that everyone makes mistakes, and the important thing is to realise that and be honest when you do,' she said in her soporific voice.

The other two nodded kindly. God, I've really screwed this up – they're giving me counselling now. But perhaps she's right. I uncrossed my arms.

Tuesday 4 May

'I think I'm going to leave,' I say to Maxine. She's not listening. 'Did you see that ankle?' she shouts out to Dr Palache. 'It's under the breast in the clinic room. Sorry Max, what did you say?'

I look at her. I desperately want to talk to someone about leaving. But now's not the time, or the place. Perhaps I should talk to the Marys. No, they never take anything

312

seriously. What about Trudy? I'm about to leave when Dr Palache walks out of his office. He's going for a cigarette and I join him round the back of A&E.

'How's the job hunt going then?' he begins. I'm sure he knows.

'I was sort of thinking,' I venture, 'that I might leave.'

'But you've only just lit your cigarette,' he replies.

'No, I mean medicine,' I explain.

He doesn't seem shocked or surprised. He just nods. 'Yeah, everyone feels like that at some point. I feel like that on a daily basis,' he laughs. 'But then I think, what other job would I do? It's interesting, you get to meet different people, and it's corny but you make a difference.'

I nod.

'I bet you can't even remember half the patients you saw last week,' he continues. 'But if I asked them, every single one of them would remember you. You were important to them. Now, to my way of thinking, that's a job worth doing.' He takes a drag of his cigarette and blows out the smoke in a fine stream like a shadowy trumpet. I tell him about Mrs Lampril.

He nods his head. 'A few years ago, when I was doing my surgery training, I killed someone,' he says.

I choke. 'What?' I say, staring at him.

He is not looking at me, but instead staring ahead.

'What happened?' I ask.

'There's not much to tell, really. I was doing an operation. I cut through a blood vessel. She bled to death on the table. There was nothing I could do. She was dead before we could even find the phone number for the vascular surgeons.'

He still doesn't look at me. 'I still remember her name: Mrs Barry,' he says quietly. 'Took me years to get over that, you know.'

'You've just lost sight of why you started all this, that's all. Just remember, when you were at medical school; all those hours studying, and how dreary it was, doing endless exams and essays. But when you graduate, you look back, and it wasn't so bad. You're pleased you stuck with it. It's the same now. You'll look back and you'll be pleased you stuck with it. Don't lose sight of that.'

He stubs out his cigarette and flicks it in front of him. It spins in the air momentarily before landing effortlessly in the bin.

'Thanks,' I say and we walk back into the hospital.

Wednesday 5 May

I first met Mr Telford a week ago when he was transferred to the stroke unit. I don't know if he can feel any pain but I stare into his eyes, looking for a flicker of emotion as he lies on the bed. I tentatively listen to his chest with my stethoscope. I can't help but think I'm doing something wrong, but, uneasily, prescribe another course of antibiotics.

A nurse comes in and begins washing him. I help the nurse tug him over on to his side while she washes his back. He is breathing heavily and each breath gurgles and bubbles with the fluid that has accumulated in his lungs. He is developing pneumonia.

I look down at his arms, almost disbelieving that only a few weeks ago he was on the local golf course, playing a round. Now his arms hang like dead weights from his body. Mr Telford never finished his game of golf. Instead, halfway round the course, he had a massive stroke, which killed off most of his brain. He was fifty-four. Cruelly, the part of his brain which controls the functions vital for life – his breathing and heart – remain intact. He is, in lay terms, 'brain dead'.

I have been covering the stroke unit for several months now but still I'm hit by the pathos of cases like this. The far end of the ward is reserved for the serious cases; those that the doctors know will never leave hospital again. Elsewhere in the hospital it is referred to as 'the vegetable patch' and a general feeling of horror surrounds it. Certainly, it is harrowing. But the medical and nursing staff do their best to liven the place up. Every patient is treated with respect, despite the fact that many are unable to communicate and require everything done for them.

It seems strange to me though to realise that while working in such a compassionate environment, I am party to something that could be considered controversial. In fact, it's something that occurs on countless hospital wards up and down the country but is not widely discussed either within the medical profession or in the public domain. Today, Mr Telford died. But if I'm honest, we killed Mr Telford, or rather we let him die. He died because we didn't treat his chest infection, something which was within our powers to cure. Undoubtedly he would have contracted another one, and then another one, and over a protracted course of infections he would have become increasingly weak until he eventually died anyway. After much discussion, it was decided that it was not in his best interests to continue treatment so the antibiotics I had prescribed were stopped.

At the time, while Dr Pike sat ashen-faced discussing options with Mr Telford's family, it seemed the most logical and humane choice. I still think it was the right choice. He had only survived this long because of medicine, and it seemed wholly appropriate that at some point medicine should re-evaluate its role in his care.

These decisions are common in hospitals. There is an argument that doctors should recognise that they regularly aid the death of their patients and it has even been suggested that in such cases we should speed up the process by involuntary euthanasia. Certainly, having watched several people die slowly after having their feeding tubes removed or treatment stopped, I'm sympathetic to this view. At the moment doctors operate in a strange moral and ethical wilderness with the ability to end life but without the legal backing to do it properly. Instead we withdraw treatment and subject the patient to a long and drawn-out death. It seems counterintuitive but sometimes, by treating people's illnesses we can, perversely, inflict more suffering. The best thing I did for Mr Telford was when, without a flicker of emotion, I crossed off the antibiotics I'd prescribed for him.

Friday 7 May

I receive a letter. It's from the hospital where I had my interview. I hold it in my hands for a moment. I suddenly feel nervous. I really want this job, despite everything. Or perhaps I just want the *offer* of the job, and I'll take the management consultant job anyway. I still don't know what to do. I do know though, that if I open the letter and they aren't offering me the job, then the decision will be made for me. I'll call Simon and accept his offer. This is it: a dangerous corner. I open the letter.

'We are pleased to be able to offer you...'

I don't read any more. I suddenly feel a wave of relief. Surely that must mean something? If I'd felt disappointed, then it would have meant that I really didn't want to stay. That I wanted to leave. But I didn't. I sit down at the kitchen table and think hard: shall I stay or shall I go? Then I see the time. I'm late already. I grab my bag and fly out of the door, the letter sitting in my pocket like a talisman.

Saturday 8 May

I was having such a good night until this point. And now she has to come along and spoil it all. I watch her talking to my friends at the other end of the table and get up under the pretext of going to the bar. I'm quite sure she doesn't recognise me, but I don't want to risk it. From a safe distance I turn around and watch her: she hasn't changed. She puts her head coquettishly on one side and smiles warmly. She's good at it,

I'll give her that. Of course, they give in. I knew they would. Having got what she wants, she heads back out into the night. I return to the table.

'Where did you go?' asks one of my friends as he puts his wallet back in his pocket.

'How much did you give her?' I ask, smiling.

'Who? That girl? I gave her five pounds. Why? You know her?' he replies.

I smile. 'Yes, I know her. She used to be one of my patients,' I say, rather ashamed of myself that I hadn't had the courage to remain in my seat while she was here.

'You didn't do a very good job of fixing her, did you?' interrupts another friend. 'She looked a right state.'

He's right, but there are some people that it's impossible to fix entirely because the problems run too deep. My friends, none of whom are doctors, don't like this.

'But there must be something you could do?' one of them asks.

They all nod; she needs help, they decide. But the idea of help is rather nebulous, especially when thinking about Gina.

Gina came in when I was working in surgery because she had abscesses in her groin where she injected drugs. We patched her up, sent her on her way.

'She's had an awful life, she told us about it,' one of my friends tells me. 'You know her father killed her mother, and the family home was repossessed to pay for his legal fees, and now she's homeless?'

'It's not true,' I reply, sorry to be shattering their illusion.

The strange thing is – that Gina's life is more horrific than any story you could make up and yet she never tells people the truth when trying to get their sympathy and money. Perhaps the truth is too painful for her. Perhaps she doesn't want to capitalise on something which has taken so much away from her. The reality is that her parents are both alive, but they, and several other members of her family, sexually abused Gina from the age of three, along with her brother. At the age of thirteen she became pregnant by her father. When her grandfather, who also sexually abused her, found out, he beat her so hard that she had a miscarriage. He also broke her jaw and she lost the sight in one of her eyes. The following year she ran away from home, and has lived on the streets ever since. She's now in her thirties. As well as begging, she works as a prostitute to help fund her addiction to crack. The sort of men who sleep with her are often violent and seriously assault her in order to get their kicks. She's been in countless hostels, but is usually evicted after a few months because of her chaotic behaviour. She's tried to kill herself dozens of times and is a frequent attender at A&E. Oh, and she's schizophrenic and HIV positive.

There's silence around the table. Everyone stares at me. Nothing like putting a dampener on the evening. 'That's horrible,' someone says. And it is.

But the really horrible thing is that after we'd changed the subject, after the mood had lightened and we'd begun to laugh and joke and enjoy the evening again, I could see Gina standing on the other side of the road, while a man, presumably her pimp, shouted at her, and eventually she got into a car, pre-sumably a punter's; the abuse she's suffered all her life being played out once more. I think of how man hands on misery to man; about how the abuse that was started as a child is perpetuated again and again for Gina, and how this has become the only form of human contact she can understand.

'You alright, Max? You're pretty quiet,' asks one of my friends. 'Stressed about work?'

'Sort of,' I reply as the car over the road drives away with Gina in it. 'Shall I get another round of drinks?' I say, as I get up to go to the bar.

Monday 10 May

'His wife is pregnant and he's not leaving

321

her,' I say and close my eyes. I've been ago-
nising over this for too long, and she has to
know. I wait for Ruby to launch her attack.

Nothing. I open them again. Ruby is standing by the sink, staring into space. 'How do
you know?' she says, not nearly as dis-
believingly as I'd have thought.

'Lewis told me. Dr Palache told him.
Sorry.'

Ruby sits down at the kitchen table. 'I
suspected something was up,' she says. 'He's
been really funny lately.'

'Sorry,' I say again, not being very adept at
this sort of thing.

These days I find it easier telling someone
they've got cancer than that the person they
love is a liar and a cheat. 'You are sure, that's
definitely what Dr Palache said?' she asks
quietly.

'Yeah I'm sure. There's no reason why he'd
make it up, is there?'

I don't think it best to inform her that it's
common knowledge in the hospital that
Housewives' Favourite makes a habit of
seducing his junior doctors.

Ruby is quiet again for a few moments,
deep in thought.

'What you going to do then?' I ask, wondering if it would involve Housewives'
Favourite attending A&E himself. 'I don't
know,' she says wistfully. 'Know any eligible
single young men?'

Wednesday 12 May

'I've got something to show you,' says The Battleaxe. If any other nurse had said this, I might have got excited. Instead, I'm expecting some form to be thrust under my nose. I follow her to the bed of Mr Kirozac. He's just been admitted from the nursing home where he lives. He's got a chest infection. He had a stroke a few years ago so can't look after himself, and is reliant on someone to help with his toileting, feeding and just about everything else. She draws the curtains round the bed. Then she pulls back the covers.

The smell knocks me in the face and I reel, taking a step back. Rotting flesh is one of those unique smells that defies definition. It is like nothing else on earth. Acrid, pungent and foul, I compose myself and examine the wound on Mr Kirozac's back from which the stench is emanating. It's a bedsore. This is where the skin has broken down because of the unrelieved pressure on one part of the body. Mr Kirozac's is so deep that the underlying bone is exposed. I have never seen anything like this. It's as though someone has gouged a piece of his flesh straight out. I look away.

'I'm going to have to report the care home. This is pure negligence,' says The

Battleaxe, sternly.

A wound this size and of this depth would have taken months to develop. It is an indication that not only is he not being turned regularly but also that the staff aren't bothered enough to try and cure it once they've failed to prevent it. I am overcome with rage that something like this could happen. That people who have others' welfare in their hands could be so cavalier and uncaring. This is abuse. 'Of course, nothing will happen, but it's the principle of the thing,' The Battleaxe says as we walk back to the nursing station.

Any fantasies I had of the nursing home being closed down, of the owners being sued and the doctors and nurses struck off quickly evaporate. 'Nobody cares about the likes of him,' she adds, meaning Mr Kirozac.

And of course she's right. It would be easy to blame the nursing staff at his care home, but I can imagine how it is. The owners, ever aware of profit margins, want to keep costs down, they employ care workers that aren't trained properly, the nurse is busy dispensing medication. It's all too easy for care to be overlooked in a care home.

Friday 14 May

The first we knew about it was the crash

team running past us in the corridor. I ignored it, as I didn't think it concerned me. An hour later, while I was on the ward, I happened to see Ruby and the crash team walk back along the corridor, silently and slowly, as though in shock. Ruby saw me and came up to me, putting her hand gently on my arm. 'Oh God, Max, I've just seen the worst thing,' she looked close to tears. Ruby is usually good at being detached; clinical. She doesn't allow things to get to her.

'What? What's happened?' I asked.

Dr Pike was charging ahead on the ward round, so before she could answer I had to race off. 'Find me at lunchtime,' Ruby called after me as I stumbled after Dr Pike and Barney.

It preyed on my mind for the rest of the morning and at lunchtime I paged Ruby and we met in the doctors' mess. I arrived to find Supriya in floods of tears, surrounded by Lewis, Ruby and a few of the crash team from that morning.

'Come on now, don't cry. It wasn't your fault,' someone was saying.

I mouthed to Ruby to ask what was happening and she stood up and I followed her to the kitchen.

'Supriya's patient died this morning. We had a crash call but we couldn't do anything to save him,' she told me, quietly.

'Oh right,' I said, still a little confused.

It is the nature of hospitals that people die while on the ward. Why was Supriya getting in such a fuss about this?

'Max, I have never seen anything like it before.' Ruby swallowed hard. 'It was horrible. That poor man. And Supriya's blaming herself.'

Supriya's patient, Ruby explained, had been admitted the previous night with a swollen stomach and was confused. The medics had said he was a surgical patient, but the surgeons had said he was medical. After some debate he had been admitted under the medics, Supriya's team, but the surgeons had asked for a CT scan of his abdomen. He had a urinary tract infection and it seemed that he also had a large hernia, with loops of bowel going into his scrotum, making it swell. He also had a large tumour growing in his liver, which they thought might have spread from his bowel. He was one of those complicated patients that make your heart sink as there is so much going on it's difficult to know where to start, or even if it is worth starting at all.

In the morning Supriya had noticed he was unwell. Her registrar had asked her to arrange the scan and to contact the surgeons asking for them to come and review the patient. Somewhere in the hectic scrum of the ward round, she had misplaced her to-do list and when it came to mid-morning, she had forgotten all about the man. When the nurses bleeped her saying that he hadn't opened his bowels, she recalled being asked to arrange something for him, but couldn't remember what. She was busy with another patient and thought it could wait. By the time the nursing staff realised how ill he was; that his bowel was obstructed and he was becoming weaker and more confused, it was too late. He deteriorated rapidly, before Supriya could phone the surgeons and her registrar. He began to vomit uncontrollably. Eventually he began to vomit faeces because of the pressure in his bowel. He inhaled them, began choking and died.

I could hear Supriya crying in the room next door. The shocking nature of his death must have made it all the worse for her. I remembered how I felt with Mrs Lampril. The crippling sensation of inadequacy and failure. Of course the man would surely have died anyway, with or without the scan. It's unlikely the results would even have been back in time to know what was going on. But I knew from Mrs Lampril that this doesn't matter. Knowing and feeling are two separate things. And I knew exactly how Supriya felt.

Monday 17 May

I saw Supriya today in the doctors' mess. I

avoided her eyes for a few minutes, not sure what to say to her. She still looked close to tears. Eventually, the silence becoming unbearable, I broached the subject. 'Look, Supriya, about that man who died on Friday,' I began.

She looked up. 'I just don't want to talk about it, Max, I'm sorry.'

But something about the way she kept looking at me, the quiver of her bottom lip, made me know that she did. Then she blurted out, 'I just feel like it was all my fault. That I failed him. That someone is dead because I was busy and stressed and stupid.'

She had signed the death certificate and had just come back that morning from viewing the body before it was sent to the undertakers, something that all doctors who sign a cremation form are required to do. 'They hadn't even cleaned up the body, Max. It was horrific. I just broke down the minute I saw him and the morgue attendant had to sit me down.'

I listened to her talk about how she felt she had failed her patient, how she hadn't realised how fragile she was and how easily something like this could topple you. How she'd spent the weekend backtracking on all her career plans and had thought about leaving medicine altogether again.

I told her about my big mistake, how I'd

felt exactly the same. That it wasn't negligence, it was just a mistake and that it
didn't take away from the tragedy of the
situation, but it didn't mean we should take
the weight of it all on our shoulders. I told
her about Dr Palache and what he had told
me. This was the first time I'd assimilated
these things into any tangible order and said
them out loud.

As I walked back to the ward, I thought
about what I'd said to Supriya and that
really it was me I'd been talking to as well. I
thought how letting the one incident, one
mistake, alter your trajectory would be, in
itself, a bigger mistake. How Supriya and I
could do more good by staying as doctors
and learning from our mistakes than by
admitting defeat and leaving. And I thought
of Mr Kirozac, and how he needed people
to help him, and that as a management
consultant, I'd never be able to do that for
him. And by the time I got back to the ward,
I'd decided that I was going to stay in
medicine. And it felt like a weight had been
lifted off me.

Tuesday 18 May

Last week I discovered a secret service that
until then, I had had no idea even existed.
There are sometimes situations you are faced

329

with that are beyond the capabilities of medicine to fix. No scans, or blood tests, or drugs at our disposal are going to help the situation. These are the cases that prey on the mind; the ones where you are powerless to help. But the service I stumbled across is the solution to the most desperate situations that can present themselves, a panacea. in the face of hopelessness. What is this miraculous cure-all? 'Dial-A-Priest'. For the beleaguered junior doctor, literally, a godsend. I used to think that it was only doctors and people who hadn't got to grips with mobile phones that had pagers. But apparently, up and down the country, day and night, with their pagers sitting next to a glass of sherry and a copy of the *Radio Times*, there are priests on call. You can even pick the denomination you want. It's like ordering a pizza. The hospital switchboard has the pager numbers, you ask to be put through, and within half an hour, bingo, your prayers are answered and a priest arrives.

Mr Bernard is one of those hopeless cases. He was found by the milkman who looked through the letterbox and saw him collapsed on the floor. He'd been lying there for three days. He was brought into hospital where it was discovered he'd had a brain haemorrhage. There was nothing that could be done, the blood vessel that had burst was still bleeding into his brain and it was only a matter of time before he died. But the really sad thing, the thing that makes this tragic, is that Mr Bernard is totally alone. There is not a single soul in the world that loves him. No one is standing by his bedside crying. There's just me and the nurses.

From his previous notes I learn that his wife died five years ago. They'd been married for sixty-six years. His next of kin is written down as his next-door neighbour, and when I call them, they don't even know his surname. 'I just came out to see what the fuss was about and the ambulance driver wrote my name down. I don't really know him that well. I'd stop and chat sometimes if we met shopping, but that was about it,' explains the neighbour.

'Does he have any family? Anyone?' I ask, disbelieving that anyone could be so totally alone.

'I don't know, I don't think so. Look, sorry, it's late; I've got to get to bed,' comes the reply.

Surely there must be someone who cares. What sort of society is this that we don't even know or care about our neighbours? It's then that I notice in his notes, above the 'next of kin' box, is a section for religious beliefs, and someone has written 'Catholic'. I've never even noticed this box before, let alone thought of acting on it. It's past midnight, Mr Bernard is deteriorating and I can't bear the idea that he'll die alone. At times like this I need people with friends in high places, so I call the switchboard and tentatively ask if they have a number for a priest.

'Oh yes, there's the on-call priest, I'll page him for you.' A few minutes later I'm talking to Father Stephen. 'I was just wondering if you could help, give him the last rites or something. Be with him,' I ask, after I've explained what's happened.

'No problem, I'm on my way,' he chirps.

Before I can say three Hail Marys, he's on the ward, holy water in one hand and a packet of Silk Cut in the other. He's a short, avuncular man with silver hair and round spectacles. He gives me a wink. 'You've done all you can, I'll take care of it now. I'll pray for him. Go and get some rest.'

Father Stephen stays by the bedside until, three hours later, Mr Bernard dies.

Father Stephen and I stand outside and smoke a cigarette as the sun rises. He's been on call since 5 a.m. yesterday. That makes me look like a part-timer. I'm amazed that anyone faced with the frailty of the human condition, day-in, day-out, can believe in God. Tennyson wrote: 'More things are wrought by prayer than this world dreams of.' And as I wave goodbye to Father Stephen and make my way back into the hospital, I hope that's true.

Wednesday 19 May

Lewis and Dr Palache join Ruby and me for a cigarette. They are nauseatingly content together despite the ongoing argument about what colour to paint their lounge. Lewis produces a swatch. Ruby rolls her eyes. For her, mocha is something to add a double espresso to, not a colour of soft furnishing.

We both avoid being drawn into their domestic bliss, although this doesn't stop Lewis concluding that we both agree with him that Butternut Cream is the only colour suitable, given that their lounge is north facing. Ruby attempts to book a head CT scan with Dr Palache, but he's clearly more concerned that Lewis is going to win in the decorating wars. Then with her usual eeriness, the miserable smoking woman materialises from around the corner and glares at us, before heading back into the A&E department. Ruby and I shudder while the other two are too engrossed in discussing floor coverings to notice her.

Thursday 20 May

I see Supriya in the doctors' office on the ward today, checking bloods. 'You all right now?' I ask as I search for some notes. Another snatched conversation conducted against the backdrop of pandemonium on the wards.

'Oh, yeah, I'm OK now. Thanks for the talk. It made me feel so much better. It's just so easy to have your confidence knocked, isn't it?'

I nod. She frantically writes down in some notes while speaking to one of the nurses outside. She's at her best when she's multi-tasking. I imagine her at home, making her bed, cooking breakfast and tackling world poverty all at once. And still finding time for a manicure.

Only a week ago Supriya was having a crisis, but now she's had to move on. This is what it's like being a doctor; constantly having to think ahead, juggle and plan the jobs that have to be done while moving effortlessly between patients, not carrying any of the drama of the previous one with you to the next. It's like this day-in and day-out. In medicine, a week is a long time.

Friday 21 May

There is a loud crash and the assembled doctors and nurses wince. Barney suppresses a giggle while someone else helpfully hands Dr Pike a tissue. He has porridge all over his trouser leg now. He carefully dabs at it, then freezes. He looks up at the patient who is lying in her bed and stares at her for a few moments. Then he picks up the toast from where it landed on the floor when he knocked over the breakfast tray. A nurse leans forward. 'We've got biscuits if you're hungry,' she offers, tactfully.

'This toast is hard,' he says and then adds, 'the porridge has gone cold.'

Clearly he's gone mad.

'It's obvious what's wrong with Mrs Hudson, isn't it?' asks Dr Pike, surveying the bemused nurses and junior doctors standing around the bed.

Mrs Hudson was admitted after having a fall. She doesn't seem to be making much progress. Of course, I realise later, I had missed a number of vital clues as to why Mrs Hudson was so frail, because while I was looking, I wasn't seeing.

Much of being a doctor is detective work. Reaching a diagnosis is not dissimilar to the deductive process employed by any good sleuth. Possible suspects are drawn up and eliminated through lines of enquiry until one culprit remains and the diagnosis is reached. It's no coincidence that one of the greatest fictional detectives was created by a doctor. Sir Arthur Conan Doyle based the character of Sherlock Holmes on a professor named Joseph Bell who he had worked for while a junior doctor. Bell used to amaze Conan Doyle by his careful analysis of apparently unrelated observations to help elucidate his patients' conditions. You can clearly see the way that this was used in the creation of Holmes. In fact, the techniques of observation and deduction form part of the training at medical school and are employed by all doctors. A thorough examination of a patient, for example, always starts with the hands to look for tell-tale signs that will help with a diagnosis. Red palms suggest liver disease; upward-turning nails indicate possible iron-deficiency anaemia, and so on. Mrs Hudson had cataracts, she had arthritis. But what was the significance of the open box on the side table which contained dentures? What had cold porridge and hard toast to do with this? Alimentary, my dear Watson (sorry, I couldn't help myself).

'Of course she's not getting better, she's not eating enough.' Hence the cold porridge and hard toast, and this in turn, Dr Pike concludes, was because she didn't have her dentures available, her eyesight was poor and the food was put out of reach. Her arthritis meant that she couldn't cut up her food properly and the food which was left in her room each mealtime was merely removed uneaten without question.

Mrs Hudson's case is by no means unique. The nurses openly admit that they don't have enough time to help patients eat. This neglect isn't out of malice, it's because nurses' time is increasingly taken up with reams of paperwork rather than the job of actual nursing. But it's not as if older people are the only ones in hospitals who have difficulty feeding themselves, and yet you don't see rows of under-fed babies when you visit a paediatric ward because they've been left with a bottle and told to get on with it. I can't help but suspect that the rate of malnourishment in older people in hospital is symptomatic of the way that we as a society ignore the elderly: another case of looking without seeing.

Sunday 23 May

Ruby and I have been avoiding mentioning Housewives' Favourite. Now we're both working in medicine we rarely see him in a professional capacity and the two of them are avoiding being seen together at work, which I'm sure is so he can continue to make his way through the rest of the female medical profession unhindered. But I'm convinced they're still meeting in some capacity or other. Her bed wasn't slept in last night again, so I can only presume that she was with him. I wonder how he managed to wheedle his way out of the fact his wife's apparently pregnant? She must really be in love with him. It's the only explanation as to why she would put up with being treated like this. And I know Ruby and I know that however hard-nosed she appears, she'd never do anything to hurt someone else, least of all a pregnant married woman.

Thursday 27 May

Teaching by humiliation used to be the mainstay of medical education. The assembled gaggle of medical students would stand by the bedside of some patient deemed 'interesting', while a grumpy consultant would pick on one poor, shaking student. They would stand there red-faced, staring at their shoes, while the consultant exposed their ignorance of a certain topic before setting about mercilessly humiliating them while the rest of the students practised making themselves look as small and inconspicuous as possible. It would soon degenerate into a general character assassination and invariably resulted in someone crying. It was thought to be character building and good preparation for life as a doctor. It was the sort of thing that put hairs on your chest, which worried a lot of the female medical students. A few noble consultants adopted a touchy-feely approach to their bedside teaching but

338

being shouted at and humiliated by an orthopaedic surgeon is only marginally worse than having a group hug with one.

Of course, since becoming a doctor I've realised that on the job, no one is interested in whether or not you know the distribution of some nerve, or the obscure presentations of an eponymous syndrome. All any of your seniors are interested in is that the results of the test they told you to book are in the notes. But this can be harder than it sounds, and can still result in plenty of going red and staring at your shoes.

Today though I can forget about this as I am on a week's holiday. Now is the time to relax, to forget about medicine and ward rounds and emergencies. It is time to sleep. I emerged from my bedroom after three days, during which I'd barely left my bed, bleary-eyed but determined to make something of the few remaining days of freedom, and decided to catch a train to visit my sister. No doubt she'll have developed some medical condition which needs my expert input.

Barely conscious as the train pulled into the station and the people began to file into the carriages, I became aware of a commotion further down the platform. 'Quick, someone, help,' a woman shouted. 'Get the guard.'

'Is he hurt?' I could hear people saying.

Then somebody said it: 'He needs a doctor.'

Ooh no, that's me. There was a crowd of people standing motionless around one of the doors. I had images of some awful scene, with me rushing to save the day, George Clooney style. Of people throwing their arms around me in thanks. Of being lauded a hero and interviewed on breakfast television. My mum would be so proud. Unfortunately after I'd had these thoughts, people were still shouting. Perhaps I should actually go and see what's the matter? But realistically what would I be able to do? It's unlikely that anyone is going to want a scan booked, which is all I'm good for. At this point the doors closed and the train's engines got louder as it prepared to pull out. There was a collective scream so loud that the driver heard and halted the train. 'Get a doctor,' someone screamed.

'I'm on holiday,' I felt like screaming back, but gave in and ran over to the scene instead.

The crowd parted. 'Are you a doctor?' someone asked.

'Yes, sort of,' I muttered. I looked around. There was nothing there.

'He's under the train,' someone says.

'Keep the mother away,' I heard someone add.

'That woman's son was getting on the

train and missed the step and has fallen down the gap, under the train.'

There was silence. Everyone had moved away from the edge of the platform and was looking at me expectantly. There was only one thing for it; I took a deep breath and peered between the platform and the train.

'I've dropped my bag of Maltesers,' came the voice of the little boy staring up at me.

'Are you hurt?' I asked.

'I've dropped my bag of Maltesers,' he repeated.

I knelt down and picked him up from where he'd fallen next to the track and put him on the platform. Quite why it required someone with a medical degree to lift him on to the platform I'm not sure. His crying mother ran forward and scooped him up. Apart from having had a bit of a surprise, he was fine. Excitement over, I got on the train and tried to make myself small and inconspicuous in my seat. Everyone was looking at me. And I went red and stared at my shoes for the rest of the journey.

Saturday 29 May

Ruby and I went out for a drink. It was the first time we had had the opportunity to celebrate our new jobs. Flora was down for the weekend and joined us after visiting her parents. 'You seem so much happier now, Max, what's happened? Don't tell me you're enjoying your job?' asked Flora.

'He's just had a week's holiday,' said Ruby drily. 'Of course he's happy.'

I smiled. 'No, it's not just that. I suppose a lot of things have happened recently and they've made me really think about what I want to do with my life. I'd lost my way a bit but then I came to the conclusion that although we love to complain, it's actually a pretty good job.'

Ruby and Flora burst into laughter. 'Don't go all smug and fulfilled on us, Max. I'd have to kill you if you did that,' said Flora, throwing a slice of lemon from her drink at me and we both laughed.

We turned to Ruby who had suddenly become very quiet. She wasn't looking at us but instead was transfixed by something out of the window. 'What's wrong, Ruby?' asked Flora, still smiling.

I followed her eyeline to the road opposite the window and took a sharp intake of breath. 'Oh, Ruby...' I said but stopped, not knowing what to say.

'What? What is it?' asked Flora as her smile quickly slipped from her face. She turned and looked at the simple scene being played out over the road.

There stood a woman, perhaps in her late thirties, in a floral print dress and cardigan, her long hair held back from her face loosely. She tossed her head back and laughed, while the man ran his hands over her stomach and kissed the back of her neck. They stopped briefly and embraced, and for that moment we could see his face clearly over the woman's shoulder. The man jokingly slapped her on the backside. Then Housewives' Favourite helped his heavily pregnant wife into the car, drove off and Ruby began to cry.

Sunday 30 May

Ruby has not come out of her room all day. Flora and I sit downstairs at the kitchen table, wondering what we should do. 'You're the psychiatrist, you talk to her,' says Flora.

I raise an eyebrow. 'Flora, I've been offered a job in psychiatry, I'm not Sigmund Freud yet.'

We both decide to see her. Flora brings a cup of tea. We knock on the door. I can hear Ruby sobbing quietly to herself. I push the door open. She doesn't look up. 'Leave me alone, please,' she says into the pillow where her face is buried.

We sit on the bed. Ruby ignores us. Flora leans forward and gently strokes the back of her head. 'Come on Rubes, you can't let him get to you like this.'

I want to say that I told her so, to say that all this was her own fault and she should have listened to everyone who told her not to get involved with him, but what good would that do now?

'He lied to me,' says Ruby, eventually. 'He said she wasn't pregnant, that I shouldn't listen to gossip. That I was the only one he loved.'

She sits up, her face red and puffy. Flora gives her a tissue which she takes and begins to pick apart. 'I can't believe he lied to me about that. He's made me feel such a fool. I was just another notch on his bedpost, and everyone but me could see it,' she says.

Flora and I give her a hug. 'Come on,' says Flora, 'have a cup of tea.'

And we sit together and talk, while I think how, even though we witness horrific things on a daily basis, and should be grateful for our lot, our own little tragedies still hurt.

JUNE

Tuesday 1 June

Ruby appears much better now, though she was noticeably quieter yesterday. She barely spoke on the way to work, and even the nurses asked me if something was wrong with her. She left work early, getting Supriya to hold her pager, claiming to be going on some important errand. When I returned from work I found her sitting at the kitchen table. She'd had her hair cut. And in the process, the last wisps of her ill-fated attempt at dyeing her hair blonde all those months ago, which had been gradually growing out ever since, had been trimmed off, leaving with her usual reddish-brown colour. She looked so much better. Back to her old self.

This morning, I woke up to the sound of the radio playing downstairs, and when I went into the kitchen, there was Ruby busy preparing breakfast. Scrambled eggs, yoghurt, grapefruit. Usually, breakfast for Ruby consists of coffee and cigarettes. I don't think she's eaten fruit since the nineties. 'Where did all this come from?' I asked.

'I got up this morning and bought it from the corner shop,' she said breezily. 'I've made you some too.'

I sat down, gingerly, wondering if indeed I had woken up at all, or if in fact I was still dreaming. I was sure this wouldn't last, so I'd better make the most of it now. I had an extra helping of eggs.

Wednesday 2 June

The shouting from outside is definitely getting louder. I peer out of the window in the nurses' office. From my vantage point I can see Dr Pike, shouting and wagging his finger at a man in a uniform. 'Have some sense, man,' I can hear him bellow.

Once again, Dr Pike's car has been clamped in the hospital car park. It seems to happen with such regularity that I'm amazed he can continue the pretence of being astounded. I am joined by a nurse. 'He's not done it again, has he?' We both roll our eyes and laugh.

But actually, it's not that funny. Dr Pike has just been clamped for parking in the hospital where he works. The man he is remonstrating with is not a council traffic warden. He's not even a hospital employee. He works for the private service company which runs the NHS hospital. Dr Pike doesn't have a parking permit; there aren't enough to go round as the trust has to pay for them. Dr Pike covers a number of hospitals and needs his car to travel between them. The fact that he's frequently here out of hours, doing work he's not paid for, doesn't exempt him from being clamped.

It's no better for patients. In fact, I'm actually embarrassed as I walk past them queueing to pay for the privilege of parking in a hospital that their taxes are funding. Only a few weeks ago, I witnessed the unbelievable sight of a man who had just seen his wife die in A&E being threatened with having his car towed away because he didn't have a ticket.

Hospitals make millions of pounds a year from car parking charges. It's part of a wider problem being witnessed in hospitals like ours up and down the country and is indicative of the way the government now sees health care. Increasingly, hospitals are beginning to resemble out-of-town shopping malls. Fast-food outlets and chain stores have slowly, insidiously replaced the League of Friends shops. When I was a student, a coffee at the hospital canteen cost me fifty pence. Yesterday, in our 'modernised' hospital after our own League of Friends shop closed a few months ago, it cost me two pounds twenty.

This transformation of our hospitals began

after the introduction of the 'internal market', when trusts were expected to supplement their income from commercial retail rentals and service contracts. Trusts sold off land, cut back on staff, and contracted out services as a way of producing revenue. It is this need to develop income-generating schemes that is behind the contracting out of car parking, as well as the privately owned restaurants, newsagents and coffee shops which litter hospital lobbies. The companies who manage these facilities, eager to increase their profit margins, can charge premium rates because they know they have a captive market. The doctors and nurses have no jurisdiction over these companies, and as a result are powerless to intervene when a little bit of common sense or compassion is called for. All we can do is stand and shout, and then pay up like everyone else.

Thursday 3 June

I didn't witness the scene in the canteen, but I have it on good authority that aubergine bake was indeed thrown and did indeed make contact with its intended target. Lewis had a ringside seat and paged me as soon as it was over to tell me what had happened. As did Maxine. And Mary 2. And Trudy. They were all in the canteen when Ruby, who had remained relatively composed until this point, happened to find herself standing next to Housewives' Favourite in the queue for lunch. He asked her why she wasn't returning his calls, at which point Ruby enlightened him on our discovery. It appears that, when confronted with what we had all seen last weekend, he continued to deny it. 'No, you must be mistaken. Must be someone else. Wasn't me,' he had protested.

Embarrassed at being exposed in so public a place, he had turned to the cashier and made reference to the fact that Ruby was probably 'hormonal', at which point Ruby was handed a plate of aubergine bake by the canteen lady.

Opinion is divided as to what exactly happened next. Mary 2 is convinced it was an accident, while Maxine is convinced of the opposite. Lewis says he doesn't care, as far as he is concerned God moved in mysterious ways and all that matters is that Housewives' Favourite had his best suit ruined. I'm not sure if God is so vindictive, but the end result was that Housewives' Favourite stormed out of the canteen humiliated, covered in food, swearing loudly in front of half the hospital staff.

'He went so red, you should have seen it, Max,' Lewis told me with glee.

Ruby refused to comment after I dragged her outside for a cigarette later that day. She would only say that she wouldn't have been so petty as to throw food over someone. But then she raised an eyebrow in a way that far from convinced me that was true.

Saturday 5 June

Flora is back for the weekend, although Ruby is on call. Flora has accepted her job in anaesthetics and will be moving back to the house in August once her current job is over. It's in the same hospital where Ruby and I have accepted jobs, so although we'll be working in different departments, we'll be back together again. This sense of future unity is remarkably comforting. 'It's the only thing that's kept me going these last few weeks,' says Flora, who is currently staying in pre-fab hospital accommodation miles from civilisation.

Flora, in anticipation of her return to the fold, is already booking up weekend art courses. No doubt most of these will have to be cancelled once we have our new rotas and discover when we're on call but she doesn't care. 'Booking them is the fun bit. Actually attending them is just a formality,' she concludes as she writes the cheques and addresses the envelopes.

We sit in the kitchen and I tell her the gory details about Housewives' Favourite and the aubergine bake. Flora nods sagely. 'I know Ruby, and that won't be the last of it,' she says and I agree. Ruby is scatty, frenetic and driven, but she has a deeply ingrained sense of justice. She is, in her own unique way, highly moral. I know that what has upset her about Housewives' Favourite is not just that she was humiliated, lied to and cheated, but that he is doing it to his wife as well. And to countless other members of staff. I wonder if he's met his match in Ruby. I hope so.

Sunday 6 June

I phone my grandparents today. Since Gran's heart attack I've desperately tried to keep in regular contact with them, ever aware that it's so easy for weeks to slip by without speaking to them. I dial the number and am taken aback to hear my sister answer the phone.

'Oh, hello, what you doing down there? I didn't know you were visiting?' I say.

'What, aren't I allowed to visit my ailing grandparents any more? Here I am, just selflessly giving my time to see Gran and Grandpa,' she begins, sardonically.

I try to imagine what she's really up to. I hear an unfamiliar voice in the background. 'Is that Granddad?' I ask.

My sister is silent for a moment.

'Ellen, are you there? Who's that I can

351

hear?' I ask.

'Erm, well, it's Toby,' she replies awkwardly, then after a brief pause, adds, 'He says hello.'

I shake my head. 'Who the hell is Toby? Are Gran and Granddad there?'

'Yes, they're sitting in the front room having tea with Toby and me. You remember Toby. He's the dermatologist who so kindly looked at my rash when Gran was in hospital. Well, it turns out it wasn't leprosy, although no thanks to you. Really, I sometimes wonder what the point of having a doctor in the family is if he can't even help his own sister.'

I ignore her provocation.

'What's he doing there?' I say, although before the words are even out of my mouth, I realise that my sister, like any good hypochondriac, was never going to let a young, attractive man who could give her ready medical advice on tap pass her by.

'Well, I just happened to be down here a few weeks ago accompanying Gran to her follow-up appointment in the hospital, and thought I'd text Toby to see if he was around...'

I chuckle as I listen to her attempts to explain herself. I have no doubt that from their first meeting my sister was intending to show Toby more than just her rash. 'Well, that was convenient,' I say.

I can imagine my sister and Gran spending hours arranging such a 'chance encounter', no doubt with wedding bells ringing in their ears (or is it tinnitus?).

Monday 7 June

Mrs Doyle's psychic, she tells me. 'You've got a very strong aura,' she says, staring into the middle distance and waving her hands around my head. It must be my aftershave. But at two o'clock in the morning, I don't need to hear about my aura. All I want to know is when her leg pain started. 'Right, anyway, what about the leg pain?' I continue, ignoring my own curiosity as to when I'll win the lottery. For my final eight weeks of life as a junior doctor, I'm also covering the medical assessment unit. This is where all the sick people from A&E are shunted if they need to be admitted or to have further investigations. It's a new government scheme in yet another attempt to try and reduce waiting times in A&E. One day someone will come up with the revolutionary idea of simply employing more doctors and nurses.

You'd think that by now I'd have experienced the worst that the junior doctor year could throw at me. You'd be wrong. Medical Assessment is your own private nightmare. You can almost guarantee that all those little things you never quite got to grips with at medical school will come back and haunt you. And the pace is ten times faster than the ward. During the day there are quite a few doctors milling around, who can be accosted for advice, but at night, there is just one senior doctor to help you, and they also have to cover the High Dependency and Intensive Care Units. So it's just me, with a constant trickle of patients being admitted into the unit, each one needing to be seen, a detailed history taken, treatment started. All of this takes time, and the patients just keep on coming. It's like *Hell's Kitchen*, only with sick people instead of soufflés.

Mrs Doyle's legs are slowing me down. She's been transferred from A&E without a diagnosis. In her notes it just says 'leg pain with rash'. Now, unfortunately we did legs at medical school during the two weeks before Christmas, when I was busy shopping and going to parties along with the rest of my year. A few years later, dermatology suffered the same fate, so the part of my brain that should be devoted to legs and rashes is instead filled with hazy memories of university Christmas balls.

'I should tell you,' she says, staring into the middle distance again, 'very soon your life will change.'

'Does it involve sleeping?' I ask.

She stares at me blankly. I don't know what's wrong with her legs, but I've managed to exclude anything life-threatening and the Mystic Meg treatment is starting to grate on me.

The morning comes and with it the joyless task of the consultant ward round. 'Oh, a classic case,' booms the consultant when he sees Mrs Doyle's leg in the morning. I stare at him. 'Erm, yes. Is it?' I say.

I'm about to be found out for a complete medical ignoramus, but Mrs Doyle comes to the rescue. 'Phlebitis,' she says.

'Pardon?' I reply.

'That's what you said it was last night, didn't you?' she continues, and winks at me. I said no such thing, so I'm perplexed.

'Yes, very good, exactly what I was thinking,' the consultant says. This woman really is a psychic: she read the consultant's mind. A shiver goes down my spine.

But then Mrs Doyle whispers to me, 'My sister's a GP. I called her this morning and that's what she said it was. Our little secret, eh?' and she smiles at me.

After the ward round I go back to Mrs Doyle to tell her how grateful I am for her help but she's already gone. Still, I'm sure she knows.

'She really liked you,' says Mary 3.

'Oh, she hasn't stopped talking about you since yesterday,' interjects Mary 1.

Mary 2 nods while she eats some Custard Creams.

'I can't thank you enough,' says Mary 1. 'Honestly, I've always said you were my favourite doctor.'

'No you haven't,' says Mary 3, laughing, having finally finished the packet of biscuits.

Through their usual impenetrable banter, I begin to realise that, unknowingly, I saw Mary 1's mother in A&E on Monday.

'You remember what you said to her, about how she shouldn't worry, and then you explained about why her heart wasn't working properly?' says Mary 1. I nod slowly and smile benignly. They have assumed that I realised it was Mary 1's mother and gave her some sort of special treatment. In honesty, though, I did no such thing.

'The nurses knew as well, I'm sure, because one of them made her a cup of tea. Everyone was so kind to her.'

I didn't like to totally shatter their illusion of nepotism on the NHS. The truth was though that I couldn't even really remember the woman, let alone what I'd said to her.

Whatever it was, though, the Marys were clearly in approval. As far as they were concerned I'd shown Mary 1's mother special treatment and they were delighted. They didn't even complain when I handed them a month's worth of dictation to type. But as I left them it slowly dawned on me that the nurses and I had treated her as we treated everyone. I felt a brief swelling of pride in myself that someone somewhere had been pleased that I'd been their doctor. I still got scared; I still felt out of my depth at times and didn't know what do to in every situation. But the Marys had, unwittingly, boosted my confidence just a little. I smiled to myself. Then my pager went off, and a nurse began to chastise me for not signing a drug chart.

Thursday 10 June

Yet more shouting in the canteen, which this time I witnessed. At first no one had particularly noticed Housewives' Favourite storm into the canteen and attempt to frogmarch Ruby outside. She resisted. He persisted. A patient interrupted and asked if Ruby was OK and would she like him to call security for her? At which point, seeing that he wasn't going to be able to forcibly remove Ruby to a place away from the prying eyes of the hospital, Housewives' Favourite gave in and began to address her in a furious whisper, in full view of everyone. Ruby stood impassively, the only evidence of her glee a wry smile gently creeping across her face as he became progressively louder and angrier.

'You told my wife, you little bitch,' he hissed.

'She already knew, she just wasn't aware of the extent of it,' Ruby said quietly, relishing every moment.

Housewives' Favourite was clearly incandescent with rage and only reined in his temper when he turned around and saw the entire canteen staring silently at him, their forks of food hovering nervously in front of their mouths while they listened intently. There was nothing he could do and seeing this, he turned on his heels and marched out of the canteen, nearly knocking into an old woman with a tray as he did so. Ruby smiled warmly, paid for her sandwich, and walked out. There was no need for any throwing of aubergine bake, accidentally or otherwise. The mess, this time, was entirely of Housewives' Favourite's making.

Saturday 12 June

'Organic morello cherry preserve, huh?' came the voice from nowhere. I looked up. I knew this man from somewhere, but where?

I smiled benignly. 'Yes, it's great with porridge,' I said, trying not to say anything too committal. 'So,' I hesitated. 'How have you been?'

He didn't answer but looked down at the jam again. I began to feel rather self-conscious about my choice of conserve. What was it saying about me? I felt as though I was being analysed. I looked at the large selection of cleaning products in my trolley, picked up in a determined effort to have a blitz-clean of the flat this weekend. I noticed him eyeing them up too, counting the number of bottles. 'I haven't got some obsessive cleaning thing or anything,' I mumbled. 'It's just I've got the car, and you know, heavy bags...' My voice trailed off.

Both our eyes fell on the four packs of jaycloths I had in my hand. 'Special offer,' I said, by way of explanation. I had a vague feeling of unease about this man, as though we had a history which wasn't altogether pleasant. I looked at him again.

'It's funny, isn't it,' he said, 'seeing you here, away from the hospital, doing normal things like, well, shopping?'

Suddenly, it came back to me who he was. He had been a patient a few months ago. He had bipolar and had been very unwell when he was admitted after he'd taken an overdose. He'd spat at me and assaulted a nurse while on the medical ward. Eventually he'd been medically cleared from his overdose and transferred to the psychiatric ward. Yes, yes, I knew him now. And he had a wife, who worked in the Post Office. Bits of his history came flooding back. He was right, it was funny seeing him out of context like this. I felt slightly embarrassed on his behalf because it's not often that you bump into someone who knows your entire life history, who has seen you at your most vulnerable, but who is, in essence, a stranger. And it was awkward for me because, in a tiny way, he now knew me a little bit better and he'd seen me at my most vulnerable – both when he'd spat at me, and now, standing here in a grubby T-shirt and messy hair.

The doctor–patient relationship has subtle but clearly defined social boundaries. It helps preserve the patient's dignity when they are unwell, because the doctor is viewed as simply a professional. But it also helps the doctor. Often situations are emotionally charged for the patient and their families, and these boundaries afford the doctor a little detachment. Certainly bumping into your local GP in the supermarket might not cause too many difficulties, but when you've been seen by someone *in extremis,* this distance is useful. Right now I feel exposed and unsure of how this can be concluded. I feel a little scared.

'Here, I'll carry your bags to your car for you,' he offers. I hear alarm bells ringing. I hesitate. 'It's a service we offer here at Waitrose,' he says, smiling. I look again at his suit, and realise that it's a uniform. 'I'm one of the managers now,' he adds, proudly. 'This any good then?' he asks, putting the jam back in the trolley, and he walks with me to the checkout.

Wednesday 16 June

Supriya and I sit in the doctors' mess, catching up on dictation. This is an incredibly tedious and laborious exercise whereby we dictate letters to the GP for every patient that has been discharged, explaining what happened and reviewing and summarising the treatment they received on the ward.

'I can guarantee that no one will ever read these letters we're dictating, will they?' Supriya says with a sigh. 'What's the point?'

I shrug my shoulders. Then her eyes fall on something, and she goes silent. 'He's really hyponatraemic,' she says to herself and calls her registrar. There is a brief discussion. Then she makes a call to the GP. Then to the ward to ensure there's a bed ready. Finally she calls the patient to ask him to come back into hospital, explaining that his blood results had come back abnormal.

She had taken some bloods the day the patient was due to be discharged, the results of which weren't back until after they'd gone home yesterday. Nobody had reviewed them because he'd already gone home. But Supriya, diligent and organised as ever, had thought she should look at them to report them to the GP so they had them on file. If she hadn't done this, nobody would ever have known that he had dangerously low sodium, until, possibly, it was too late. I look at the pile of dictation I have sitting by me, and pick up my dictaphone and start dictating with a new energy, like my, or at least a patient's, life depended on it.

Thursday 17 June

Walking down the corridor this morning I am met by two familiar faces: Sad Sack and Daniel. They are both dressed in surgical scrubs and look even more tired and harassed than I remember. I smile and wave and they do the same as we pass each other. My time in surgery seems so long ago. Time is distorted for doctors. It races by because you are so busy, but because each day is so full, so long, and so much happens it has the effect of making, in retrospect, weeks seem like months, and months like years. I've changed so much since I last saw them, but here are two people come back from the dim and distant past to remind me. I think all this in the time it takes to walk past the two of them and wave.

Sunday 20 June

On call again this weekend and I am overjoyed to hear the door of the doctors' mess open bright and early this morning and be greeted with Maurice's cheery whistling. He wheels his bicycle in, parks it in the hallway and immediately sets about clearing up and putting the kettle on. He's frailer now, slower in the way he moves about. He still has a faint scar on his head from when he was mugged. 'Here,' I say, 'I'll do that,' and get up and take the kettle from him. 'You sit down for a bit.'

To my amazement he does. I make him a cup of tea and rinse the few cups that have been left on the side for washing. I steal a clandestine glance at him while I take down the sugar and notice him tremble slightly, wobbling as he goes to sit down. I know that it won't be long before he'll be unable to keep coming here to clean up our mess. It's not really fair on him how much we've come to rely on him anyway. He shows me the new trousers he bought with the money left over after we'd bought the bicycle. He's still incredulous that we should have helped him, when he felt so indebted to us. I tidy up around him briefly and then head for the ward. Later that day, when I go back to the mess, Maurice is asleep in one of the chairs, the television quietly chattering in the background. I close the door and leave him to it.

Tuesday 22 June

Somewhere along the way, things have gone horribly wrong. It wasn't supposed to be like this. I did what my mum told me: I worked hard at school, I tried hard in my exams. J thought that if you worked hard, then everything would be OK. Now I'm supposed to be reaping the benefits.

This, I now realise, is not going to be the case. I'm working harder now than I ever have done. I've spent the best years of my life studying so I can make sick people better again, and the best I can hope for in return is a box of Milk Tray. While all my friends who dropped out of school, flunked their A-levels or spent the majority of their three years at university studying the bottom of beer glasses are busy sunning themselves on holiday, travelling the corners of the earth or sponging off their parents, here am I stuck in the windowless Medical Assessment Unit not even sure if it's night or day. A&E is so full of drunks though that

I could almost imagine I was in Ibiza.

Miss Talbot has been beaten up. 'My name's Rosie,' she corrects me. I get the feeling that respect is not going to be gained by using surnames. She's the same age as I was when I went to medical school, eighteen. She's lying on her bed and I notice a heart-shaped tattoo on her ankle. She's painfully thin. She was found unconscious in the doorway of a shop. She's ostensibly been admitted as she had a head injury and needs to be kept in for observation. While she was in A&E though, she asked to be tested for HIV and hepatitis, and so we've also kept her in so we can tell her the results when we get them in the morning. It's not normal practice, but sometimes protocol has to go out the window, even if the department is windowless.

There's also the problem of her pimp. She's lost her night's earnings and the A&E staff are worried about discharging her because she was so scared of what he might do to her when he finds out. We sit and talk. She tells me about being sexually abused, about running away from home, about taking drugs, about becoming a prostitute. Her story is nothing new, nothing surprising. I read about it in the papers, see it on television all the time. But it's different to talk to people for whom this isn't a statistic or a news item. For whom it's real.

The morning comes and with it the results of Rosie's blood tests. They're negative. I go and give her the good news.

'Can I have a certificate or something? Have it written down that I haven't got anything?' she asks.

I've never been asked this before. 'Erm, why do you want that?' I ask.

She looks at me and suddenly I feel very naive and stupid. 'You can charge more if you can prove you haven't got anything,' she says.

I feel sick. In my ignorance I thought that this would be some cathartic event for her, some moment of realisation, a reprieve. But for her, it's economic. Nothing's changed. She still has to get money and now she'll be able to get a bit more for it. I want to bundle her up and take her somewhere safe, where people have respect for each other, where she's not just a piece of meat to be bought and sold. But I can't and instead I discharge her. As she walks away, I think about how someone's life can end up like this. About the choices that other people made for her. And how somewhere, along the way, things went horribly wrong.

Friday 25 June

Only a few weeks left and then it's all over.

I think back to my first few days on the wards: the pure fear of it all – the utter, unbridled panic that would overtake me when required to do even the simplest of things. Things that I take for granted now were mysterious and unfathomable back then and the prospect of ever getting to grips with them was a distant fantasy.

I remember standing on the ward, with a nurse in front of me gently sneering, and the patient's relatives standing around me, looking expectantly at me. 'She's got a headache, Doctor, please do something,' repeated the patient's son. My pen hovered over the drug chart. I broke out in a sweat. Eventually I looked at the nurse and confessed what she'd already guessed: I didn't know how to prescribe paracetamol.

My mum, for goodness' sake, with not a day's medical training in her life, could successfully give someone paracetamol. I knew what paracetamol looked like, I knew what you gave it for, I even knew the pharmacology behind how it worked. But how to actually prescribe – the doses, what to write and where, how often it should be given and so on – is something that doctors aren't taught at medical school. The nurse looked at me, and barely able to control her smugness whispered, '1g QDS.' I scribbled it down and scampered off.

Recently on the ward the nurses have

begun to talk about a memo that they have been sent. It concerns proposals that nurses would be allowed to prescribe medication without supervision from a doctor. It is with some wariness that I dip my toe into these murky waters. Any perceived criticism by a doctor of a nurse is pounced upon as evidence of their arrogance and lack of respect for other health professionals. On the contrary, my argument is actually based on what nurses are good at: nursing.

Medical school did not prepare me for life on the wards. While it pumped my head full of facts and figures, the day-to-day running of the ward, where to find X-rays, how to fill out blood forms, and indeed how to prescribe drugs, were omitted. Nurses have played a major part in my transition from a bumbling idiot into someone who at least knows roughly what is going on.

Instead, medical school works as an extended aptitude test to weed out those that aren't going to be able to stand it on the wards. All doctors worth their salt know their limits and consult the *BNF* – the medications' bible – when they're out of their depth. And let's not forget that junior doctors are very rarely expected to make a decision as to what drug actually has to be given. These decisions are made on ward round by the consultant, who has usually amassed several decades' worth of experience. We aren't taught how to prescribe drugs, because that's not the hard bit. The hard bit is knowing how they work, why they work, why some interact with others, how the body breaks them down. The hard bit is working out what's wrong with someone in the first place. It's easy to prescribe paracetamol when someone's got a headache when you know how. It's differentiating between a sub-arachnoid brain haemorrhage and a headache that takes six years at medical school and countless years of training afterwards. To isolate prescribing and pluck it from the range of doctors' skills as though it were a Woolworths pick 'n' mix fails to realise that it's part of a far wider and more complex process. It's dangerous. One profession needs to take responsibility for this otherwise there will be confusion and chaos and it's the doctors that are given this responsibility. Conversely, I don't know how to dress a wound and I'm jolly pleased nurses do.

Allowing nurses or other health professionals to prescribe drugs isn't about valuing their contribution to patient care or their clinical abilities. It's about cutting corners to reduce waiting times, to meet targets and to do so at no extra cost. Respecting nurses is about realising that the job they do – looking after patients, making sure the wards run smoothly and tending to patients' needs – is vital. Without nurses nursing, the wards would fall apart. Adding the responsibility of prescriptions to their list is simply a cost-cutting exercise and will end in a headache for staff and patients alike that no tablet can take away, whoever prescribes it.

Saturday 26 June

Today has been a glorious day. Today has confirmed to me something many people already know and that I now have proof of: doctors are hypocrites.

Ruby and I went to the pub this evening, in celebration of the fact that neither of us were on call or so tired that we couldn't speak. In fact, so energised were we by the prospect of only one month to go in this job that we cleaned the bathroom this afternoon. Well, I cleaned the bathroom while Ruby perched on the sink and pointed out the bits I'd missed. Then we went out for dinner and then for a drink with a few other friends. As the evening drew to a close, Ruby and I went outside to wait for a taxi. We sat down on a bench in the now-deserted pub garden, smoked a cigarette and looked up at the stars. After a few minutes it became apparent that we weren't alone. There was a noise coming from behind us, a slight creak of someone shifting on a bench accompanied by the sound of a cigarette lighter. I turned round. In the darkness I could make out a shadowy figure sitting a few hundred yards away, and could see the small, glowing embers of a lit cigarette in the figure's hand.

Ruby turned round as well. 'Ooh, that sent shivers down my spine,' she whispered. 'I didn't realise there was someone sitting over there. Where did they appear from?'

I looked back at the shape, which began moving towards us until Ruby and I could clearly recognise it: the mysterious non-smoking woman who had haunted us round the back of A&E all these months. She was clearly drunk, as well as having a cigarette in her hand, and had moved closer to inspect us.

'Hello again, you two,' she said, slightly slurring her speech. 'I'm just... I've just... I'm going home now,' and she tottered off into the darkness.

We both sat in stunned silence. 'I cannot believe she is a closet smoker. After all the hassle she's given us. What a hypocrite!' said Ruby, clearly delighted. And she took a long drag on her cigarette.

JULY

Thursday 1 July

Mrs Mycek has worked hard and saved all her life. She's ninety-four years old next week. 'Just let me die at home, would you daring?' she says to Dr Pike. 'I don't want to go into a home, I've got a perfectly good home.'

He ignores this request. 'You're not safe there,' says Dr Pike.

This is heartbreaking. Mrs Mycek has had several falls at home and now, on this, her fourth admission in under a year, it's been decided that she can't go back to the little townhouse she's lived in all her adult life. She's forgetful and vague, but still knows her home and wants to go back there. 'You just can't, I'm afraid,' says Dr Pike. Although, if anyone is afraid, it's Mrs Mycek, and I can understand why.

Dr Pike turns away and seeing my face, shrugs his shoulders. 'That's show business,' he says. I grit my teeth. There is part of me that thinks, why can't we just let her go home, and if she falls and dies at home, rather that than rotting away in some home, away from everything that is familiar to her. Wouldn't she rather live a possibly shorter life surrounded by memories in an environment she knows, than a longer one where she doesn't? But I understand that in the present climate of litigation, defensive medicine and institutional care, this isn't an option. And once she has gone into the home, there'll be no going back. Her house, which she owns, will be sold off to pay for the care she receives.

So why is it that, depending on where you live or what your diagnosis is, you may be required to pay for your care, while others are not? For old people who are unable to live independently and require care, it would seem that the founding principle of the NHS – that care is free at the point of access – has been largely abandoned.

But the current crisis has its roots in the early days of the NHS and to understand what's gone wrong today, it's important to understand what happened in the past. The post-war Labour government, filled with utopian ideologies, wanted to create the kind of care for older people that had previously been the preserve of the rich. Before state provision, those that could afford it lived in hotels, with private nurses tending them if necessary, while the majority lived at home with only basic care provided by family members, or were at the mercy of charitable organisations. The 1946 NHS Act and the 1948 National Assistance Act promised that the inequalities of the past would forever be put asunder. Or so it was thought. What it actually did, unintentionally, was create two parallel systems of care. The NHS would provide a universal system of health care which was free at the point of access, while the National Assistance Act meant that local authorities would provide a supplementary system for those in need of 'care and attention' or 'personal care'. The latter category was meant to be for those who, a bit weary and tired of life alone, wanted to move into 'hotel-like' accommodation where they could be looked after, and was therefore means tested. It was never intended that this would include those who were infirm, like Mrs Mycek. While the motivation for these two pieces of legislation were honourable, they, unfortunately left a loop-hole which subsequent governments would exploit.

By drawing a distinction between those that were medically 'sick' and those that wanted 'care and attention', an artificial line was drawn that has been slowly shifted over the past few decades to force more people to pay for their care. With NHS trusts desperate to keep expenditure down, the arbitrary line between what constitutes medical care and what constitutes personal care has shifted. Someone who has had a stroke, for example, may be left requiring help with washing and dressing. This, now, constitutes personal care and is therefore means tested, despite the fact that it's clearly because of a medical problem. If someone has an ongoing, complex medical need, however, they may be eligible for NHS long-term care, in which case they won't be required to pay a penny. As NHS provision for people with long-term medical needs was cut, so the eligibility criteria for medical care has shifted so that it is retermed personal care and therefore becomes means tested.

Mrs Mycek needs prompting with washing and dressing and the occasional bit of help. Because of her falls she's also considered a risk, and therefore needs nursing input. This is all because of medical problems, but she falls on the wrong side of the line for funding because the care she needs is considered to be 'personal care'. Hence we are in a situation where those who have worked hard all their lives, paid into the NHS and then become infirm, enter a lottery where they may be forced to pay for their care depending on where the arbitrary distinction is drawn in their area. Which hardly provides much of a motivation to work hard and save.

Friday 2 July

Maxine is grabbing me by the arm quite hard in her excitement. 'Dr Palache just told me. I can't believe it!' She's wide-eyed. 'I'm so pleased he's finally come a cropper.'

It seems Maxine has only just learnt about Ruby's showdown with Housewives' Favourite in the canteen and his subsequent disgrace. 'I knew something was up. He's been keeping himself to himself, we've all noticed it. Not so much of his swaggering about, thrusting his crotch in everyone's face,' she says, swinging back on her chair and playing with her hair like a schoolgirl. 'Honestly, practically nothing in a skirt could get away from him. That's why I always hated him.'

'I don't think anyone liked him and I'm not surprised, the way he carried on,' I say while searching for yet more X-ray films.

'Oh, don't get me wrong, I didn't dislike him cos he perved on me. He never touched me, never tried anything on with me, not even so much as a wink. That's what really annoyed me, little jumped-up wotsit. I mean, what's wrong with me, huh?' she says, snorting loudly.

I think it rude to begin a list so don't say anything.

Monday 5 July

Doctors are supposed to have a fantastic memory. This is reinforced at medical school where we are given reams of facts and figures to memorise which we then have to regurgitate in exams. Of course, everyone then promptly forgets all the lists of useless Latin names they've learnt as they walk out of the exam hall and fall into the nearest pub. But it's good training for when you're a junior doctor, as we are expected to retain the most unbelievable amount of arbitrary facts about each of our patients. Nowhere is this more publicly evident than on ward rounds where every morsel of information about each of my patients is expected to be at my fingertips.

Mrs Hughes was admitted with pneumonia a few weeks ago. She's improved on the antibiotics we've given her, but her chronic problem is arthritis, which has destroyed her joints. She's bed-bound because of it, and has been for the past five years. She takes morphine so that the pain is kept under control and so that she can have limited movement in some of her joints. But because of the pneumonia, we've had to reduce the amount of painkillers she's receiving and predictably the pain has come back. Last week Dr Pike decided that we needed to get a specialist in pain management to come and see her. And so it was left to me to make the referral to Dr Brook, the pain specialist.

Now, you'd think that someone who specialised in pain would be keen to reduce suffering. Unfortunately, his desire to end suffering doesn't extend to junior doctors. I called him and almost immediately the barrage of questions intended to trip me up began: I dredged up some numbers from the recess of my memory while I desperately flicked through the notes. 'Has the rheumatologist seen her? Who is her rheumatologist? What's his fax number?' he continued before I'd had a chance to reply. 'Come on, come on, do you want me to see her or not?'

The questions just kept coming. It wasn't going very well. Thankfully Gill, the physiotherapist, was nearby and, sensing that I needed help, rummaged through the notes while I stalled Dr Brook on the phone. Our combined efforts meant that eventually he agreed to come and see Mrs Hughes. Buoyed up by this success I suggested to Gill that she paid Mrs Hughes a visit as well, to see if she could help, and I got in touch with the rheumatologist, who also came and adjusted some of her medication. I was on a roll, so I also arranged for the occupational therapist to see her.

Today, as I walk past Mrs Hughes' room,

Gill pops her head round the door.

'There's someone in here that wants to speak to you,' she says.

I go into the room and Mrs Hughes is sitting up, doing exercises with a big rubber ball. I barely recognise her. The transformation is remarkable.

'Thank you so much, Max, for your help. All these people have been to see me and I feel marvellous,' she says.

She then reels off all the new medications she's taking, and shows me some of the exercises Gill has taught her. 'I can't thank you enough for all the trouble you went to,' she says. 'Don't be silly, it's a pleasure,' I reply. I walk away feeling a once unknown but increasingly familiar sensation: the satisfaction of having done a good job.

Tuesday 6 July

Ruby and I sneak outside for a cigarette after the ward rounds are over. Her alcoholic liver patients aren't getting any easier. 'One spat at me today because I told him he couldn't drink his whisky on the ward. The woman next to him threw her newspaper at him and told him to behave,' she says drolly. 'He's got gangrene and the surgeons will probably have to take his leg off, so you can't be too punitive with him, really.'

We both slouch on a wooden pallet that someone has left leaning against the wall next to the bin. Ruby's pager goes off and she lets out a sigh. 'What do they want now?' she wails. 'It's like being a school teacher on that ward trying to keep them all under control.' Her ward actually has only a few patients with alcoholic liver disease, the rest of them suffering from a variety of ailments unrelated to drink. But it's the alcoholic ones that cause her the trouble.

'Two of them just got in a fight,' she says, returning from A&E where she'd answered her pager. 'One of them has now got a cut on his head I have to look at, as if I don't have enough to do.' She looks down at the long list of jobs she has scribbled from the ward round on a piece of paper. 'They can't be that unwell if they can get out of bed and fight.'

A shiver goes down my spine, and I turn round. Once again, the white-coated woman is standing behind us, having apparently materialised out of nowhere. This time, though, she doesn't say anything. She glares at us for a moment, and then the tiniest corner of her mouth moves up in the faintest of smiles. Then she goes again. Ruby and I consider this a victory and we get a coffee to celebrate.

'We can't discharge her, she might be murdered,' says Supriya passionately down the phone in the doctors' office. She's come on to my ward because she needed to make a sensitive phone call. I'd assumed she was ordering some underwear or something. I try not to listen, but the thought of someone being murdered is too much. 'She's my patient and I've got to have her best interests at heart,' she continues.

It's definitely nothing to do with underwear. After some time she slams the phone down. Her teeth are clenched and she's flushed. 'What on earth is wrong?' I ask.

'It's just this woman who's come in,' she says reluctantly, as though retelling this story only makes it worse for her. 'She had a head injury and so we just admitted her over night for neuro obs. She was a bit concussed but she's fit now and we're supposed to discharge her.'

'And?' I say, feeling there's nothing particularly remarkable enough to warrant her behaviour on the phone.

'That was the police and they said they won't do anything unless she makes a formal statement,' she adds.

'About what?' I ask, confused.

'Her husband. She's covered in scars from where he's hit her. She's got cigarette burns on her arms. He broke her finger last year. He's going to kill her if it continues. I don't know what to do,' she says, her whole body tensing.

'So why doesn't she just report him to the police?' I ask.

'I don't know. She's scared, she says she loves him, she says he's not always like it. I know if can just have a bit more time with her I can get her to see sense. I just can't believe there's nothing we can do.'

The woman is medically cleared and so her consultant is saying she should be discharged. The police won't do anything unless the woman makes a statement, which she won't do. I can see how it's hard for Supriya to take any action, much as she wants to. 'I just can't bring myself to discharge her back to that environment. What if the next time he hits her she's not so lucky? What if...' Her voice trails off.

This is the problem with medicine. In theory, its boundaries are clear. But in practice, health and illness are tied up with so many other factors. Domestic violence is not medical. A head injury is. But teasing the two apart is incredibly difficult to do. It doesn't seem right. It's like just patching up a soldier to go once more into battle without trying to stop the war, or in Supriya's case, discharging a woman to inevitably get beaten up by her husband again.

Monday 12 July

I sit in the lecture hall while the lecturer drones on. Photographs of smiley faces are projected on to the screen and they look down at me, benignly. Keywords are flashed up in bright colours. The man in front of me is explaining how there will be fewer doctors being employed in the trust this time next year. He smiles. This, he concludes, is going to be beneficial to patients and help improve patient care.

All the junior doctors are assembled this morning for a talk on government schemes to modernise the NHS. I feel like spooning my own eyes out. Lewis is asleep. But as I listen to the lecturer I become increasingly enraged. He's saying something about delivering a modernised and focused career structure. Streamlining. Flagships. Supporting real patient choice. But none of this really *means* anything. It's just gobbledygook non-words. There is talk of the medical profession's competence, while, from the junior to the senior, we're treated as though we're all incompetent. There is talk of responsibility, while responsibility is taken away from us and handed to men with clipboards and business acumen. Of choice, where there is none. Suddenly I am fifteen years old again and sitting in an English class. 'War is Peace. Freedom is Slavery. Ignorance is Strength,' I remember reading as we ploughed our way through George Orwell's *Nineteen Eighty-Four*.

Increasingly the language used about, and within, the NHS appears to be designed to obscure what's really going on, what's really being said. While people protest at the planned closures, we have our ministers and leaders telling us, earnestly, that this is what patients want. Departments will close and lives will be saved. Jobs aren't lost, instead services are 'streamlined' and 'restructured'. Resources are 'redistributed' and 'modernised' rather than reduced; valuable services are improved by being axed. In this 'collateral damage' era, wordplay is ever important. Bad things are renamed and rebranded as being good, and repeated again and again in the hope that, in some way, we will begin to believe it.

This isn't just jargon, it's a new way of viewing the world – a happy world of smiling faces, looking down benignly while the NHS is slowly destroyed.

Wednesday 14 July

Late night and I'm on call. Craig, the young man in front of me, doesn't look right. He's breathing funny. I know that doesn't sound very medical, but it's 3 a.m., give me a break. The nurse called me. 'He's really short of breath,' she said over the phone. 'He can barely speak. He's not asthmatic or anything.' She read me his obs over the phone. His heart rate was very high and his blood pressure was worryingly low. The pulse oximeter which measures the amount of oxygen in the blood was only at seventy-five per cent, when it should have been near one hundred per cent. 'You're going to have to come quick,' said the nurse.

I run to the ward, and immediately see him. He is sitting up in bed, breathing fast and very distressed. The veins in his neck are bulging. The other patients on the ward are asleep and the light over his bed illuminates his face, which is pale and sweaty. What on earth is going on? I try and remain calm. First things first. The nurse tells me his history while she puts an oxygen mask on him and I examine him. He's come in because of his Crohn's disease. He's been having a number of investigations and currently has a tube going into his stomach with a drip attached. I wonder if this could be causing these symptoms? At this point I remember Mrs Lampril and my Big Mistake and remember that I mustn't be distracted from the clinical signs as I was with her. I mustn't allow myself to be sidetracked. I examine him. I listen to his chest. On the right side I can clearly hear the air going in and out of his lung. On the left hand side though, it's silent. I tap his chest and on the left hand side, instead of sounding dull, it is resonant, like an empty barrel. I look at his windpipe and it's been pushed to the right. I stand motionless, feeling sick as it dawns on me what's happening. He has developed a tension pneumothorax and will be dead in a matter of minutes unless I do something. His left lung has collapsed and in the process a one-way valve has developed in the gap between his lung and chest wall. With every breath he takes air rushes into the gap and can't escape, causing the space to get bigger and further collapse the lung. As the pressure increases, it pushes on the heart and stops it being able to pump. Then he'll die.

There's no time for a chest X-ray to confirm the diagnosis – he'll be dead before I've finished filling out the form. This is a medical emergency and I've got to do something, and quick. But I've never seen a tension pneumothorax before, let alone treated one. I think back to medical school and desperately try to remember everything I'm supposed to do. My hands are shaking. I turn to the nurse and ask her to page Barney and explain what's happened and tell him he has to come to help. I can't wait for him to come, though. I run to the clinical room and grab a cannula and some gloves. 'I need to do a needle decompression,' I tell the nurse. I open the cannula and explain to Craig what I'm going to do to him: 'I've got to push this needle into your chest to allow the trapped air which is pressing on your lung and heart to come out.'

He just stares at me while he fights for breath. 'Second rib, mid-clavicular line,' I say to myself as I count down the ribs on his chest. I am trying to keep calm. I locate the place I am supposed to insert the needle but I hesitate. If I am wrong, I will puncture his lung. I begin to doubt myself. The needle hovers over the spot. But if I do nothing and my diagnosis is correct, he will die in front of me. I take a deep breath and plunge the needle into his chest. There is a small hiss of air from the end of the needle. This is the air from the gap in his lungs escaping, and it means I was right: he did have a tension pneumothorax. I breathe a sigh of relief

Almost immediately Craig's breathing improves. The colour comes back to his face and I watch his oxygen levels steadily increase on the machine next to him. This is only a temporary reprieve though. Now he must have a chest drain inserted. The nurse explains that Barney is on his way but was dealing with an emergency in A&E. I'm going to have to make a start on the chest drain on my own, despite having never done one before on a live person.

I leave the nurse with Craig and run back to the clinical room to get the things I need. I return and cover his chest in a drape, a small window in it exposing the chest wall underneath. I sterilise the skin with beta-dine and put on sterile gloves. I inject local anaesthetic and make a small incision above the sixth rib. The nurse hands me forceps and I use them to make a hole in the muscle between the ribs and I push a tube into the hole and attach it to a bottle on the floor filled with water. This will ensure that air can escape but cannot re-enter the lung.

As I finish, Barney arrives. 'Oh, well done, Max,' he says, seeing how far I've got. I look up at him and smile. 'You've got everything under control here, it seems,' he says and helps me finish off.

Craig's obs are now back to normal and the nurse comes up to me. 'Well done Max, good call,' she says.

'Thanks,' I say as I leave the ward. And as I walk down the corridor, my smile breaks into a wide beam.

Thursday 15 July

'Do you have to?' asks Mrs Goldsworthy. She's pleading with me.

388

'I do really, I'm sorry. It will be over in a jiffy,' I chirp. At some point since becoming a doctor I've become numbed to the daily indignities I have to subject my patients to. Nothing is sacred any more. With all the patients I've seen, there is now no orifice in the human body I haven't explored, no bodily function I haven't enquired about, no intimate area that has been left unexamined. You name it, I've been there. If you're eating your breakfast while reading this, I apologise.

The first time I had to examine someone's back passage, I was mortified. My hands were shaking and beads of perspiration formed on my forehead as I explained to the male patient sitting in the cubicle in A&E what I was going to do. The examination is called a PR, a name conjuring up glamorous images of *Absolutely Fabulous*, champagne cocktails and canapés but which belies the true meaning, which stands for *per rectum*, and roughly translates from the Latin to mean 'up the bottom'. Considering that we often have to discuss our findings openly on the ward, this is one instance where I feel doctors' penchants for obscuring what they're talking about by using acronyms and dead languages is perfectly justified.

'Oh, don't worry,' the man said. 'It has to be done, I understand.'

I smiled nervously while desperately fiddling with the rubber gloves in an attempt to get them over my clammy hands. Whoever it was that designed rubber gloves didn't have junior doctors performing their first examination in mind. The more nervous you are, the harder they are to get on, and the more you struggle with them, the worse it looks in front of the patient, so the more nervous you get. Once it's got to this stage, there's little that can be done except perform the examination with whatever digits have managed to be covered in latex, regardless of whether or not they're in their corresponding finger on the glove.

There was a momentary pause as the patient looked around the cubicle. Just as I was ready to begin he gave a little cough and looked over his shoulder at me as he lay on the couch. 'You might want some lubricant?' he suggested helpfully, but with the look of someone calculating how quickly he could pull his trousers up and run for the hills.

The whole experience was far more humiliating for me than it was for him.

Now nearly a year into the job, I've become so used to doing unspeakable things to people, I barely bat an eyelid. All patients like to think that they're special, that their case is unique. The fact that they might be the tenth heart attack I've seen that morning is of little comfort to them. But when they realise that you've done more of these examinations than Kilroy-Silk's had sun-beds, they can relax a little; suddenly they're pleased they're not so special. It might come as some consolation to anyone who has had to undergo such an examination that the doctor is thinking about far more important things than what they're doing to you, like where they put their car keys and what they're going to have for tea that evening. While there's a time and a place for seeing patients as individuals, there's also definitely a case for sometimes seeing them as just another exam that has to be done. Not only does this keep the doctor sane, but it makes the whole thing more bearable for the patient.

Having dispelled any images of *All Creatures Great and Small* she may have had, I examine Mrs Goldsworthy. 'There, over and done with. Not so bad, was it?' I say as I straighten her bed sheets.

'I suppose not. It must be worse for you having to do it,' she laughs.

Just as I leave, she calls after me, 'Don't forget your car keys.'

I turn round to see them lying on her table. 'Oh, there they are,' I say. 'I'd been wondering where I'd put them.'

Saturday 17 July

I go home to visit my mum. I'm greeted at the door, though, by my sister. 'Oh, hello,

Ellen, you coming out for lunch with us then?' I say as I walk into the house. 'Yes, we thought we'd come and see you,' she says.

'We?' I question.

'Yes, me and Toby. He's come up to see me for the day. We're going to go shopping afterwards and he's going to buy me a dress I've seen in town. He doesn't know about that bit yet, obviously, so don't say anything to him, will you?'

Toby emerges from the lounge and shakes my hand. We talk briefly about medicine before my mum commandeers him. 'I'm sure I've got asthma. Or maybe it's just hay fever. How can you tell the difference?' she says, giving a few wheezes for good measure.

'He's a dermatologist,' I say. 'Give him a break.' Although secretly I'm rather pleased that someone else is taking the brunt of my family's hypochondria.

He's on his best behaviour though, clearly attempting to make a good impression on the matriarch. 'Oh, it's OK,' he says, smiling at my mum, 'I don't mind.'

'Well in that case,' I say, rolling up my sleeve to show him a mark on my arm, 'do you think that's contact dermatitis?'

Friday 23 July

Lewis is going on annual leave next week, so

392

this is his last day. We say goodbye in the doctors' mess. 'Once our lounge is decorated, Mark and I are going to have a party and you and Ruby must come, OK?' he says.

I nod. 'Course we will. It will probably be the first time I'll see Dr Palache without having to try to get some scans arranged.'

I look at Lewis, with his stethoscope hanging round his shoulders, and realise how much he, and in fact all of us, have grown in confidence since we started last year. Ruby, Supriya and I hug him goodbye before following him outside to where Dr Palache is waiting in the car. 'Thanks so much for all your help over the past year,' I say to Dr Palache.

'Have a good holiday,' shouts Supriya as they drive away, with Lewis waving out of the window.

Saturday 24 July

Doctors are not renowned for their grace and elegance, particularly when it comes to dancing. More funky chicken than Fonteyn. But there is something at which we excel – a rare piece of choreography, beautifully executed night and day up and down the country, in a hospital near you: the Doctors' Dance. This is a highly specialised, site-specific performance that few outside the health-care profession are able to witness. It is charged with tension and passion and is the result of a collaboration between doctor and cleaner. I am only just managing to perfect its subtle and nuanced moves.

Those of you hoping to catch this wonder are most likely to do so late at night in the A&E department, preferably on a Friday. This is when cleaners are out in force, and doctors are at their most stressed. The result would put Nureyev to shame.

After seeing patients, doctors write up their notes standing at those desks which have been infuriatingly designed so that they are too high to sit at, but too low to comfortably stand and write on. Ideally we would have bar-stool type chairs to sit on but we don't. Instead we stand and adopt various poses which mean we can write without resulting in a slipped disc. Then the cleaners come. Everyone who can, vacates the area, but that rarely includes the doctor who has a mounting list of patients to see and isn't going to be delayed by house-keeping. Cleaners are equally single-minded: the floor needs to be mopped, so it will get mopped, regardless of the fact that there are people standing on it at the time. First, the cleaners clean round the doctor's shoes and then gently nudge them with their mops. Then they start battering them, and as a result the doctor is forced to perform the Doctors' Dance as they hop from one foot to the next while the increasingly frustrated cleaner tries to clean under their feet. All this is in complete silence. It reaches truly balletic proportions when the cleaner attempts to push the mop between the doctor's legs in order to clean the floor under the desk where the doctor is standing.

It was during one of these performances that I met Saidi. He's a cleaner and had just soaked one of my shoes. It's a sad fact that doctors and cleaners don't usually talk in hospitals. But on this occasion, as I was wringing disinfectant from my sock, Saidi turned to me and said, 'It's so great to work here, isn't it, Doctor?'

I was a little taken aback. He was cleaning up other people's dirt and I'd just been threatened with a knife by a patient. What's great about that? I wondered. He introduced himself, and explained that he came from Ethiopia. 'I've been here four years now, and it's such a privilege to work in the NHS.'

I stared at him. Privilege? Not the word I'd immediately have chosen at two in the morning. 'Where I come from, there's nothing like this. We're so lucky here.'

And the part of me that had made me apply to medical school, to want to be a doctor in the first place, began to wake. He was right. The NHS is amazing. It's easy to complain about it, and certainly there are lots of things that are wrong and don't work. But it's a fantastically British institution, quirky and daft at times but based on a heart-felt idea of equality. A nurse standing at the computer piped up: she was born in the US, but came to the UK six years ago specifically to work in the NHS. 'I believe in everything it stands for, and I wanted to support it. Health care in the US is a disgrace. Sure it's fine if you've got money, but if you don't have insurance, it's worse than the third world.'

In fact, over 40 million Americans don't have health insurance. For a few brief moments, three people representing three continents stood and marvelled at the marvellous NHS. We've become a bit complacent about our health service, particularly those who were born knowing nothing else. But every so often I think we should remember just how lucky we are to have an NHS. Perhaps we should even do a little dance.

Wednesday 28 July

Supriya and I go to see Mrs Crook in the administration block to pick up some forms for our next job. We walk into her office to find her head lolled back in the chair, and snoring loudly. Supriya tactfully makes a noise and Mrs Crook gives a start. Her glasses have slipped down the side of her face, so when she puts her head forward they sit wonky over her nose. She straightens them while pretending she was examining the ceiling. 'Yes, what can I do for you two?' she says blinking at us.

'We've come to get our forms. We're leaving this time next week to start in different trusts.'

She looks at us. 'That's nice, dear.'

Silence. 'Well, can you give us them?' I ask.

'Who? Me?' she says bewildered.

Given that there are only three of us in the room, and it's her office, I wonder who else she thinks I could mean.

'Where is it you work?' she asks.

I sigh. 'We work here, Mrs Crook. We're supposed to get some forms from you for payroll.' She stares at us, smiling benignly. Silence again. Supriya and I look at each other. 'Don't worry about it,' I say, 'I'm sure we'll manage without them.'

And we leave her to resume her sleep.

Friday 30 July

I walk past Trudy's office on my way to visit the Marys with some more dictation for them to type. Trudy calls out to me, and I pop in. 'I'm on holiday next week, so I won't see you before you go,' she says. 'Hope everything goes well for you, Max.'

I hover by the door, wanting to articulate how much her kindness and friendship over the past year has meant to me, but don't know how to without it sounding naff and sentimental.

'Fancy some Battenberg? For old time's sake?' she says. 'Kettle's just boiled.'

I smile and sit down. We talk about my new job and where's she's going on holiday until my pager goes off.

'Allow me,' she says, dialling the number. 'Dr Pemberton is in a meeting at the moment...' she begins.

'Thank you,' I mouth.

Saturday 31 July

Flora came home this weekend, laden down with boxes and bags. She's moving all her belongings back in time for next week when she finishes her job.

'There's one more thing,' she says as she surveys the pile of stuff in the hallway. She pops outside and from the car she brings a large rectangular object, draped in a bed sheet.

'What's that?' Ruby asks, as she descends

the stairs having only just woken up.

'It's Daedalus,' says Flora triumphantly, as she whips off the bed sheet to reveal a birdcage.

Ruby and I stare inside. 'It's a budgie,' says Ruby disappointedly, 'why have you got a budgie?'

'I bought him a few months ago to cheer me up. It was so lonely and miserable living in that hospital accommodation, I thought it would be nice to have a pet,' says Flora defensively.

Ruby peers suspiciously through the bars of the cage. 'He's looking at me.'

The bird flaps its wings in disapproval at being stared at. We leave him in the hall while we put the kettle on. As we settle down round the kitchen table, though, we are disturbed by the sound of a pager going off. We all, as a reflex, glance down to our belts and then remember it's the weekend and that we aren't at work.

'Must be your pager going off,' I say to Ruby, as I know mine's upstairs. It does it again. Ruby gets up to investigate. It sounds slightly strange though. There's something not quite right about it.

Flora looks sheepish. 'Erm, the thing is, I haven't told you about Daedalus. Well, he's got a bit of an annoying habit. I suppose it could be viewed as a talent really...

'It's the bloody bird,' says Ruby coming

back in holding the cage aloft. 'It mimics the sound of the pagers.'

'He just started doing it, I think because he could hear it going off all the time in my room when I wasn't working,' says Flora desperately. 'He's a nice budgie really.'

'It's going to drive us mad,' replies Ruby sternly.

'It's OK, Max is training as a psychiatrist,' jokes Flora.

Ruby and I don't laugh.

'Perhaps he'll grow out of it?' says Flora hopefully.

The bird flaps its wings and makes the sound once more. Ruby rolls her eyes. 'Can we never escape that sound?' she says, glaring at the bird. He flaps his wings again.

HOME STRETCH

Tuesday 3 August

The countdown has begun. Somewhere, the fat lady is preparing to sing. Like all good things, my first year as a junior doctor has come to an end. Unlike all good things, it's been hell on earth. But while there were times when every sinew in my body ached to run away, I stayed. While I've never worked so hard in my life, or survived before on so little food and sleep, it's also been an amazing experience, made all the more amazing by the fact that I survived it in one piece. I've been privy to people's most intimate, personal moments. While I've held people's hands as they've died and seen some real human tragedies, I've also had some of the happiest memories anyone could hope for from a job. The learning curve has been exponential. My greatest achievement though has to be that I'm now a dab hand at cannulas, which caused me, and every other junior doctor I know, so many problems at the beginning. I can now insert them in my sleep, and in fact I'm sure there were times during night shifts when I did.

The day races by. I say goodbye to Maxine and the Marys in the morning. 'You won't forget us, will you?' says Mary 2 as I hand over some chocolates. But I know that tomorrow there'll be a whole throng of new doctors to compete for their attention, and in a short while we'll all be distant memories, rarely thought of or talked about. It is they that will forget me first. Dr Pike gives me a pat on the back which nearly knocks me over and wishes me luck for the future. Barney shakes my hand.

As the day progresses I continue to say my farewells. I stay late to tie up loose ends and see Supriya on my way back from the laboratory, as she frantically finishes up seeing the last of her patients. We hug each other and promise to keep in touch. 'Thanks for everything, Max,' she says.

'It's been great working with you,' I reply.

We look at each other for a few seconds, and I know exactly how she feels. While I barely knew Supriya before starting work, we have both grown up together here on these wards.

I explain to the patients that I'm leaving. Mrs Paterson is nearly as excited as I am. 'Ooh, so tomorrow you'll become a proper doctor,' she exclaims. 'Your mum will be proud.'

'No,' I correct her in a rather stern voice. 'I'm a proper doctor now, just very junior.'

But, I go on to explain, from tomorrow, I will no longer be the scrawny chick in the medical profession's pecking order. A horde of bright-eyed fledgling doctors, fresh out of medical school, will be cast on to the wards, to sink or swim, and I will become a slightly more senior junior doctor. 'And I'll be registered with the General Medical Council,' I say in an attempt to make it sound more impressive.

'Ooh!' Her eyes light up. 'What does that mean?'

Now she's got me. 'Erm, I pay them two hundred and ninety pounds and they put my name on a register and if I'm unprofessional they can take it off again.' When put like this, registration with the GMC is not a particularly exciting reward for having endured the past year.

'Well, don't you worry about that dear,' she says, 'I think you're great.'

I suspect that this view is more to do with the painkiller I've just given her, rather than any reflection on my abilities as a doctor, but never mind.

Despite six years at medical school, I had no idea what it meant to be a doctor twelve months ago. Now, while I've got an idea, I'm still no nearer knowing if I'm any good at it. It's difficult because being a good doctor isn't just about knowledge or technical ability. There are some doctors who are academically brilliant but who have the people skills of an enema. The really good doctors that I've worked with, the ones where it's been a privilege to watch them in action, have a quality that can't be easily quantified or tested for. Each of them has had their own style, so there can be no set formula that can be easily copied. But each of them approaches their patients with a certain humility and a desire to understand that person in their entirety, rather than just grapple with the reason they are in hospital.

I say goodbye to Mrs Paterson and finish the hand-over notes for the doctors starting tomorrow. I leave my pager on the desk next to the computer and Ruby comes in. 'I've finished. Are you done yet?' she asks. I nod.

We walk out of the ward, and I wave goodbye to the nurses. We walk through A&E where we have spent so many hours of our lives over the past twelve months. Someone is vomiting in one of the cubicles, and it seems strange to think that this is no longer any of our concern. We walk out of the back of A&E, past the ambulance bays and by the bins where we spent so many furtive minutes smoking and arranging scans with Dr Palache. We walk down the lane towards the bus stop, the evening sky in front of us illuminated bright red. We both turn to each other and smile.

'Can't believe that's all over with,' says Ruby.

I think of how a year ago I could only have imagined the things I'd see, the situations I'd find myself in, and the incredible array of people I'd meet. Would I go through it again? Not on your life.

Author's Note

Medicine is always changing and doctors are required to adapt rapidly. Treatments and procedures are re-evaluated and political decisions impact directly on the way that doctors practise. In recent years the training of junior doctors has been in upheaval. The hours and on-call requirements have been reduced, mostly in response to EU pressure to improve the working lives of doctors. Initially the European Working Time Directive was side-stepped by many trusts, as was the case when I began work a few years ago, but more recently the government has imposed penalties on trusts that do not comply with working times and the situation has officially improved. There remains a clear incentive, of course, for hospitals to manipulate this data and put pressure on junior doctors to lie on their monitoring forms, but certainly the days of 100-hour working weeks are a thing of the past.

In the summer of 2007 the government introduced a new initiative called modernising medical careers (MMC) and junior doctors were rebranded 'Foundation Year' doctors. It turned out to be a chaotic reshuffle, which relied on a Kafkaesque on-line application service called MTAS and saw all junior doctors forced to re-apply for their jobs. From the beginning the process was fraught with technical glitches, delays and conflicting information. The result was utter confusion, and it saw the total numbers of junior doctor positions reduced, with thousands facing unemployment. At the time of writing, the situation has still not been satisfactorily resolved. Many junior doctors cut their losses and left the country while others left medicine altogether. Those that remain face an uncertain future. MTAS has now been abandoned following a parliamentary investigation into the fiasco. No doubt it will simply be replaced with another acronym.

Finally, a note on the text: is it a work of fiction or an autobiography? I suppose it's both. Everything that happens in this book is based on something that happened in real life. But I retained the bits that were important to the story, and changed the rest so as to protect the identity of patients and staff. But I've tried to remain as faithful to my feelings in that year as possible. And no, Ruby's taste in men hasn't improved.

Max Pemberton
London, November 2007

Acknowledgements

It is hard to know who to thank, as so many people over such a long period of time have helped me survive both that first year of being a doctor and writing this book. Sarah, Anna and the People's Republic of Old Street: what would I ever have done without you? Emily, Justin and Isi, who gave me so many happy memories of that first six months; Beth, who I hope is grateful that I didn't mention the time when she wet herself on a ward round; Toby, a brilliant doctor and a wonderful friend; Ben and Becky. Dr Katz – I've still got your laptop, thank you so much. Nan, Pop. My beautiful sister (I changed your name so you can't hate me). Tasha, who has been the best friend I could ever have hoped for and Rhiannon: perfect in every way. And Katharine and all my non-medic friends who put up with me in that first year and who tried to keep me entertained despite my pleas to be allowed to sleep. The anthropologists: Nadine, Ellie, Rob, Kate and Susie. Sister Mary Stephen. Gill Scurr. Enormous thanks of course to Anne Hughes, without whom I would never have become a doctor. Warm thanks to all those who gave me support, friendship, or, in the case of some, food, during that first year: Gill and Tony, Jose and Bill, Jeannie and Tod, Ann, Eileen, June and David, Zoe and Tania, the Burbridges, Christine and David; Jill (I dread to think what my BMI would be without you), Flora and Thomas, Andrew, Sue, Dorothy, the Gardiner family, Hilary and Sarah, Auntie Cis, the Murphy family, Mrs Burns, Prof Robertson, the Davies family, the Lennards, the Barry clan, the Barlows, Keith.

Thanks to all the consultants I've worked with. You have all, in your own ways, taught me an immense amount and I'm very grateful. And to the nurses who made me tea late at night and held my hand. And the secretaries and legions of admin staff who made it all run smoothly and who covered for me when I messed up and it didn't. And of course, not forgetting the patients.

The staff at the *Daily Telegraph*, both past and present: George Cover, Chloe Rhodes, Izzy Shirlaw, Becky Pugh, Paul Davies, Richard Preston, Rachel Forder and Rachel Simhon, Genevieve Fox, Fiona Hardcastle and Liz Hunt, all of whom are, or have been, a real joy to work with. And to the subs, who make my late-night copy readable. And thanks to Charles Moore who took a chance on me. And of course the readers of my column whose support and loyalty has been astounding. Thanks to those at Hodder: Jocasta Brownlee who has been so kind and patient and Nicola Doherty who was wonderful and didn't shout at me when this was late and Henry Jeffreys. And Heather Holden-Brown, without whom I would never have got organised enough to write this. And to Elly James, apologies for being a bit scatty at times.

Lastly, Neil, who has read everything I have ever written, and for whose unwavering support I am eternally grateful. You cooked for me, you looked after me. You've always been so understanding. Thank you.

The publishers hope that this book has given you enjoyable reading. Large Print Books are especially designed to be as easy to see and hold as possible. If you wish a complete list of our books please ask at your local library or write directly to:

Magna Large Print Books
Magna House, Long Preston,
Skipton, North Yorkshire.
BD23 4ND